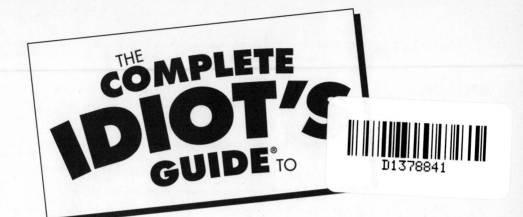

THE
COMPLETE IDIOT'S GUIDE TO

Cooking for Two

Merry XMAs Roommate!
Not that you're an Idiot......

L.
Pat

by Ellen Brown

ALPHA

A member of Penguin Group (USA) Inc.

This book is dedicated to my dear sister, and brother-in-law, Nancy and Walter Dubler, who have been such a support for me through many reinventions of my life.

ALPHA BOOKS

Published by the Penguin Group

Penguin Group (USA) Inc., 375 Hudson Street, New York, New York 10014, U.S.A.

Penguin Group (Canada), 10 Alcorn Avenue, Toronto, Ontario, Canada M4V 3B2 (a division of Pearson Penguin Canada Inc.)

Penguin Books Ltd, 80 Strand, London WC2R 0RL, England

Penguin Ireland, 25 St Stephen's Green, Dublin 2, Ireland (a division of Penguin Books Ltd)

Penguin Group (Australia), 250 Camberwell Road, Camberwell, Victoria 3124, Australia (a division of Pearson Australia Group Pty Ltd)

Penguin Books India Pvt Ltd, 11 Community Centre, Panchsheel Park, New Delhi—110 017, India

Penguin Group (NZ), cnr Airborne and Rosedale Roads, Albany, Auckland 1310, New Zealand (a division of Pearson New Zealand Ltd)

Penguin Books (South Africa) (Pty) Ltd, 24 Sturdee Avenue, Rosebank, Johannesburg 2196, South Africa

Penguin Books Ltd, Registered Offices: 80 Strand, London WC2R 0RL, England

International Standard Book Number: 978-1-59257-607-4
Library of Congress Catalog Card Number: 2006936704

09 08   8 7 6 5 4 3 2

Interpretation of the printing code: The rightmost number of the first series of numbers is the year of the book's printing; the rightmost number of the second series of numbers is the number of the book's printing. For example, a printing code of 07-1 shows that the first printing occurred in 2007.

Printed in the United States of America

Note: This publication contains the opinions and ideas of its author. It is intended to provide helpful and informative material on the subject matter covered. It is sold with the understanding that the author and publisher are not engaged in rendering professional services in the book. If the reader requires personal assistance or advice, a competent professional should be consulted.

The author and publisher specifically disclaim any responsibility for any liability, loss, or risk, personal or otherwise, which is incurred as a consequence, directly or indirectly, of the use and application of any of the contents of this book.

Most Alpha books are available at special quantity discounts for bulk purchases for sales promotions, premiums, fundraising, or educational use. Special books, or book excerpts, can also be created to fit specific needs.

For details, write: Special Markets, Alpha Books, 375 Hudson Street, New York, NY 10014.

Publisher: *Marie Butler-Knight*
Editorial Director: *Mike Sanders*
Managing Editor: *Billy Fields*
Acquisitions Editor: *Michele Wells*
Development Editor: *Nancy D. Lewis*
Production Editor: *Megan Douglass*

Copy Editor: *Nancy Wagner*
Cartoonist: *Richard King*
Book Designer: *Trina Wurst*
Cover Designer: *Bill Thomas*
Indexer: *Heather McNeill*
Layout: *Ayanna Lacey*
Proofreader: *Mary Hunt, Donna Martin*

Contents at a Glance

Contents

▲ Fast
● Healthy
■ Make-ahead
+ Vegan

Part 3: Saucing to Success   71

7 Poultry with Panache   73

8 Sensational Seafood   87

9 The Meat of the Matter   101

Appendixes

Introduction

If you're cooking for two—or just cooking for you—you're hardly alone. You're one of millions of cooks who may hate leftovers because recipes are always written for at least four servings. Or you've rebelled at the concept of cooking, and you're living on take-out and a freezer stocked with entrees ready to nuke in the microwave.

Perhaps you're nesting for the first time in an apartment with a real kitchen instead of stir-frying on a hot plate in your dorm room. One- and two-person households are the part of American society growing at the fastest rate. At least one in three new households created during the 1990s was for a single person, and those new nesters account for 26 percent of U.S. households. That's up from less than 10 percent in 1950.

Or maybe you're cooking for two at the other end of the spectrum. Now that you've emptied your nest, you need a refresher course in cooking for less than a crowd. If so, you're not alone either. The Baby Boomers, those 76 million Americans born between 1946 and 1964, now have children who are setting up kitchens, and many of them are down-sizing from the family house. Along with professional couples without children, these empty nesters have created the market for luxury condominiums in all American cities.

This growth of smaller households isn't confined to the United States. A study in Britain revealed that in the 30 years from 1971 to 2001, the percentage of one-person households grew from 17 percent to 31 percent. In Australia the number of households of families with children declined from 60 percent in 1976 to 50 percent in 1996.

So as household size has decreased, why haven't cookbooks kept up with the trend? Perhaps some authors believed that the only time one- and two-person households cooked was when they were cooking for company.

But all of that has changed, and you're now holding a book dedicated to delicious meals geared to your lifestyle. Here you'll learn to buy just what you need and cook just what you want for *one* meal. All the recipes in this book were formulated for two servings without leftover ingredients spoiling in the refrigerator or leftover casseroles filling your freezer only to be thrown out in a few months.

The first step is to become a savvy shopper, and you'll learn those tips in Chapter 1. The supermarket scene is looking brighter for smaller sizes, and you'll learn tips on keeping yourself in the Express Lane.

And once you have the small bag of groceries home, you'll find a wealth of ways to use them. The dishes in this book are "real food." They're not made with convenience products that list more chemicals on their labels than words recognizable as foods.

In these chapters, you'll find recipes for quickly-cooked stir-fried and sautéed dishes that you can have on the table in minutes, and they're drawn from cuisines that span the globe. Balancing this yin is the yang of dishes that cook more slowly and add luscious anticipatory aromas to your house.

But cooking for two doesn't mean you have to reinvent the wheel every time you enter the kitchen. In Part 3, "Saucing to Success," you'll find a cache of chapters with dishes that are made in large batches, with only one third served that night. These sauces and bases can replace the frozen entrées as your "dinner insurance," and the quantities all fit in a one-quart bag. Unlike a thawed leftover, you'll complete these recipes with fresh food so there's no tired taste.

I also know there are times that it's nice to know that the chicken or pork loin you're slowly roasting on a Sunday afternoon will have a second life during the week. In Part 6, "Reveling in Roasts," you'll learn how to roast all sorts of meats, and then the following chapter presents a cornucopia of ways to transform food already cooked into an exciting option.

And do save room for dessert. I've included three chapters of sweet ways to end a meal, and all of them are formulated for two servings. So there won't be that half a pie turning soggy on its third day.

You'll find so many ways to cook healthful fruits—from simply poaching them to creating crumbles and cobblers. And no dessert section would be complete without many ways to enjoy chocolate!

When you're cooking for two, there's a basic assumption that the second person is one you cherish, be it a spouse, lover, friend, or relative. And what better way can there be to show love than with a luscious meal!

How This Book Is Organized

The book is divided into seven parts:

Part 1, "Ready, Set, Cook!" gives you some basic knowledge concerning both equipment and ingredients. Each recipe chapter (in Parts 2 through 7) contains introductory material concerning the foods that serve as the foundation for the recipes, but the useful information in Part 1 concerns cooking in general. In the first chapter you'll get tips for savvy shopping to minimize waste when cooking for two, and the next chapter details appropriate size pots and pans for small batch cooking and ways to cut down the quantities in recipes from other cookbooks.

Part 2, "Casual Fare," includes recipes to make everyday meals special many times of day. Here you'll find recipes for breakfast and brunch dishes, many of which would also work as a supper. The rest of the recipes are divided by categories of dishes. There are recipes for hearty soups and hot sandwiches that need just a small salad to complete the meal. Then you have a chapter for entrée salads that combine many types of vegetables and fruits with poultry, seafood, or chicken.

Part 3, "Saucing to Success," gives you "dinner insurance," which takes the form of small bags in the freezer that you can transform into full meals in a matter of minutes. Here you'll find recipes for dishes that make a base for three separate meals. That's the part you freeze, and then you finish the dish by adding fresh poultry or seafood to flavorful sauces or vegetables to almost-tender stews. This part concludes with a chapter on pasta sauces.

Part 4, "Fast Food: Stir-Fries and Sautés for All Seasons," gives you ways to have dinner on the table from start to finish in 30 minutes or less. The recipes are divided by flavors, with chapters comprising Asian, Mediterranean, and the rest of the world. A chapter of vibrantly flavored international vegetarian recipes ends this part.

Part 5, "Anticipatory Aromas: Slow Roasts, Casseroles, and Braises," contains recipes that still have you out of the kitchen in 30 minutes, but with time to enjoy a glass of wine or magazine while reveling in the aromas coming from the kitchen before the meal is ready. The recipes for poultry, seafood, and meat dishes all include a large proportion of fresh vegetables.

Part 6, "The Second Time Around: Luscious Leftovers," presents you with innovative ways to roast foods and then ways to give leftovers an exciting second life. You'll discover exotic ways to flavor simple roasted poultry, fish, and meat in the first chapter. The delicious recipes for already-cooked foods in the second chapter will encourage you to make a bigger roast.

Part 7, "Just Desserts," is full of easy recipes for sweets that don't leave you with unwanted leftovers because you're only making small batches. One chapter is tailor-made for chocoholics, and other chapters offer a wide range of baked goods including homey cakes and cobblers, haute tortes, and quick breads for all occasions.

Following the dessert chapters, you'll find some useful appendixes. A glossary will add to your knowledge of foods, and an appendix of charts will help you convert measurements to or from the metric system. The other two appendixes are about food. One gives you weights and measures of ingredients to ease your shopping, and the other gives you a list of pantry staples for which to shop.

Extras

In every chapter you'll find boxes that give you extra information that is either helpful, interesting, or both.

Double Feature

In these boxes you'll find tips. Some are specific to the recipes they accompany, but others will boost your general cooking knowledge and its ingredients, give you ideas for presentation, or teach you ways to preserve ingredients left over when cooking a recipe for two. These tips are meant to make your life easier and your time in the kitchen more pleasurable.

Duet Dialogue

Cooking has a language all its own, and some of the terms and ingredients can be intimidating if you don't know what they mean. Look to these boxes for technique and ingredient definitions if you don't want to flip to the glossary.

Déjà Two

Check out these boxes for amusing tidbits of food history. They're fun to read and share with friends, and they'll make you sound like a real gourmet.

Double Trouble

It's always a good idea to be alerted to potential problems in advance. These boxes provide just such a warning, either about cooking in general or the recipe in particular.

A Note on Recipe Timing

You'll notice that the times given with each recipe are broken into two segments. Cooking is like sports; there are participants and spectators, and these two time measurements are similar.

The first is the "active time." That's the time you actually have to be in the kitchen chopping, sautéing, or stirring. In all cases this time is less than 30 minutes. You're not going to be spinning swans from sugar or boning tiny quail. When you're the cook, this is the measurement you need to factor into your day.

The second measurement is simple enough to understand—"start to finish" means just that. It's the combination of the active time with the cooking time and then any additional time that's needed for marinating before cooking or chilling after cooking. But during most of this time you can be reading a book in the living room. The start to finish time is so you know when to begin a dish in order to have it ready by a particular time.

Acknowledgments

Writing a book is a solitary endeavor, but its publication is always a team effort. My thanks go to …

Michele Wells of Alpha Books for proposing this interesting project.

Ed Claflin, my agent, for his constant support and great humor.

Nancy Lewis and Megan Douglass for their eagle-eyed editing.

Karen Konopelski for her sensible nutritional analyses.

Grace Skinger Lefrancois for her editorial assistance.

My many friends whose palates aided me in recipe development, including Suzanne Cavedon, Janet Morell, Vicki Veh, Nick Brown, Heidi Howard, Dan Potter, Constance Brown, Kenn Speiser, Edye DeMarco, and Tom Byrne.

Tigger and Patches, my furry companions, who personally approved all seafood recipes.

Special Thanks to the Technical Reviewers

The Complete Idiot's Guide to Cooking for Two was reviewed by experts who double-checked the accuracy of what you'll learn here, to help us ensure that this book gives you everything you need to know. Special thanks are extended to Karen Konopelski and Dr. Mario Ciani.

Trademarks

All terms mentioned in this book that are known to be or are suspected of being trademarks or service marks have been appropriately capitalized. Alpha Books and Penguin Group (USA) Inc. cannot attest to the accuracy of this information. Use of a term in this book should not be regarded as affecting the validity of any trademark or service mark.

Part 1

Ready, Set, Cook!

The theme for these chapters is "think small." The considerations of shopping—both for food and pots and pans with which to cook—is different for two people and two servings than for a larger group.

The first chapter in this part is a guerilla guide to savvy shopping. You can bet it rarely leads you to a warehouse store! You'll learn about shopping from bulk bins, fruit carts, and supermarket salad bars. You'll also get more tricks to prevent food you don't need wasting away—literally—in your refrigerator.

The second chapter in this part gives you a guide to the sizes of pots and pans that work best with the recipes that follow. There's also a section on how to "down-size" recipes for larger yields on your own.

Savvy Shopping

In This Chapter

- ◆ Buying what you need
- ◆ Salad bar shopping
- ◆ Food safety

You know the pitfalls of cooking for one or two from traditional cookbooks; that's why you're holding this one in your hand. In this book I've tailored the recipes to buying what you need without leftovers, and in this chapter I give you hints to make that promise come true.

One- or two-person households are small players in our super-size world. Just look at the size of packages of meats in the supermarket case! Even nature works against us. A bunch of celery is as small as it gets, or is it?

And cooking the food you've bought is the logical next step after shopping. So at the end of this chapter, I'll give you some pointers on basic food safety to ensure your good food is good for you.

Thinking Small

When you buy for one or two, the tendency is to "overbuy," and what seems like a good bargain is truly not because you'll end up throwing much of it out. So the first rule of smart shopping is to stop looking for bargains, and start buying just what you need.

Begin by making a list that includes quantities for the recipes you're planning on making. If you see celery on the list, don't be tempted to buy a whole bunch when all you need is ½ cup.

Ring That Bell!

Getting help might take you a few extra minutes, but the biggest waste for small households is buying large packages of meat, fish, and poultry. And that's all you'll find pre-packaged in the case.

Take the extra time to ring the bell and ask the real live human who will appear for *exactly* what you want. If you need two (6-ounce) chicken breast halves, buy two. If you want only ½ pound of ground beef, then buy that amount, and you won't be throwing out the other half pound a few days later.

Double Feature

Make sure you shop at a supermarket that doesn't charge a premium price—more than that of pre-packaged foods—for custom service. Many supermarkets do offer discounts for large-quantity purchases, but just make sure you're not paying more than for a regular package.

Many supermarkets do not have personnel readily available in departments like the cheese counter, but if wedges of cheeses are labeled and priced, then someone is in charge. It might be the deli department or the produce department, but find someone and ask for a small wedge of cheese if you can't find one the correct size.

Another advantage to interaction with the store personnel is they'll get to know you, and you'll get to know them. These folks are a font of knowledge, and once you know them, you won't feel awkward asking a question or two to become a more knowledgeable cook.

Buying from the Bins

The concept of buying just what you need extends to shelf-stable foods, too. An increasing number of supermarkets offer foods, like grains, beans, pastas, and dried fruit, from bins rather than packages. And that's where you should head.

Each of these departments has scales so you can weigh ingredients, such as dried mushrooms or pasta. If a recipe calls for a quantity rather than a weight, you can usually "eyeball" the quantity. If you're unsure of amounts, take a 1-cup measure with you to the market. Empty the contents of the bin into the measuring cup rather than directly into the bag.

One problem with bulk food bags is that they are difficult to store in the pantry; shelves were made for sturdier materials. So wash out plastic deli containers or even plastic containers that once contained yogurt or salsa and use these for storage once the bulk bags arrive in the kitchen.

Smaller Sizes

Because more and more manufacturers are beginning to realize that the average American household isn't the *Brady Bunch*, you'll find different sizes of packaged foods for everything from flour and sugar to grated cheeses.

But don't look at the price per pound side of the label because it's always going to be higher. Go for the smaller size because you won't waste it. All of the recipes in this book give you can sizes, and with rare exceptions, you'll have no leftovers.

Double Trouble

Always label your containers of bulk foods, both at the supermarket and if you're transferring the foods to other containers at home, so you know what they are, especially if you're buying similar foods. Basmati and Arborio rice look very similar in a plastic bag but are totally different grains and should not be substituted for each other.

Double Feature

Canned stock only comes large (14.5-ounce) and larger (1 quart). But you can save unused stock by freezing it into cubes. Measure the capacity of your ice cube tray with a measuring tablespoon, then freeze leftover stock as cubes. When you encounter the next recipe that requires just a few tablespoons, you're ready to go.

Salad Bar Shopping

There's no question that supermarkets charge a premium price for items in those chilled bins in the salad bar, but the amount of time saved—and the lack of potential waste—makes shopping the salad bar appealing for these recipes.

The salad bar has done all the vegetable prep work for you, and that means you can substantially decrease the active time needed for any of these dishes. The carrots are already peeled and sliced; the onions are pre-chopped; and the spinach is rinsed and stemmed. Check those tasks off the list! But what's equally important is that you're buying just the amount you need.

Salad bars offer more than produce that makes them treasure troves. Want to make egg salad? You'll find hard-cooked eggs already peeled. Want just a few beans rather than a 15-ounce can? You'll almost always find garbanzo beans and frequently other options.

>
>
> **Double Trouble** _____
>
> One fear of shopping from salad bars, and eating from salad bars, too, is that the produce might have been sprayed with chemicals to prevent discoloration and wilting. Question the supermarket about this practice if it concerns you.

Other Options

In general, pre-packaged produce works to the disadvantage of small households. But there are exceptions to this rule. And bags of pre-mixed vegetables for stir-frying save both time and money.

All of the stir-fried recipes in this book list individual vegetables. But remember that recipes are guidelines and not laws. If you see an appealing mix of vegetables pre-trimmed for you, it's probably the right volume for these recipes.

I've geared all the hints thus far in this chapter to supermarket shopping. But an alternative, at least during the summer months in even large cities, is the farmers' market.

I'm addicted to farmers' markets. There you'll find an incredible variety of the freshest possible ingredients, and you need to buy only what you want. Most of the time carrots and other vegetables are sold by the pound rather than the bunch, so you can purchase only what you need.

The first cousin of farmers' markets for small quantities of fruits is the sidewalk vendors in many cities. One great advantage to buying from them is that their fruit is usually ripe and ready to eat or cook.

> **Déjà Two** _____
>
> The U.S. Dept. of Agriculture began publishing the National Directory of Farmers' Markets in 1994, and at that time the number was less than 2000. It's now double that figure, and to find a farmers' market near you, go to www.ams.usda.gov/ farmersmarkets.

The Organic Alternative

Whenever you have the chance, it's always best to buy produce that is certified organic. Organic agriculture is about growing foods without synthetic fertilizers and chemical biocides. And it's also about using agricultural practices that benefit the planet, such as recycling.

When this method of healthy farming began about 20 years ago, the only way to ensure that food was organic was to purchase it directly from a reputable farmer. Luckily, that's no longer the case.

In 2002 the National Organic Program (NOP) became law. The U.S. Department of Agriculture administers this program which upholds the prohibitions against chemicals first spelled out in the Organic Food Production Act of 1990. The NOP states that it believes in "optimizing the health and productivity of interdependent communities of soil life, plants, animals, and people. Management practices are carefully selected with an intent to restore and then maintain ecological harmony on the farm, its surrounding environment, and ultimately the whole planetary ecosystem."

Wanting to eat organic food is another reason to buy food in season rather than imported food. Many European countries also have strict standards as to the meaning of "organic," but most of those countries share our climates. Unfortunately strict standards are not applied in most Asian and Latin American countries, and they are the source of most crops that are out of season in the United States.

If you use produce that is conventional rather than organic, always pay attention to the skin to see if it's been treated with wax. This is especially true of cucumbers and citrus fruits. While citrus fruits need to be peeled before juicing, cucumbers do not. But if cucumbers are waxed, peel them.

> **Double Feature** _____
>
> Make buying organic your shopping goal when you're looking for shelf-stable food as well as fresh. There are now organic options for everything from canned tomatoes and chicken stock to tortilla chips made from organic corn. These are all good choices.

Bargain Buddies

There's no question that supermarkets try to lure customers with "buy one, get one free" promotions. And there's no reason why small households shouldn't enjoy the same cost savings. The answer? Find a bargain buddy. Perhaps it's the neighbor down the hall or a friend across town, but chances are you know someone who is also shopping for small amounts of food.

The bargain buddy system can work in two ways. The first is to take the cost of the item, split it in half, and each person pays half the cost. If you think that's too labor-intensive for a few dollars savings, the alternative is to take turns. Maybe this week you drop off the free package of chicken breasts, and next week your buddy will bring you the spoils of that week's shopping spree.

The system also works well for disposable products like paper towels. When the 12-packs are on sale, split one between the two of you.

> **Double Feature** _____
>
> Those thin plastic bags for bulk foods and produce can be useful in the kitchen, but they usually end up messing up a drawer. Instead, save an empty paper tissue box and stuff the bags into it. They'll be handy and not messy.

Safety First

The first—and most important—requirement for good cooking is knowing the basic rules of food safety. This begins with trips to the supermarket and ends with leftovers refrigerated or frozen at the end of a meal.

The following sections may seem like common sense, but after many decades as a food writer who has heard horror stories about very sick people, please believe me, they're not.

> **Double Feature** _____
>
> If you have any questions about food safety, the U.S. Department of Agriculture is the place to go. The Food Safety Inspection Service was designed to help you. The website, www.fsis.usda.gov, provides a wealth of information in a very user-friendly format.

Safe Shopping

Most supermarkets are designed to funnel you into the produce section first. But that's not the best place to start. Begin your shopping with the shelf-stable items from the center, then go to produce, and end with the other refrigerated and frozen sections.

Never buy meat or poultry in a package that is torn and leaking, and it's a good idea to place all meats and poultry in the disposable plastic bags available in the produce department.

Check the "sell-by" and "use-by" dates, and never purchase food that exceeds them. For the trip home, it's a good idea to carry an insulated cooler in the back of your car if it's hot outside or if the perishable items will be out of refrigeration for more than one hour. In hot weather, many seafood departments will provide some crushed ice in a separate bag for the fish.

Banishing Bacteria

Fruits and vegetables can contain some bacteria, but it's far more likely that the culprits will grow on meat, poultry, and seafood. Store these foods on the bottom shelves of your refrigerator so their juices cannot accidentally drip onto other foods. And keep these foods refrigerated until just before they go into the dish.

Bacteria multiply at room temperature. The so-called "danger zone" is between 40°F and 140°F. As food cooks, it's important for it to pass through this zone as quickly as possible.

If you want to get a jump-start on dinner by browning meats or poultry or cutting up vegetables in advance, that's fine. Just refrigerate all foods separately until it's time to combine them and cook the finished dish. Like all rules, this one has exceptions. It's fine to pre-mix batters for pancakes in advance, even though they contain raw eggs.

Don't Cross-Contaminate

Cleanliness is not only next to godliness, but it's also the key to food safety. Wash your hands often while you're cooking, and never touch cooked food if you haven't washed your hands after handling raw food.

Double Feature

A good way to prevent food-borne illness is by selecting the right cutting board. Wooden boards might be attractive, but you can never get them as clean as plastic boards that you can run through the dishwasher. Even with plastic boards, it's best to use one only for cooked food and foods such as vegetables that are not prone to containing bacteria, and devote another one to raw meats, poultry, and fish.

The "cooked food and raw food shall never meet" precept extends beyond the cook's hands. Clean cutting boards, knives, and kitchen counters often. Or if you have the space, section off your countertops for raw foods and cooked foods, as many restaurant kitchens do. Don't place cooked foods or raw foods that will remain uncooked (such as salad) on cutting boards that you have used to cut raw meat, poultry, or fish. Bacteria from raw animal proteins can contaminate the other foods.

The Least You Need to Know

◆ It's possible to ask supermarket personnel for exactly the amount of protein you need for a recipe rather than buying pre-packaged food.

◆ Shopping for small quantities of produce from supermarket salad bars ensures you'll have no wasted food from recipes listing small quantities.

◆ Sharing food with friends makes it possible to take advantage of the cost savings offered as supermarket promotions.

◆ Cooked food should never come into contact with any surface that held the food raw.

The Efficient Epicure

In This Chapter

- Pots and pans
- Kitchen gadgets
- Retooling larger recipes

Now it's time to realize that we're the 9×9-inch folk in a world of 9×13-inch recipes! In Chapter 1, I discussed the food you're going to cook, and in this chapter, you'll find pertinent information on what you need at home to cook the food.

We'll begin with equipment lists, called the *batterie de cuisine* in classic French cooking if you want to sound classy and say it in French. This comprises both pots and pans and the other essential equipment you need.

At the end of the chapter, you'll find some guidelines on how to successfully adapt recipes for a crowd to your one- or two-person kitchen.

Panpoly of Pans

If you're an empty-nester, there's a good chance that you have more kitchen space than you need for your now smaller household. In that case, you can skip most of this chapter because it's intended for cooks at the other end of the spectrum who might be operating out of cramped apartment kitchens; that's why I give a lot of space-saving tips with many recipes.

Using the size pot or pan listed in a recipe is important to the success of the dish, and most often cooks make mistakes by using a pan that is too large rather than too small.

It's easy to know if a pot is too small; the food won't fit in it. But if you're sautéing one shallot in a 12-inch skillet, it's also a problem because you can't control the food well and keep it stirring. That task needs a 6-inch skillet.

When it comes to selecting pots and pans, the heft and durability matters more than the material. I personally prefer enameled iron, but stainless-steel and anodized cast aluminum are other good choices.

One aspect of selection is whether or not you plan to wash the pots in the dishwasher. Such upscale brands as Calphalon should not be washed in the dishwasher, and you also can't wash pots with wooden handles in the dishwasher because the handles will rot and break off.

Double Trouble

When it comes to pots and pans, being penny wise is being pound foolish. You only buy them a few times in a lifetime, and while the quality of your can opener doesn't matter, the quality of your pots does. Flimsy pans have hot spots that can cause food to stick and burn.

Here's the list of pots I think you need, along with some suggestions for what you'll do with them:

- 1-quart saucepan with a lid for just about everything
- 2-quart saucepan with a lid for stews, soups, and small roasts
- 4-quart stockpot with a lid for pasta and party cooking
- 7-inch skillet for sautéing vegetables
- 10-inch skillet for browning food
- 12-inch skillet with a lid for stir-frying
- 9×9-inch glass or metal baking pan for baking casseroles
- 9×13-inch glass or metal baking pan for roasting meats and vegetables

- Metal colander to drain pasta

- Broiler pan with a rack that fits on top

- ½-size sheet pan with 1-inch sides for toasting nuts and general baking

- 1-quart soufflé dish for soufflés and casseroles

- 6-ounce and 8-ounce ovenproof ceramic or glass ramekins

- 1-quart mixing bowl

- At least two 2-quart mixing bowls

- 4-quart mixing bowl

Double Feature

If you haunt yard sales and thrift shops, you might uncover treasure troves of inexpensive kitchen items. When people move, they part with "stuff." And "stuff" is what you want. I don't trust used electrical equipment as it can lead to fires, but a mixing bowl is a mixing bowl.

The Electrical Aisle

Very few small appliances are truly essential in the kitchen. The most important is a food processor. Even if you're shopping off the salad bar, chances are you may have to do additional dicing, mincing, and fine chopping.

The on and off action of the food processor has revolutionized formerly laborious tasks. When I test recipes, I do the chopping by hand to calculate the active time, and I'm always amazed at how long it takes!

My food processor has a permanent spot in the dishwasher because I use it every day. Here are some other good additions to the electric arsenal:

- An immersion blender with a whisk attachment is excellent for beating small quantities that would get lost in the beaters of an electric mixer.

- A hand-held electric mixer is the size you'll need even if you're very interested in cake baking; the capacity of a standard mixer is just too large for these recipes.

Double Feature

Don't bother spending money on a toaster; you can toast anything your heart desires underneath the oven broiler. The same is true for a blender. While it may make smoothies better than a food processor, a blender can't chop and dice for you. So if you're only going to buy one appliance, make it a food processor.

♦ A hinged-top grill is the new kid on the block, and the most prominent brand is the George Forman. Great for pressed sandwiches and indoor grilling, it comes in a 10-inch size perfect for these recipes.

♦ An electric or battery kitchen scale is extremely important for weighing food for recipes; your scale doesn't have to be top-of-the-line, but a middle-of-the-road that digitally registers weight is important.

The Pots' Pals

Pots and pans don't exist in a vacuum, and any cook who has had to improvise a soup ladle from a mug or tried to do without a slotted spoon knows that it's the inexpensive equipment that makes cooking efficient.

This list of miscellaneous odds and ends completes your kitchen list:

♦ Measuring spoons, graduated from ¼ teaspoon to 1 tablespoon

♦ Dry measuring cups, graduated from ¼ cup to 1 cup

♦ 2-cup liquid glass measuring cup

♦ A few plastic cutting boards

♦ Glass and stainless-steel mixing bowls

♦ Some long-handled cooking spoons

♦ Heatproof rubber spatula

♦ 8-inch tongs

♦ 12-inch tongs

♦ Slotted spatula

♦ Offset spatula with a handle higher than the blade

♦ Slotted spoon

♦ Sturdy meat fork

♦ Soup ladle

♦ Garlic press

♦ Vegetable peeler

- Instant-read meat thermometer
- Wire mesh strainer that can double as a sifter
- Puncture bottle opener for opening cans of liquid
- Manual can opener
- Corkscrew

Double Feature

A corkscrew comes in handy even if you don't drink wine. It's great for opening bottles of vinegar and fancy olive oils, too.

The Cutting Edge

Knives are so important to cooking that chefs travel with their own sets. You don't have to go nuts and buy a huge knife set with a wooden block to take up counter space. What's important is that the knife is made from carbon steel and that the blade goes the entire way to the end of the handle. That's called full tang, and it makes knives sturdier.

You need these basics:

- At least one paring knife with a 4-inch blade for peeling, slicing, and dicing small foods, like shallots
- A chef's knife with an 8- to 12-inch blade for chopping, mincing, dicing, etc.
- A serrated knife with a 12- to 14-inch blade for slicing bread, tomatoes, and meats
- A sharpening steel to keep the knives razor-sharp

People cut themselves with a poorly sharpened knife much more often than with a sharp knife. A dull knife makes the job of cutting harder and can detract from the appearance of the food, so make sure you've got some way of keeping knives sharp.

A steel rod or sharpening stone is much less expensive than the electric gizmos and serves the same function with the aid of a little elbow grease.

Double Feature

If you're setting up your first "real" kitchen, you might ask for knives as a special graduation or birthday gift. A set of three knives from Sabatier, Wüsthof, or Henckels—the three market leaders—are in the $200 and up range.

Recipe Retooling

While you think of a recipe as linear, it really exists on many different levels because quantities, times, and volumes are involved. With a few exceptions for roasted meats in Chapter 18, I have written all the recipes in this book for two servings. If you want to cut down on a recipe from another cookbook, use these guidelines:

◆ Know your measurements. If you remember that 1 tablespoon is 3 teaspoons and 1 cup is 16 tablespoons, you're on your way to success. So if a recipe for six servings used ½ cup of liquid, the two-serving version would require 2 tablespoons and 2 teaspoons.

◆ Round measurements to the nearest ¼ or ⅓ cup. If a recipe for four servings calls for ¾ of a cup, then your closest measurement for two servings would be ⅓ cup. It's sometimes easier if you transform fractions into percentages.

◆ Scale back the size of the pan. This is especially important for skillets. It's better to use a small skillet than the one specified in the recipe for a larger yield. While it's not as crucial with saucepans, do realize that the larger the surface area of liquid, the faster it will evaporate and reduce.

◆ Vary cooking times with quantity. It only makes sense that reducing 4 cups of liquid by half will take far longer than reducing 2 cups of liquid by half. Recipes are written for the quantities listed, so don't go by those times if you're scaling back the quantity.

Double Trouble

Notice that the tips in this chapter are for cooking and not for baking, and there's a reason for that. Baking is both a science and an art, and specific temperatures are involved in the formulation. For foods such as muffins you can cut back the batch size, but don't try to redo cake recipes.

The Least You Need to Know

◆ Using the right size pot is essential to the success of a recipe.

◆ You need smaller equipment to cook smaller batches of food.

◆ Keeping knives sharp is important to prevent accidents in the kitchen.

◆ You must adjust quantities and cooking times when cutting back on the number of servings for a recipe.

Part 2

Casual Fare

Sure, you might want to cook the fancy dinner with candles lit and silver gleaming a few nights a week. But what about Sunday brunch? And those nights when what hits the spot is a hearty bowl of soup or a light entrée salad? Those are the times you'll be perusing the recipes in this part.

There's a chapter with goodies for breakfast and brunch, but don't relegate them to the morning. Many of them can do double duty as a light supper, too.

The other chapters contain recipes for those great stalwarts of casual cooking—soups, entrée salads, and sandwiches. But do look closely. While the categories are casual, the dishes are sophisticated as well as delicious.

Reasons to Rise: Dishes for Breakfast and Brunch

In This Chapter

◆ Frittatas: Italian baked omelets

◆ Strata: Savory bread puddings

◆ International egg dishes

Many cooks feel overwhelmed—and understaffed—when preparing breakfast or brunch for even two people. And I know this is true because I'm one of them.

But this need not be the case, as you'll discover when cooking the recipes in this chapter. You'll find a selection of vibrantly flavored egg dishes that can double as light supper, if you wish.

Sizing the Situation

The size of eggs (jumbo, extra large, large, medium, and small) is determined by how much the eggs weigh per dozen. All the recipes in this book, and in most cookbooks, specify large eggs, the ones stocked most often in supermarkets. Although you can substitute in these recipes, it's important to use the correct size egg when preparing batters for baked goods.

If you're using small eggs, increase the number by 1 for every 4 large eggs specified in a recipe. If you're using medium eggs, increase the number by 1 for every 6 large eggs. On the other side, decrease the number of eggs called for by 1 for every 4 jumbo eggs used and by 1 for every 8 extra large eggs used.

Egg Chemistry 101

It's a misnomer to say something is "as easy as boiling an egg." Although anyone can cook eggs, achieving a light, velvety texture takes some care. The basic principle for cooking all egg dishes is to use gentle, low heat so the eggs do not toughen.

At high temperatures, the proteins don't just solidify; they toughen. That's why the baking temperature given for scrambled eggs is lower than that given for eggs that are baked whole. Also, covering egg dishes produces a lighter texture, because covering a pan creates a more even heat inside the pan.

Cutting Cholesterol

Eggs have gotten a bad nutritional reputation because of the fat and cholesterol in the yolk, not in the white. The white, that which gives eggs their ability to bind, is made up primarily of protein and water.

If you want to be judicious about cutting cholesterol, you can use any of the egg substitute products on the market; the best known one is Egg Beaters. These products are essentially egg whites tinted yellow. But you can also make your own by using two egg whites for each whole egg, or if a recipe calls for several eggs, use two egg whites and one whole egg for every two whole eggs listed.

Potato, Onion, and Bacon Frittata

Smoky bacon is joined with sautéed crispy onions and potatoes for this hearty dish.

¼ lb. bacon, cut into 1-inch lengths

1 cup frozen hash-brown potatoes

1 small onion, peeled and diced

1 garlic clove, peeled and minced

4 large eggs

2 TB. half-and-half

Salt and freshly ground black pepper to taste

Active time: 20 minutes

Start to finish: 30 minutes

Each serving has:

539 calories

341 calories from fat

38 g fat

13 g saturated fat

22 g protein

27 g carbohydrates

1. Preheat the oven to 425°F. Place bacon in an ovenproof 10-inch skillet over medium-high heat. Cook for 5 to 7 minutes or until bacon is crisp. Remove bacon from the pan with a slotted spoon and set aside.

2. Discard all but 2 tablespoons of bacon fat from the skillet. Add potatoes and cook until tender, scraping them occasionally with a heavy spatula. Add onion and garlic to the skillet and cook for 5 minutes, stirring occasionally, or until onion is soft.

3. Whisk eggs with half-and-half and season to taste with salt and pepper. Return bacon to the skillet and pour egg mixture into the skillet. Cook for 4 minutes over medium heat.

4. Transfer the skillet to the oven and bake for 10 minutes or until the top is browned. Remove the skillet from the oven and run a spatula around the sides of the skillet and underneath the frittata to release it from the pan. Slide the frittata onto a platter, and cut it into wedges. Serve immediately.

Variation: You can substitute ham or sausage for the bacon, and cook ½ cup diced red bell pepper along with onion and garlic.

Double Feature

If you have trouble separating individual slices of bacon when it's cold, here's an easy solution. Peel off the total number of slices you need, and place the block into the hot pan. Within a few minutes the slices will naturally separate from the heat, and you can pull them apart.

Spicy Corn Frittata

Jalapeño Jack cheese adds its zesty flavor to this herbed brunch dish.

Active time: 10 minutes

Start to finish: 20 minutes

Each serving has:

540 calories

373 calories from fat

41.5 g fat

23 g saturated fat

29 g protein

15 g carbohydrates

¾ **cup frozen corn kernels**

4 large eggs

2 TB. half-and-half

½ **tsp.** *Herbes de Provence*

Salt and freshly ground black pepper to taste

1 cup grated jalapeño Jack cheese

2 TB. unsalted butter

1. Preheat the oven to 425°F. Cook corn according to package directions and drain well.

2. Whisk eggs with half-and-half and herbes de Provence. Season to taste with salt and pepper and stir in jalapeño Jack cheese. Melt butter in an ovenproof 10-inch skillet over medium-high heat. Pour egg mixture into the skillet. Cook for 4 minutes over medium heat.

3. Transfer the skillet to the oven and bake for 10 minutes or until the top is browned. Remove the skillet from the oven and run a spatula around the sides of the skillet and underneath the frittata to release it from the pan. Slide the frittata onto a platter and cut it into wedges. Serve immediately.

Variation: Substitute frozen chopped spinach or chopped broccoli for corn, and Swiss cheese, Monterey Jack, or cheddar cheese for jalapeño Jack cheese.

Duet Dialogue

Herbes de Provence is a dried blend of sunny flavors popular in the south of France which includes basil, fennel, marjoram, rosemary, sage, and thyme. While it's easy to find in supermarkets, if you don't have any, use a combination of those herbs you have in your pantry.

Spanish Tortilla

In Spain a tortilla is similar to a frittata, and this one contains vegetables, cheese, and ham.

2 TB. olive oil

1 large red-skinned potato, scrubbed and cut into ½-inch dice

½ red bell pepper, seeds and ribs removed, thinly sliced

½ small sweet onion, such as Vidalia or Bermuda, peeled and thinly sliced

½ cup chopped serrano ham or prosciutto

1 garlic clove, peeled and minced

1 tsp. fresh thyme or ¼ tsp. dried

Salt and freshly ground black pepper to taste

4 large eggs

2 TB. freshly grated Parmesan cheese

2 TB. shredded mozzarella cheese

2 TB. unsalted butter

Active time: 20 minutes

Start to finish: 45 minutes

Each serving has:

555 calories

357 calories from fat

40 g fat

15 g saturated fat

23 g protein

27 g carbohydrates

1. Preheat the oven to 425°F. Heat olive oil in a heavy 10-inch skillet over medium-high heat. Add potatoes and cook, stirring occasionally, for 5 minutes or until potatoes are browned. Add red bell pepper, onion, ham, garlic, and thyme to the skillet. Cook, stirring constantly, for 3 minutes or until onion is translucent. Reduce the heat to low, cover the pan, and cook vegetable mixture for 15 minutes or until vegetables are tender. Season to taste with salt and pepper and let cool for 10 minutes. (You can do this a day in advance and refrigerate, tightly covered. Before baking, reheat vegetables to room temperature in a microwave-safe dish, over low heat, or leave them out at room temperature for at least 3 hours.)

2. Whisk eggs well, stir in Parmesan cheese and mozzarella, and season to taste with salt and pepper. Stir cooled vegetable mixture into eggs. Melt butter in an ovenproof 10-inch skillet over medium-high heat. Pour egg mixture into the skillet. Cook for 4 minutes over medium heat.

3. Transfer the skillet to the oven and bake for 10 minutes or until the top is browned. Remove the skillet from the oven and run a spatula around the sides of the skillet and underneath the frittata to release it from the pan. Slide the frittata onto a platter and cut it into wedges. Serve immediately.

Double Feature

Unlike the plate of leftover poached eggs that should be destined for the trash, save and refrigerate leftover slices of frittatas or this Spanish tortilla, which is a first cousin. Take them on picnics or cut the leftovers into small squares as an hors d'oeuvre.

Three-Cheese Strata

The combination of cheeses gives this bread pudding a complex as well as creamy flavor.

Active time: 10 minutes

Start to finish: 55 minutes

Each serving has:

529 calories

266 calories from fat

30 g fat

15 g saturated fat

36 g protein

28 g carbohydrates

3 large eggs

1 cup whole milk

Salt and freshly ground black pepper to taste

½ cup grated mozzarella cheese

½ cup grated Swiss cheese

¼ cup freshly grated Parmesan cheese

2 large French or Italian rolls, cut into ½-inch slices

1. Preheat the oven to 350°F. Grease a 9×9-inch baking pan. Combine eggs, milk, salt, and pepper in a mixing bowl and whisk well. Stir in mozzarella, Swiss, and Parmesan cheeses. Arrange bread slices in the prepared baking pan and pour egg mixture over them, pressing down so bread will absorb liquid. Allow mixture to sit for 10 minutes.

2. Cover the pan with aluminum foil and bake in the center of the oven for 20 minutes. Remove the foil and bake for an additional 10 minutes or until a toothpick inserted in the center comes out clean and top is lightly browned. Allow to rest for 5 minutes and serve by scooping strata from the pan with a heavy spoon.

Variation: Use cheddar, Gruyère, or Monterey Jack cheese in place of cheeses listed, and add ¾ cup diced ham or cooked chicken.

Double Feature

Grating cheese is a snap in a food processor fitted with a steel blade. If you're grating by hand with a box grater, spray the grater with vegetable oil spray, and the cheese will grate far more easily.

Dilled Shrimp and Corn Strata

The custard for this strata is flavored with aromatic dill, and the sweet flavors of corn and shrimp meld with each other.

3 large eggs

1 cup whole milk

Salt and freshly ground black pepper to taste

½ cup grated mozzarella cheese

2 large French or Italian rolls, cut into ½-inch slices

1 TB. unsalted butter

1 large shallot, peeled and thinly sliced

¼ lb. cooked, peeled, and deveined shrimp, cut into ¼-inch pieces if large

¾ cup frozen corn kernels, thawed

2 TB. chopped fresh dill or 2 tsp. dried

Active time: 15 minutes

Start to finish: 50 minutes

Each serving has:

536 calories

226 calories from fat

25 g fat

12 g saturated fat

37 g protein

41 g carbohydrates

---

1. Preheat the oven to 350°F. Grease a 9×9-inch baking pan. Combine eggs, milk, salt, and pepper in a mixing bowl and whisk well. Stir in mozzarella. Arrange bread slices in the prepared baking pan and pour egg mixture over them, pressing down so bread will absorb liquid.

2. Melt butter in a small skillet over medium heat. Add shallot and cook, stirring frequently, for 3 minutes or until shallot is translucent. Stir shallot, shrimp, corn, and dill into bread mixture.

3. Cover the pan with aluminum foil and bake in the center of the oven for 20 minutes. Remove the foil and bake for an additional 10 minutes or until a toothpick inserted in the center comes out clean and top is lightly browned. Allow to rest for 5 minutes and serve by scooping strata from the pan with a heavy spoon.

Variation: Substitute crab meat or diced lobster for shrimp, and to give the strata a Mexican flavor, substitute jalapeño Jack cheese and chopped cilantro for mozzarella and dill.

 Déjà Two

Author Clifton Fadiman said it best when he described cheese as "milk's leap toward immortality."

Mexican Scrambled Eggs (*Migas*)

Smoky bacon, pieces of crisp tortilla, and vegetables add flavor and texture to this easy breakfast dish.

Active time: 25 minutes

Start to finish: 25 minutes

Each serving has:

598 calories

311 calories from fat

34.5 g fat

12 g saturated fat

32 g protein

44 g carbohydrates

4 (6-in.) corn tortillas

4 slices bacon, cut into 1-inch pieces

3 TB. vegetable oil

½ small red onion, peeled and finely chopped

2 garlic cloves, peeled and minced

1 small jalapeño chili, seeds and ribs removed, finely chopped

½ red bell pepper, seeds and ribs removed, finely chopped

4 ripe plum tomatoes, rinsed, cored, seeded, and coarsely chopped

½ tsp. ground cumin

4 large eggs, lightly beaten

½ cup grated Monterey Jack or mild cheddar cheese

Salt and freshly ground black pepper to taste

Double Feature

This method for making scrambled eggs will produce very light and fluffy eggs, and you can use it for all scrambled dishes. For making scrambled eggs for a crowd, bake the pan, covered with aluminum foil, in a 350°F oven for 15 minutes. Stir, recover the pan, and cook at 10 minute intervals until the eggs reach the proper consistency.

1. Tear tortillas into 1-inch pieces and set aside. Cook bacon in a heavy skillet over medium-high heat, turning occasionally, for 5 to 7 minutes or until bacon is crisp. Remove bacon from the pan with a slotted spoon and drain on paper towels. Discard bacon grease from the skillet.

2. Heat oil in the skillet over medium-high heat. Fry tortilla pieces a handful at a time, turning them frequently, until pale golden, 2 to 3 minutes. Transfer to paper towels to drain.

3. Add onion, garlic, chili, and red bell pepper to the skillet and cook, stirring frequently, for 5 minutes or until onion is soft. Add bacon, tomatoes, and cumin. Cook, stirring occasionally, for 2 to 3 minutes or until tomatoes begin to soften. (You can do this a day in advance and refrigerate, tightly covered. Reheat in the skillet before continuing.)

4. Add tortilla pieces and stir until well combined. Pour eggs over tortilla mixture, stir in cheese, and season to taste with salt and pepper. Reduce the heat to low and cover the pan. Cook for 2 minutes, stir, recover the pan, and cook for an additional 1 to 2 minutes or until eggs are just set and cheese is melted. Serve immediately.

Baked Eggs with Herbed Cheese

This dish is a variation on classic shirred eggs, which are baked with cream and in this case, a bit of herbed cheese.

1 TB. unsalted butter

3 TB. heavy cream

4 large eggs

2 TB. herbed chèvre or Boursin cheese

Salt and freshly ground black pepper to taste

1 TB. chopped fresh chives or parsley

Active time: 5 minutes

Start to finish: 15 minutes

Each serving has:

306 calories

239 calories from fat

26.5 g fat

13.5 g saturated fat

15 g protein

2 g carbohydrates

1. Preheat the oven to 450°F and bring a kettle of water to a boil.

2. Divide butter and cream into the bottoms of 4 (6-ounce) oven-proof ramekins. Break 1 egg into the center of each ramekin and dot top of each egg with ¼ of cheese. Sprinkle eggs with salt and pepper.

3. Arrange ramekins in a baking pan and pour boiling water into the pan so it comes half way up the sides of the ramekins for a *bain marie*. Bake eggs for 7 to 10 minutes or until whites are set. Serve immediately. Garnish with chives or parsley if desired.

Variation: Substitute grated cheddar, dilled Havarti, or jalapeño Jack for cheeses listed.

Duet Dialogue

Bain marie is the French term for a water bath that cooks food gently by surrounding it with simmering water. The water temperature is actually lower than the oven temperature because water only reaches 212°F, so delicate egg dishes and custards set without getting rubbery.

Mexican Fried Eggs with Salsa (*Huevos Rancheros*)

This dish, with fried eggs topping corn tortillas and a spicy tomato sauce, is a hearty way to begin a day.

1 TB. olive oil

1 small onion, peeled and diced

2 garlic cloves, peeled and minced

1 TB. chili powder

1 tsp. ground cumin

½ tsp. dried oregano

1 (8-oz.) can tomato sauce

Salt and cayenne to taste

4 (6-in.) corn tortillas

¾ cup grated Monterey Jack cheese

1 TB. unsalted butter

4 large eggs

Freshly ground black pepper to taste

Active time: 20 minutes

Start to finish: 30 minutes

Each serving has:

615 calories

345 calories from fat

38 g fat

16 g saturated fat

29 g protein

42 g carbohydrates

Double Feature

If your tortillas become hard in the refrigerator, place them in a resealable plastic bag with a damp paper towel. Seal the bag, microwave the tortillas for 20 seconds, and they'll be pliable again.

1. Preheat an oven broiler. Heat olive oil in a heavy 1-quart saucepan over medium-high heat. Add onion and garlic and cook, stirring frequently, for 3 minutes or until onion is translucent. Stir in chili powder, cumin, and oregano. Cook, stirring constantly, for 1 minute.

2. Add tomato sauce and bring to a boil, stirring occasionally. Reduce the heat to low and simmer sauce, uncovered, for 10 minutes, stirring occasionally. Season to taste with salt and cayenne. Keep warm. (You can do this a day in advance and refrigerate, tightly covered. Reheat sauce before continuing.)

3. While sauce is simmering, arrange tortillas on a baking sheet and sprinkle each with Monterey Jack cheese. Broil for 1 to 2 minutes or until cheese melts. Remove the pan from the broiler and set aside.

4. Melt butter in a heavy 10-inch skillet over medium heat. Break eggs into the skillet and season eggs to taste with salt and pepper. Cook eggs to desired doneness.

5. To serve, place 1 egg on each tortilla and top with sauce. Serve immediately.

Variation: Stir bits of fried chorizo, bacon, or ham into sauce; ⅓ cup per person is a good amount.

Smoked Salmon Hash

Salty smoked salmon enlivened with capers, horseradish, and mustard is joined with hash-brown potatoes in this sophisticated hash.

1 TB. unsalted butter

1 TB. olive oil

½ lb. frozen hash-brown potatoes, not thawed

1 large shallot, peeled and finely chopped

¼ lb. smoked salmon, cut into thin strips

1 TB. *capers*, drained and rinsed

3 TB. sour cream

2 tsp. bottled horseradish

2 tsp. Dijon mustard

Salt and freshly ground black pepper to taste

Active time: 10 minutes

Start to finish: 20 minutes

Each serving has:

330 calories

178 calories from fat

20 g fat

8 g saturated fat

15 g protein

25 g carbohydrates

1. Heat butter and olive oil in a large skillet over medium-high heat. Add potatoes and shallots, cover the pan, and cook for 5 minutes. Uncover the pan, turn potatoes and shallots with a metal spatula, and cook for an additional 5 to 10 minutes or until golden brown. While potatoes are cooking, combine smoked salmon, capers, sour cream, horseradish, and mustard in a small mixing bowl.

2. Reduce heat to low and stir in salmon mixture. Cook, stirring gently, for 2 minutes or until heated through. Season to taste with salt and pepper.

Duet Dialogue

Capers are the flower buds of a bush native to the Mediterranean, ranging in size from tiny nonpareil to about the size of your thumbnail. They are dried and then usually packed in brine, which makes them quite salty. Be sure to rinse them before using.

Corned Beef Hash with Baked Eggs

Buying corned beef and mashed potatoes at the supermarket make this hash easy to get on the table.

Active time: 20 minutes
Start to finish: 45 minutes
Each serving has:
598 calories
361 calories from fat
40 g fat
13 g saturated fat
30.5 g protein
29 g carbohydrates

1 TB. unsalted butter

1 TB. vegetable oil

½ sweet onion, such as Bermuda or Vidalia, peeled and diced

½ red bell pepper, seeds and ribs removed, chopped

1 garlic clove, peeled and minced

½ lb. thickly sliced cooked corned beef, coarsely chopped

1 cup mashed potatoes (homemade or purchased from the supermarket's refrigerated aisle)

½ tsp. fresh thyme or pinch dried

Salt and freshly ground black pepper to taste

2 to 4 large eggs

Déjà Two

Hash is a general term for food that is finely chopped. The English word first appeared in the mid-seventeenth century and comes from the French word *hacher*, which means "to chop." Because hash was frequently made with leftovers, inexpensive restaurants became known as "hash houses."

1. Preheat the oven to 400°F. Grease an 8×8-inch baking pan. Heat butter and oil in a large skillet over medium heat. Add onion, red bell pepper, and garlic. Cook, stirring frequently, for 10 minutes or until vegetables are soft. Add corned beef, mashed potatoes, and thyme and mix well. Season to taste with salt and pepper. (You can do this a day in advance and refrigerate, tightly covered. If chilled, add 15 minutes to the initial covered baking.)

2. Spread hash in the prepared baking pan and cover with aluminum foil. Bake for 15 minutes or until hot. Remove the pan from the oven, remove the foil, and create 2 to 4 indentations in the top of hash, evenly spread apart. Break 1 egg into each indentation and sprinkle eggs with salt and pepper. Return the pan to the oven, uncovered, and bake for an additional 10 minutes or until egg whites are set. Serve immediately.

Chapter 4

Soup-er Suppers: One Dish Dinners in a Bowl

In This Chapter

- Soups with chicken and meats
- Seafood stews
- Hearty vegetarian soups

On a chilly night, few foods are as comforting as a big bowl of steaming soup. When the aroma from its broth reaches your nose, the world seems calmer and so do you! And these are the types of soups you'll find when cooking this chapter's recipes.

A bonus is that one can of stock is the perfect volume for a soup for two, and with rare exceptions, all these soups can be on the table within an hour. So while the soup is simmering, you can be relaxing.

Strengthening the Stock

I'm a realist, and that's why these recipes specify a can of stock. While I as a "foodie" might save up chicken bones and vegetables past their prime to simmer stock for hours, I know most cooks wouldn't consider it.

But there is a middle ground if you wish to enrich the flavors of your soups. You can make a large batch and parcel it out for a few different soups, and it only takes 20 minutes!

Double Feature

The flavor and composition of canned stocks varies greatly, with the best known national brands not very high on the list. Whenever possible, buy organic stocks because the sodium content is much lower. And stocks found in whole foods markets usually have a better flavor.

Pour 1 quart canned stock into a large saucepan or stock pot and add 1 small peeled and quartered onion, 1 scrubbed and sliced carrot, 1 rinsed and sliced celery rib, 3 parsley sprigs, 2 thyme sprigs, 2 peeled garlic cloves, 12 black peppercorns, and 1 bay leaf. Bring the mixture to a boil, reduce the heat to low, and simmer for 20 minutes. Then strain the stock, pressing with the back of a spoon to extract as much liquid as possible, and discard the solids.

Once this enriched stock cools, parcel it out by 14½-ounce servings in 1-quart resealable plastic bags and freeze them until you need them.

Sides for Soups

All these soups are a meal in a bowl and quite filling. But the star does need some supporting players.

A crunchy salad of some type and perhaps some sort of bread are the perfect partners, and what's fun is to theme the added attractions to the flavors of the soup. For example, some herbed focaccia and a tossed salad with Italian dressing would work well with a minestrone, while all-American cole slaw and corn bread works well with any chowder.

Mexican Turkey Meatball Soup

Flavorful balls of lean ground turkey with crushed tortilla chips added for texture float in this lusty broth.

Vegetable oil spray

1 (1-oz.) bag tortilla chips

1 large egg, lightly beaten

2 TB. milk

2 garlic cloves, peeled and minced

3 TB. chopped fresh cilantro

1 tsp. ground cumin

½ tsp. dried oregano

½ lb. ground turkey

Salt and freshly ground black pepper to taste

2 TB. olive oil

1 small onion, peeled and diced

1 celery rib, rinsed, trimmed, and sliced

1 carrot, peeled and sliced

1 TB. chili powder

1 (14.5-oz.) can diced tomatoes, undrained

1 (14.5-oz.) can chicken stock

½ cup frozen corn

½ cup frozen peas

Active time: 20 minutes	
Start to finish: 45 minutes	
Each serving has:	
568 calories	
260 calories from fat	
29 g fat	
5 g saturated fat	
37 g protein	
45 g carbohydrates	

1. Preheat the oven to 450°F, cover a baking sheet with aluminum foil, and spray the foil with vegetable oil spray. Place tortilla chips in a heavy resealable plastic bag and crush them with the back of a small skillet. Set aside.

2. Combine egg, milk, 1 garlic clove, 1 tablespoon cilantro, cumin, and oregano in a medium mixing bowl. Whisk well. Add turkey and tortilla chips, season to taste with salt and pepper, and mix well. Form turkey mixture into balls the size of walnuts and arrange them on the prepared pan. Bake turkey balls for 20 minutes or until an instant-read thermometer registers 170°F.

3. While meatballs are baking, heat olive oil in a heavy 2-quart saucepan over medium-high heat. Add onion, celery, carrot, and remaining garlic. Cook, stirring frequently, for 3 minutes or until onion is translucent. Stir in chili powder and cook for 1 minute, stirring constantly. Stir in tomatoes and stock.

4. Bring to a boil and simmer soup, uncovered, for 20 minutes or until vegetables are tender. Add meatballs, corn, and peas to soup along with remaining cilantro and simmer for 5 minutes. Season to taste with salt and pepper and serve immediately. (You can do this up to two days in advance and refrigerate the soup, tightly covered. Reheat over low heat, stirring occasionally, until it comes to a simmer.)

Variation: Substitute beef, pork, or veal for ground turkey.

Double Trouble

Be careful when adding salt to dishes that contain a salted food such as tortilla chips. Chances are the meatball mixture will need very little, if any, salt because the salt from the chips is part of the mixture.

Greek Lemon Egg Soup with Chicken and Orzo (*Avgolemono*)

This is a satiny soup thickened with egg custard in which you'll find cubes of lean chicken, tender pasta, and vegetables.

Active time: 10 minutes

Start to finish: 25 minutes

Each serving has:

313 calories

58 calories from fat

6.5 g fat

2 g saturated fat

34 g protein

28.5 g carbohydrates

1 (6- to 8-oz.) boneless, skinless chicken breast

1 (14.5-oz.) can chicken stock

⅓ cup orzo

1 small carrot, peeled and thinly sliced

1 celery rib, rinsed, trimmed, and thinly sliced

1 large egg

1 large egg yolk

¼ cup freshly squeezed lemon juice

Salt and freshly ground black pepper to taste

1. Rinse chicken and pat dry with paper towels. Trim chicken of all visible fat and cut into ½-inch cubes.

2. Combine stock, chicken, orzo, carrot, and celery in a heavy 2-quart sauce pan. Bring to a boil over high heat, stirring occasionally. Reduce the heat to low and simmer soup, covered, for 10 to 12 minutes or until orzo is tender.

3. While soup is simmering, whisk together egg, egg yolk, and lemon juice. When orzo is tender, remove soup from the heat and stir constantly for 1 minute. Soup should no longer be bubbling at all. Stir in lemon mixture, cover the pan, and allow soup to sit for 5 minutes to thicken.

4. Season to taste with salt and pepper and serve immediately. (You can do this up to two days in advance and refrigerate soup, tightly covered. Reheat over low heat, stirring frequently, until it is hot. Do not let soup boil.)

Double Feature

The reason for stirring the liquid cool before adding the egg is to prevent the egg from curdling and turning the soup into a Greek version of Chinese Egg Drop Soup. Eggs thicken at 180°F while the boiling point of liquid is 212°F. That's why you have to stir it.

Asian Cream of Squash Soup with Chicken

Chinese seasonings and heady bourbon flavor this thick and creamy soup.

1 (6 to 8-oz.) boneless, skinless chicken breast

1 (10-oz.) pkg. frozen winter squash, thawed

1 (14.5-oz.) can chicken stock

2 TB. *hoisin sauce*

1 TB. bourbon

½ tsp. Chinese five-spice powder

2 tsp. balsamic vinegar

½ cup half-and-half

Salt and freshly ground black pepper to taste

Active time: 10 minutes
Start to finish: 25 minutes
Each serving has:
341 calories
79 calories from fat
9 g fat
5 g saturated fat
30 g protein
33 g carbohydrates

1. Rinse chicken and pat dry with paper towels. Trim all visible fat from chicken and cut into ½-inch cubes.

2. Combine squash, stock, chicken, hoisin sauce, bourbon, five-spice powder, and balsamic vinegar in a heavy 2-quart saucepan and stir well. Bring to a boil over medium-high heat, stirring occasionally.

2. Reduce heat to low and cook soup uncovered for 10 minutes. Stir in half-and-half and simmer for an additional 5 minutes. Season to taste with salt and pepper. Serve immediately. (You can do this up to two days in advance and refrigerate soup, tightly covered. Reheat over low heat, stirring occasionally, until it comes to a simmer.)

Duet Dialogue

Hoisin sauce (pronounced *hoy-ZAN*) is a soybean-based thick sauce with a sweet and spicy flavor. It's used in many Chinese dishes and also includes garlic, chili peppers, and some form of sugar or honey.

Nantucket Clam Chowder

This recipe won contests when I was a caterer on Nantucket. It contains celery and herbs in addition to the usual potatoes and onions.

Active time: 20 minutes
Start to finish: 30 minutes
Each serving has:
615 calories
179 calories from fat
20 g fat
10 g saturated fat
49 g protein
58 g carbohydrates

½ lb. red-skinned potatoes, scrubbed and cut into ½-inch dice

1 celery rib, rinsed, trimmed, and diced

1 (8-oz.) bottle clam juice

1 pt. fresh minced clams, drained with all clam juice reserved

2 TB. chopped fresh parsley

2 tsp. fresh thyme or ½ tsp. dried

1 bay leaf

3 TB. unsalted butter

1 onion, peeled and diced

2 TB. all-purpose flour

1 cup whole milk or half-and-half

Salt and freshly ground black pepper to taste

1. Combine potatoes, celery, bottled clam juice, reserved clam juice, parsley, thyme, and bay leaf in a heavy 2-quart saucepan. Bring to a boil over high heat. Reduce the heat to medium and cook for 15 minutes or until potatoes are tender and liquid is reduced by half.

2. While potatoes are boiling, melt butter in a small saucepan over medium heat. Add onion and cook, stirring frequently, for 5 minutes or until onion is soft. Reduce the heat to low. Stir in flour and cook for 2 minutes, stirring constantly. Whisk in milk and bring to a boil over medium heat, stirring constantly. Simmer for 2 minutes. Set aside until potatoes are tender.

3. Add cream mixture to potato mixture and bring to a boil over medium heat. Stir in clams and simmer for 5 minutes, stirring occasionally. Season to taste with salt and pepper and serve immediately. (You can do this up to two days in advance and refrigerate soup, tightly covered. Reheat over low heat, stirring occasionally, until it comes to a simmer.)

Variation: Many versions of chowder include either corn kernels, crisp crumbled bacon, or both. For this size batch, ½ cup corn kernels and 3 tablespoons crumbed bacon would be good additions.

Déjà Two

In Melville's *Moby Dick,* Ishmael and Queequeg land on Nantucket and are sent to Hosea Hussey's Try Pots Inn. The name of the inn comes from the iron cauldrons used to melt blubber into whale oil. Melville writes that the two had "chowder for breakfast, chowder for dinner, and chowder for supper."

Spanish Seafood Soup with Garlicky Mayonnaise (*Caldo de Perro*)

Healthful Swiss chard adds color and texture to this vibrantly flavored soup topped with a garlicky sauce.

2 TB. olive oil

1 onion, peeled and diced

4 garlic cloves, peeled and minced

2 cups fish stock or bottled clam juice

⅓ cup dry white wine

2 tsp. freshly squeezed lemon juice

¼ lb. red-skinned potatoes, scrubbed and cut into ½-inch dice

1 TB. chopped fresh parsley

2 tsp. fresh thyme or ½ tsp. dried

1 bay leaf

¼ cup mayonnaise

½ tsp. grated lemon zest

¼ lb. Swiss chard, rinsed, stemmed, and sliced

½ lb. halibut, cod, or monkfish fillet, rinsed and cut into 1-inch cubes

Salt and freshly ground black pepper to taste

Active time: 20 minutes

Start to finish: 35 minutes

Each serving has:

604 calories

363 calories from fat

40 g fat

7 g saturated fat

32 g protein

21 g carbohydrates

1. Heat olive oil in a heavy 2-quart saucepan over medium-high heat. Add onion and 2 garlic cloves and cook, stirring frequently, for 3 minutes or until onion is translucent. Add fish stock, wine, lemon juice, potatoes, parsley, thyme, and bay leaf. Bring to a boil and simmer, uncovered, for 15 minutes or until potatoes are tender.

2. While soup is simmering, combine remaining garlic, mayonnaise, and lemon zest in a small bowl. Stir well and refrigerate until ready to serve.

3. Add Swiss chard and halibut to soup. Bring back to a boil and simmer, covered, for 3 minutes. Remove and discard bay leaf and season to taste with salt and pepper. Serve immediately and pass sauce separately. (You can do this up to two days in advance and refrigerate soup, tightly covered. Reheat over low heat, stirring occasionally, until it comes to a simmer.)

Double Trouble

Because all fish and seafood cooks very quickly using any cooking method, overcooking is a great danger. While a general rule for cooking fish is 10 minutes per 1 inch of thickness, this rule does not apply to small pieces in stews. They need far less time.

Beef and Barley Soup with Two Mushrooms

Aromatic wild mushrooms are joined with fresh mushrooms in this hearty soup perfect for a cold winter evening.

Active time: 20 minutes

Start to finish: 1 hour

Each serving has:

623 calories

300 calories from fat

33 g fat

7 g saturated fat

40 g protein

47 g carbohydrates

2 TB. finely chopped dried porcini mushrooms	1 small carrot, peeled and diced
½ cup boiling water	1 garlic clove, peeled and minced
½ lb. beef, chuck or round	1 (10-oz.) pkg. sliced fresh mushrooms, rinsed
Salt and freshly ground black pepper to taste	1 (14.5-oz.) can beef stock
3 TB. olive oil	½ tsp. dried thyme
1 onion, peeled and diced	⅓ cup pearl barley
1 celery rib, rinsed, trimmed, and sliced	2 TB. chopped fresh parsley

Double Feature

A French press coffee maker has a second life for rehydrating mushrooms or any ingredient. The top of the pot keeps the food submerged, and the screen that keeps coffee grounds from spilling into cups strains the soaking liquid.

1. Soak mushrooms in boiling water for 10 minutes, pushing them down into water with the back of a spoon. Drain mushrooms, reserving soaking liquid. Strain soaking liquid through a sieve or coffee filter, and set aside. Rinse beef and pat dry with paper towels. Trim beef of all visible fat, cut beef into ½-inch dice, and sprinkle with salt and pepper.

2. Heat 2 tablespoons olive oil in a heavy 2-quart saucepan over medium-high heat. Add beef and cook, stirring frequently, for 3 minutes or until beef is no longer pink. Remove beef from the pan with a slotted spoon and set aside.

3. Heat remaining 1 tablespoon olive oil in the pan. Add onion, celery, carrot, garlic, and fresh mushrooms. Cook, stirring frequently, for 5 minutes or until mushrooms are soft.

3. Add beef, dried mushrooms, soaking liquid, stock, thyme, and barley to the pan. Bring to a boil, reduce the heat to low, cover the pan, and simmer soup, stirring occasionally, for 1 hour until beef is tender.

4. Stir in parsley and season soup to taste with salt and pepper. Serve immediately. (You can do this up to two days in advance and refrigerate, tightly covered. Reheat over low heat, stirring occasionally, until soup comes to a simmer.)

Variation: Use chicken and chicken stock in place of beef and beef stock.

Chili with Beans

There's nothing like a bowl of chili, redolent with spices and tomatoes, and this one fits the bill!

2 TB. vegetable oil

½ lb. lean ground beef

1 medium onion, peeled and diced

1 garlic clove, peeled and minced

1 small jalapeño chili, seeds and ribs removed, finely chopped

½ green bell pepper, seeds and ribs removed, and finely chopped

2 TB. *chili powder*

2 tsp. ground cumin

1 (14.5-oz.) can diced tomatoes, undrained

1 (8-oz.) can tomato sauce

1 (15-oz.) can red kidney beans, drained and rinsed

Salt and cayenne to taste

Condiments:

Sour cream

Chopped onion

Grated Monterey Jack cheese

Active time: 15 minutes
Start to finish: 1 hour
Each serving has:
656 calories
250 calories from fat
28 g fat
6.5 g saturated fat
38 g protein
66 g carbohydrates

1. Heat 1 tablespoon oil in a medium skillet over medium-high heat. Add ground beef and cook, breaking up lumps with a fork, for 3 to 5 minutes or until beef is browned. Transfer beef with a slotted spoon to a heavy 2-quart saucepan and discard grease from the skillet.

2. Heat remaining 1 tablespoon oil over medium-high heat and add onion, garlic, jalapeño, and green bell pepper. Cook, stirring frequently, for 3 minutes or until onion is translucent. Stir in chili powder and cumin. Cook for 1 minute, stirring constantly. Scrape mixture into the saucepan with beef and stir in tomatoes, tomato sauce, and kidney beans. Season to taste with salt and cayenne.

3. Bring to a boil over medium heat, stirring occasionally. Simmer chili, partially covered, stirring occasionally, for 45 minutes or until thickened. Serve immediately, passing sour cream, onion, and cheese separately. (You can do this up to two days in advance and refrigerate the soup, tightly covered. Reheat over low heat, stirring occasionally, until it comes to a simmer.)

Variation: Use ground turkey in place of ground beef without changing the cooking time.

Duet Dialogue

Chili powder is really a blend of herbs and spices, and if you make it yourself, you can personalize the taste. Use ground red chilies and ground cumin for the base. Then add as much paprika, ground coriander, cayenne pepper, and oregano as you like. Some brands also include garlic powder and onion powder.

Hot and Sour Soup with Pork

Slivers of exotic wild mushrooms and feathery eggs join lean pork in a fiery broth that's a classic in Szechwan cooking.

Active time: 20 minutes

Start to finish: 40 minutes

Each serving has:

395 calories

204 calories from fat

23 g fat

4 g saturated fat

29 g protein

15 g carbohydrates

⅓ lb. boneless pork chops

⅓ cup shiitake mushrooms

½ cup boiling water

1 TB. vegetable oil

1 TB. Asian sesame oil

3 scallions, rinsed, trimmed, and thinly sliced

2 garlic cloves, peeled and minced

1 (14.5-oz.) can chicken stock

2 TB. soy sauce

2 TB. rice vinegar

1 TB. dry sherry

¼ to ½ tsp. freshly ground black pepper

¼ lb. firm *tofu*, drained, rinsed, and cut into ½-inch cubes

1 TB. cornstarch

2 TB. cold water

1 large egg, lightly beaten

Salt to taste

1. Rinse pork and pat dry with paper towels. Trim off all visible fat and cut pork into thin slices against the grain. Combine mushrooms and boiling water, pushing mushrooms into water. Soak for 10 minutes. Then drain mushrooms, reserving soaking liquid. Discard stems and slice mushrooms thinly.

2. While mushrooms are soaking, heat vegetable oil and sesame oil in a heavy 2-quart saucepan over medium-high heat. Add pork and cook, stirring frequently, for 3 minutes or until pork is browned. Add scallions and garlic and cook, stirring frequently, for 1 minute.

3. Stir in stock, soy sauce, vinegar, sherry, and pepper. Bring to a boil, and simmer soup, covered, for 15 minutes. Add mushrooms, reserved soaking liquid, and tofu. Simmer for 5 minutes.

4. Combine cornstarch and cold water in a small bowl. Add to soup and simmer for 2 minutes or until soup lightly thickens. Slowly add egg while stirring. Simmer 1 minute, season to taste with salt and pepper, and serve immediately. (You can do this up to two days in advance and refrigerate soup, tightly covered. Reheat over low heat, stirring occasionally, until it comes to a simmer.)

Duet Dialogue

Tofu, sometimes called bean curd, is a white custard-like food made in a manner similar to that of cheese. Iron-rich soy milk is curdled and then the curds are pressed to extract the whey. The texture depends on how much whey is removed and can range from very soft (silken) to hard.

Moroccan Lamb and Garbanzo Bean Soup

Aromatic seasonings like cumin and coriander flavor this rich soup that contains tomatoes and other vegetables.

½ lb. boneless leg of lamb

2 TB. olive oil

1 onion, peeled and diced

2 garlic cloves, peeled and minced

1 small carrot, peeled and sliced

½ tsp. ground coriander

½ tsp. ground cumin

1 (14.5-oz.) can beef stock

2 ripe plum tomatoes, rinsed, cored, seeded, and chopped

1 (15-oz.) can garbanzo beans, drained and rinsed

½ cup water

2 TB. freshly squeezed lemon juice

2 TB. chopped fresh parsley

Salt and freshly ground black pepper to taste

Active time: 15 minutes	
Start to finish: 1 hour	
Each serving has:	
624 calories	
203 calories from fat	
22.5 g fat	
5 g saturated fat	
40 g protein	
67 g carbohydrates	

1. Rinse lamb and pat dry with paper towels. Trim all visible fat and dice lamb into ½-inch pieces.

2. Heat olive oil in a heavy 2-quart saucepan over medium-high heat. Add lamb and cook, stirring occasionally, for 5 minutes or until lamb is browned. Remove lamb from the pan with a slotted spoon and set aside.

3. Add onion, garlic, and carrot to the pan and cook, stirring occasionally, for 3 minutes or until onion is translucent. Stir in coriander and cumin. Cook, stirring constantly, for 1 minute.

4. Return lamb to the pan and stir in stock, tomatoes, and half of garbanzo beans. Bring to a boil over medium heat, stirring occasionally.

5. While soup begins to simmer, combine reserved garbanzo beans, water, and lemon juice in a blender or food processor fitted with a steel blade. Purée until smooth. Stir mixture into soup.

6. Simmer soup over low heat, covered, for 45 minutes or until lamb is tender. Stir in parsley, season to taste with salt and pepper, and serve immediately. (You can do this up to two days in advance and refrigerate soup, tightly covered. Reheat over low heat, stirring occasionally, until it comes to a simmer.)

Variation: Substitute beef for lamb. Add 15 minutes to the cooking time if using beef.

Déjà Two

There's an old Spanish proverb: "Of soup and love, the first is best."

Tuscan White Bean Soup with Sausage

The flavors from the sausage are infused into this thick and hearty soup that also contains Swiss chard.

Active time: 20 minutes

Start to finish: 45 minutes

Each serving has:

761 calories

354 calories from fat

39 g fat

15 g saturated fat

41 g protein

62 g carbohydrates

½ lb. bulk Italian sausage (sweet or hot)

1 onion, peeled and diced

2 garlic cloves, peeled and minced

2 celery ribs, rinsed, trimmed, and diced

1 carrot, peeled and diced

1 (14.5-oz.) can chicken stock

1 (15-oz.) can white beans, drained and rinsed

2 TB. chopped fresh parsley

½ tsp. dried thyme

1 small bay leaf

½ cup water

¼ lb. Swiss chard, rinsed, stemmed, and thinly sliced

¼ cup freshly grated Parmesan cheese

Salt and freshly ground black pepper to taste

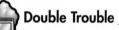 **Double Trouble**

If you can't find bulk sausage, you can always find sausage links at the market, but push the sausage out of the casings before browning it. You'll think you're chewing rubber bands if the casings end up in the soup.

1. Place a heavy 2-quart saucepan over medium-high heat. Add sausage, breaking up lumps with a fork. Cook, stirring occasionally, for 3 minutes or until sausage is browned and no longer pink. Remove sausage from the pan with a slotted spoon and set aside. Discard all but 1 tablespoon sausage fat from the pan.

2. Add onion, garlic, celery, and carrot to the pan. Cook, stirring occasionally, for 3 minutes or until onion is translucent. Add stock, ½ of beans, parsley, thyme, and bay leaf to the pan. Bring to a boil over medium heat and simmer, partially covered, for 20 minutes or until carrots are soft.

3. While soup begins simmering, combine reserved beans and water in a blender or food processor fitted with a steel blade. Purée until smooth. Stir mixture into soup.

4. Add Swiss chard to soup and simmer for 5 minutes. Remove and discard bay leaf and stir in Parmesan cheese. Season to taste with salt and pepper and serve immediately. (You can do this up to two days in advance and refrigerate soup, tightly covered. Reheat over low heat, stirring occasionally, until it comes to a simmer.)

Southwest Sweet Potato and Corn Chowder

Fiery chipotle chilies add the Hispanic accent to this creamy chowder.

2 TB. olive oil

½ red bell pepper, seeds and ribs removed, finely diced

1 small onion, peeled and diced

1 garlic clove, peeled and minced

1 large sweet potato or yam (12-oz.), peeled and cut into ½-inch dice

1 (14.5-oz.) can vegetable stock or chicken stock

2 canned *chipotle chilies* in adobo sauce, finely chopped

2 tsp. adobo sauce

1 (8-oz.) can creamed corn

½ cup frozen corn

1 cup half-and-half

Salt and freshly ground black pepper to taste

Active time: 15 minutes

Start to finish: 30 minutes

Each serving has:

508 calories

257 calories from fat

29 g fat

11 g saturated fat

12 g protein

58 g carbohydrates

1. Heat olive oil in a heavy 2-quart saucepan over medium-high heat. Add red bell pepper, onion, and garlic. Cook, stirring frequently, for 3 minutes or until onion is translucent.

2. Add sweet potato, stock, chipotle chilies, and adobo sauce to the pan. Bring to a boil over high heat, reduce the heat to a simmer, and cook chowder uncovered, stirring occasionally, for 12 to 15 minutes or until sweet potato is soft.

3. Stir creamed corn, corn, and half-and-half into chowder, bring back to a boil, and simmer for 3 minutes. Season to taste with salt and pepper, and serve immediately. (You can do this up to two days in advance and refrigerate soup, tightly covered. Reheat over low heat, stirring occasionally, until it comes to a simmer.)

Duet Dialogue

Chipotle (pronounced chee-POOT-lay) are dried jalapeño chilies that have then been smoked. They are canned in a spicy sauce similar to a hot red pepper sauce made from chilies, vinegar, and salt.

Vegetarian Minestrone with Pasta

You'll be enjoying a cornucopia of vegetables as well as pasta in this herbed tomato broth.

Active time: 15 minutes

Start to finish: 45 minutes

Each serving has:

360 calories

157 calories from fat

17.5 g fat

4 g saturated fat

14 g protein

41 g carbohydrates

2 TB. olive oil

1 small onion, peeled and diced

1 celery rib, rinsed, trimmed, and diced

1 small carrot, peeled and diced

1 garlic clove, peeled and minced

1 (14.5-oz.) can vegetable stock or chicken stock

1 (8-oz.) can tomato sauce

1 TB. chopped fresh parsley

½ tsp. dried oregano

½ tsp. dried thyme

1 medium zucchini, trimmed and sliced

1 medium yellow squash, trimmed and sliced

¼ cup orzo or other small pasta

¼ cup freshly grated Parmesan cheese

Salt and freshly ground black pepper to taste

Double Feature

Save the rinds from Parmesan cheese and use them for flavoring dishes such as soups and sauces. The rind will not melt into the dishes, but it will impart flavor. Remove and discard it before serving.

1. Heat olive oil in a heavy 2-quart saucepan over medium-high heat. Add onion, celery, carrot, and garlic. Cook, stirring frequently, for 3 minutes or until onion is translucent. Add stock, tomato sauce, parsley, oregano, and thyme.

2. Bring to a boil, reduce the heat to low, and cook, partially covered, for 15 minutes. Add zucchini, yellow squash, and orzo. Simmer for an additional 15 minutes or until vegetables are tender.

3. Stir in Parmesan cheese and season to taste with salt and pepper. Serve immediately. (You can do this up to two days in advance and refrigerate soup, tightly covered. Reheat over low heat, stirring occasionally, until it comes to a simmer.)

Salad Daze: Entrée Salads for All Seasons

In This Chapter

◆ Stir-fried salads with fruits

◆ Cold salads with hot proteins

◆ Salads with distinguished dressings

One category of foods that continues to grow in popularity is the entrée salad, especially for the warm summer months. These visually attractive and colorful mixtures of raw lettuces and other greens with cooked chicken, seafood, or meats are refreshing as well as healthful to eat, and this chapter gives you the recipes to make them from.

Entrée salads are a great way to ensure you're getting all nine daily servings of fruits and vegetables into your diet. And they can be on the table in a matter of minutes.

Learning Lettuce

We are long past the days when salad meant a wedge of iceberg lettuce. The produce section of most supermarkets is expanding daily with options. Not only will you find a wide range of green hues, but also reds, whites, and even dots of color from edible flowers. Here's a guide to salad greens:

◆ Arugula: Small, tender, and pungent, the elongated, smooth, dark green leaves have fairly long stems and grow in small clusters. It is excellent when combined with sweet or bitter greens, adding a decidedly spicy taste.

◆ Belgian endive: The spear-shaped leaves form a small, compact head. They're pale green, almost white, with slightly ruffled, pale yellow edges. The texture is crisp and juicy, the flavor pleasantly bitter.

◆ Bibb: This small version of Boston lettuce has loosely furled, green leaves that are often darker and have a crunchier texture. Mild dressings complement its delicate, sweet flavor.

◆ Boston or butter: Its moderately sized, loosely furled leaves form a tight core. They're pale green (almost white near the center rib), soft, and delicate.

◆ Curly endive: A type of chicory, it has large, lacy (almost prickly), dark green outer leaves and tender, pale green inner ones. The outer leaves often are blanched and served, warm or cold, with olive oil and lemon juice or vinegar. Use the inner leaves in salads.

◆ Escarole: Also a member of the chicory family this large head has dark green outer leaves that are loosely packed and slightly furled. It has a tender, pale green inner heart. The flavor is bitter with a slightly sweet edge.

◆ Frisée: This is the mildest of the chicory family and has pale green, slender curly leaves with the heart almost a yellowish-white.

◆ Iceberg: This remains the largest selling salad green in the United States. It's appreciated primarily for its crunchy texture, making it a nice addition to a salad with arugula, escarole, or chicory.

◆ Leaf or red leaf: Its frilly-edged leaves are delicate in texture and flavor. Available in green and red-tipped types. Leaf lettuces are best in a mixed salad.

◆ Mâche (corn salad): Mâche is a dark green, delicate cluster of leaves that grows from a small center stem. This mild and sweet green is a true specialty item—expensive and very perishable.

◆ Oakleaf: Its large leaves resemble those of an oak and are arranged loosely around a central core. It is available in a red leaf (also called ruby) and pale green leaf.

◆ Radicchio: Developed in Italy, it is a member of the chicory family. The head ranges from the size of a golf ball to a grapefruit. The beautifully veined rather bitter leaves are any shade from bright red to dark maroon.

◆ Romaine: Also called Cos (after the Greek island where it originated), it has crisp, oblong leaves that are dark green with a thick white rib down the center. The inner leaves usually are pale yellow-green and more tender than the outer ones. Its flavor is a little more pronounced than those of other mild greens.

◆ Watercress: A member of the cabbage family, its peppery-flavored sprigs have 5- to-6-inch crisp, succulent stems with tender, green leaves.

Other Options

Although these vegetables aren't part of the list of lettuces, they are used in salads. Here's some information on additional ingredients you can add to the salad bowl:

◆ Bean Sprouts: Look for pale, crisp sprouts 1½-to 2-inches long with moist and tender tips. Generally, the shorter the sprout, the more tender it will be.

◆ Bok choy: This Asian cabbage comes both in large bunches and tiny baby varieties. It resembles celery more than green cabbage because the ribs are attached at the base as a stalk. The ribs are snowy white with bright deep green leaves, and it has a delicate flavor. Use both the ribs and leaves.

◆ Napa (Chinese) cabbage: This long, light green cabbage has large ribbed leaves and a crinkly texture. Napa cabbage has a delicate, almost sweet taste.

◆ Spinach: Spinach, with its richly toned dark green leaves and slightly bitter flavor, is one of the most versatile vegetables because it can be eaten raw or cooked. Baby spinach leaves are preferable for salads because they're more tender.

Stir-Fried Chicken and Papaya Salad

Creamy avocado and luscious papaya are joined with stir-fried chicken in dressing that contains sunny orange juice.

Active time: 20 minutes

Start to finish: 20 minutes

Each serving has:

929 calories

620 calories from fat

69 g fat

10 g saturated fat

47 g protein

41 g carbohydrates

Double Feature

Always add granular seasonings like salt or sugar to a salad dressing before adding the oil. These ingredients dissolve in liquid but not in oil.

2 (6-oz.) boneless skinless chicken breast halves

1 navel orange

2 TB. sesame seeds

1 shallot, peeled

1 garlic clove, peeled

2 TB. sherry vinegar

2 tsp. fresh ginger, peeled and sliced

Salt and freshly ground black pepper to taste

½ cup vegetable oil

1 head Boston lettuce, rinsed, dried, and broken into 1-inch pieces

1 ripe avocado, peeled and cut into ¼-inch slices

1 ripe papaya, peeled, seeds removed thinly sliced

1 red bell pepper, seeds and ribs removed and thinly sliced

1 TB. soy sauce

1. Rinse chicken and pat dry with paper towels. Trim all fat and slice chicken into ¼-inch slices against the grain. Cut all rind and white pith off orange and then cut between sections to free orange segments from membranes.

2. Place sesame seeds in a dry medium skillet. Toast seeds over medium heat for 2 minutes or until lightly browned and fragrant. Remove seeds from the skillet and set aside.

3. Place orange segments, shallot, garlic, sherry vinegar, ginger, salt, and pepper in a blender or food processor fitted with a steel blade. Purée until smooth. Add ⅓ cup vegetable oil and blend again. Set aside. Arrange lettuce, avocado, and papaya on two dinner plates.

4. Add remaining oil to the skillet and heat it over medium-high heat. Add chicken and red bell pepper and cook, stirring constantly, for 3 minutes or until chicken is cooked through and no longer pink. Add soy sauce to the skillet and stir well. Turn off heat and add dressing to the skillet. Stir to warm dressing, but do not let mixture boil.

5. Mound chicken mixture on top of greens and fruits and sprinkle with sesame seeds. Serve immediately.

Variation: Instead of chicken, substitute ½ pound extra large (16 to 20 per pound) shrimp, peeled and deveined.

Chicken Salad with Fennel and Oranges

Oranges and anise-flavor fennel are a classic Italian salad, and they're joined with grilled chicken for this salad.

2 (6-oz.) boneless, skinless chicken breast halves

1 small fennel bulb

¾ cup freshly squeezed orange juice

2 garlic cloves, peeled and minced

Salt and freshly ground black pepper to taste

½ cup olive oil

1 TB. dry Marsala wine

1 romaine heart, rinsed, dried, and sliced

1 navel orange, peeled and sliced

2 shallots, peeled and chopped

2 TB. vegetable oil

Active time: 20 minutes

Start to finish: 50 minutes, including 30 minutes for marinating

Each serving has:

661 calories

393 calories from fat

44 g fat

6 g saturated fat

43 g protein

27 g carbohydrates

---

1. Rinse chicken and pat dry with paper towels. Trim fat and cut chicken into thin strips 2 inches long and 1 inch wide. Rinse, trim, and discard stem end and green stalks from fennel bulb. Cut bulb in half, remove and discard core. Slice bulb thinly and set aside.

2. Combine orange juice, garlic, salt, and pepper in a jar with a tight-fitting lid. Shake well. Add olive oil and shake well again. Pour half of dressing into a heavy resealable plastic bag. Add chicken and marinate at room temperature for 30 minutes, turning the bag occasionally. Add wine to remaining dressing and set aside.

3. Divide romaine between two plates and arrange orange and fennel slices on top. Scatter shallots on top of all.

4. Heat vegetable oil in a medium heavy skillet over medium-high heat. Drain chicken from marinade and pat dry on paper towels. Discard marinade. Cook chicken, stirring constantly, for 3 minutes or until chicken is cooked through and no longer pink. Divide chicken between two plates, *drizzle* salad with remaining dressing, and serve immediately.

Variation: Substitute ½ pound extra large (16 to 20 per pound) shrimp, peeled and deveined, or ½ pound pork tenderloin, thinly sliced, for chicken.

Duet Dialogue

To **drizzle** is to pour a liquid very slowly in a fine stream over food. Salad dressings are drizzled and often glazes are drizzled over cakes as decoration.

Asian Chicken Salad

Sharp mustard and heady sesame oil flavor the dressing for this Asian salad using leftover chicken.

Active time: 15 minutes

Start to finish: 15 minutes

Each serving has:

355 calories

164 calories from fat

18 g fat

3 g saturated fat

37 g protein

11 g carbohydrates

1 medium cucumber

2 TB. soy sauce

2 TB. rice vinegar

2 TB. vegetable oil

1 TB. Asian sesame oil

1 TB. Dijon mustard

1 TB. grated fresh ginger

¼ tsp. dried hot red pepper flakes

1½ cups cooked chicken, coarsely shredded

2 cups shredded Napa cabbage

3 scallions, trimmed and finely chopped

¼ cup chopped fresh cilantro

1. Peel cucumber and halve lengthwise. Discard seeds, cut each half in half, and slice thinly. Set aside.

2. Combine soy sauce, vinegar, vegetable oil, sesame oil, Dijon mustard, ginger, and red pepper flakes in a jar with a tight-fitting lid. Shake well and set aside.

3. Combine chicken, cabbage, cucumber, scallions, and cilantro in a large mixing bowl. Toss salad with dressing and serve immediately.

Variation: Substitute shredded cooked beef or pork for chicken.

Double Feature

Many a cook has suffered a scraped knuckle when grating fresh ginger. A solution to this problem is to peel only a small portion of the rhizome, and then hold on to the unpeeled portion as a handle.

Warm Shrimp and Fruit Salad

The contrast between warm shrimp and refreshing fruits make this salad special.

1 bunch mâche or watercress, rinsed, dried, and stemmed

1 cup sliced romaine, rinsed and dried

1 ripe avocado, peeled and cut into ¼-inch slices

1 navel orange, peeled and sliced

1 mango, peeled and thinly sliced

2 TB. freshly squeezed lime juice

2 TB. chopped fresh cilantro

Salt and freshly ground black pepper to taste

⅓ cup extra-virgin olive oil

½ lb. extra large (16 to 20 per lb.) raw shrimp, peeled and deveined

> **Active time:** 15 minutes
>
> **Start to finish:** 15 minutes
>
> **Each serving has:**
>
> 643 calories
>
> 422 calories from fat
>
> 47 g fat
>
> 7 g saturated fat
>
> 27 g protein
>
> 37 g carbohydrates

1. Toss mâche and romaine together and divide mixture onto two plates. Arrange avocado, orange, and mango on top of greens.

2. Combine lime juice, cilantro, salt, and pepper in a jar with a tight-fitting lid. Shake well, add ¼ cup olive oil, and shake well again. Set aside.

3. Heat remaining olive oil in a medium skillet over medium-high heat. Add shrimp and cook, stirring frequently, for 3 minutes or until shrimp are bright red. Turn off the heat, add dressing, and allow dressing to warm.

4. Spoon shrimp onto the plates with a slotted spoon and drizzle dressing over all. Serve immediately.

Variation: Substitute bay scallops, sea scallops cut into quarters, or 1-inch cubes of a firm-fleshed white fish like cod or halibut for shrimp.

> **Double Trouble**
>
> While you want a salad dressing on a warm salad to be warmed, it shouldn't come to a boil. Not only will the dressing, which you've just shaken to emulsify, separate, but you'll also be over-cooking the food it's on.

Thai Shrimp Salad

This authentic Thai recipes deliver quite a spicy flavor from its combination of lemongrass, chilies, and basil.

Active time: 20 minutes

Start to finish: 20 minutes

Each serving has:

395 calories

191 calories from fat

21 g fat

3 g saturated fat

28 g protein

27 g carbohydrates

1 small fresh *lemongrass* stalk

1 lime

3 TB. freshly squeezed lime juice

2 scallions, rinsed, trimmed, and finely chopped

1 fresh serrano chili, stem discarded, finely chopped

1 TB. Asian fish sauce (*nam pla*)

1 TB. granulated sugar

Salt and freshly ground black pepper to taste

3 TB. vegetable oil

1 TB. Asian sesame oil

½ lb. extra large (16 to 20 per lb.) cooked shrimp, peeled and deveined

2 cups baby spinach leaves, rinsed and dried

1 ripe beefsteak tomato, rinsed, cored, and cut into 1-inch wedges

1 small cucumber, peeled and thinly sliced

1 cup bean sprouts, rinsed

½ cup loosely packed fresh Thai basil leaves

¼ cup loosely packed fresh cilantro leaves

Duet Dialogue

Lemongrass looks like a tan, dried-out scallion. This herb, used extensively in Thai and Vietnamese cooking, contains citral, an oil also found in lemon zest. This oil gives lemongrass its characteristic lemony flavor and fragrance.

1. Trim lemongrass to 3 inches and discard tough outer leaves. Finely chop remaining bulb. Cut peel and white pith from lime with a sharp knife and discard. Cut lime segments free from membranes, then finely chop segments. Combine chopped lime, minced lemongrass, lime juice, scallions, serrano chili, fish sauce, sugar, salt, and pepper in a jar with a tight-fitting lid. Shake well. Add vegetable oil and sesame oil and shake well again. Set aside.

2. Combine shrimp, spinach, tomato, cucumber, bean sprouts, basil, and cilantro in a large mixing bowl. Toss with dressing and serve immediately.

Variation: Substitute diced cooked chicken or turkey for shrimp.

Grilled Tuna Salade Niçoise

This is a salad that includes green beans, tomatoes, potatoes, hard-cooked eggs, and seared fresh tuna.

6 small (1- to 2-inch) new potatoes, scrubbed and halved

2 TB. red wine vinegar

1 shallot, peeled and minced

1 tsp. Dijon mustard

1 garlic clove, peeled and minced

½ tsp. anchovy paste

1 tsp. fresh thyme or ¼ tsp. dried

1 TB. chopped fresh basil or 1 tsp. dried

Salt and freshly ground black pepper to taste

⅓ cup extra-virgin olive oil

¼ lb. fresh green beans, rinsed and trimmed

2 (6- to 8-oz.) tuna steaks, rinsed and patted dry with paper towels

Vegetable oil for brushing

2 cups sliced romaine, rinsed and dried

⅔ cup cherry tomatoes, rinsed

¼ cup Niçoise or other small brine-cured black olives

2 hard-cooked large eggs, peeled and quartered

1 TB. capers, drained and rinsed

2 TB. chopped fresh parsley

Active time: 40 minutes
Start to finish: 45 minutes
Each serving has:
768 calories
260 calories from fat
29 g fat
5 g saturated fat
60 g protein
69 g carbohydrates

1. Place potatoes in a heavy 2-quart saucepan and cover with cold water. Add salt to water and bring to a boil over high heat. Cook potatoes uncovered for 10 to 12 minutes or until tender when pierced with the tip of a paring knife. Combine vinegar, shallot, mustard, garlic, anchovy paste, thyme, basil, salt, and pepper in a jar with a tight-fitting lid. Shake well. Add olive oil and shake well again. Set aside. Remove potatoes from water with a slotted spoon and toss with 2 tablespoons dressing. Set aside.

2. Add beans to boiling water and cook for 2 minutes. Drain and plunge beans into ice water to stop the cooking action. Drain again and set aside.

3. Preheat a grill or oven broiler. Brush tuna with oil and season to taste with salt and pepper. Grill for 2 to 4 minutes on a side or to desired doneness. Remove tuna from grill and set aside.

4. Place romaine in a mixing bowl and toss with half of dressing. Divide romaine onto 2 plates and arrange tuna, potatoes, green beans, tomatoes, olives, and eggs on top. Sprinkle capers and chopped parsley over all and serve immediately, passing additional dressing in a bowl.

Variation: Substitute swordfish, cod, or chicken breast for tuna.

 Déjà Two

Niçoise (pronounced *knee-SWAHZ*) is a French phrase that means "as prepared in Nice," the resort on the Riviera. Tomatoes, black olives, garlic, and anchovies are always part of the definition, and the salad always contains potatoes, green beans, and hard-boiled eggs as well.

Moroccan Salmon and Lentil Salad

Spice-rubbed salmon fillets are joined by savory lentils and olives in this salad with Middle Eastern flavors.

Active time: 15 minutes

Start to finish: 40 minutes

Each serving has:

755 calories

261 calories from fat

29 g fat

4 g saturated fat

60 g protein

63 g carbohydrates

3 scallions

1 cup dry lentils

3 cups water

2 TB. freshly squeezed lemon juice

3 TB. olive oil

2 TB. chopped fresh cilantro

Salt and freshly ground black pepper to taste

1 tsp. ground cumin

1 tsp. ground coriander

½ tsp. ground cinnamon

Pinch cayenne

2 (6-oz.) skinless salmon fillets, rinsed and patted dry with paper towels

2 cups arugula, rinsed and dried

6 black oil-cured Moroccan olives, pitted and chopped

1. Rinse and trim scallions and discard all but 2 inches of green tops. Slice scallions thinly and set aside. Combine lentils and water in a heavy 2-quart saucepan. Bring to a boil over high heat, reduce heat to medium-low, and cook lentils for 20 minutes or until they are firm but tender. Drain lentils and while they are still warm, add 1 tablespoon lemon juice, 2 tablespoons olive oil, and cilantro. Season to taste with salt and pepper and keep warm.

2. Mix together cumin, coriander, cinnamon, and cayenne. Dust one side of the fillets with spice mixture. Season with salt and pepper.

3. Preheat oven to 400°F. Heat a large, heavy, ovenproof skillet over high heat. Add remaining olive oil to the pan and place salmon in the hot pan, spice side down. Cook over high heat for 3 minutes or until spice side is well browned and beginning to crisp.

4. Turn salmon over in the pan with a spatula and place the entire pan in the oven. Cook for 7 minutes or until salmon is cooked through but not flaking apart. Remove salmon from the pan and blot with a paper towel.

5. Arrange arugula on two plates. Divide lentils to one side of plate and place salmon on other side. Sprinkle salmon with remaining lemon juice, scallions, and olives. Serve immediately.

Variation: Substitute swordfish or tuna steaks or thick cod fillets for salmon.

Déjà Two

For centuries lentils have been used in India and the Middle East as a substitute for meat. These tiny, lens-shaped pulse can be yellow, red, or brown. All taste the same and cook the same, and they're a good source of iron, phosphorous, and other vitamins and minerals.

Teriyaki Pork Tenderloin Salad

Lean pork is marinated with Asian ingredients and then roasted to top a bed of crunchy greens.

1 (¾-lb.) pork tenderloin

½ cup snow peas

2 TB. soy sauce

2 TB. rice vinegar

2 TB. dry sherry

2 TB. grated fresh ginger

½ tsp. Chinese five-spice powder

1 garlic clove, peeled and minced

Freshly ground black pepper to taste

¼ cup vegetable oil

1 cup packed baby spinach leaves, rinsed and dried

1 cup shredded Napa cabbage, rinsed and dried

1 small cucumber, halved and sliced into ¼-inch slices

2 scallions, rinsed, trimmed, and sliced

½ cup bean sprouts, rinsed

¼ cup salted peanuts, chopped

2 TB. chopped fresh cilantro

Active time: 20 minutes

Start to finish: 2 hours, including at least 1 hour for marinating

Each serving has:

435 calories

188 calories from fat

21 g fat

4 g saturated fat

45 g protein

16 g carbohydrates

1. Trim tenderloin of visible fat and scrape off iridescent *silver-skin*. Rinse and stem snow peas and cut diagonally into 1-inch pieces. Set aside.

2. Combine soy sauce, vinegar, sherry, ginger, five-spice powder, garlic, and pepper in a jar with a tight-fitting lid. Shake well, add vegetable oil, and shake well again. Reserve ⅓ cup for salad. Pour remaining mixture into a heavy resealable plastic bag and add pork. Marinate pork, refrigerated, for 1 to 3 hours, turning bag occasionally.

3. Bring water to a boil in a heavy 2-quart saucepan. Add snow peas and cook for 30 seconds. Drain and plunge snow peas into ice water to stop the cooking action. Drain again and set aside.

4. Preheat oven to 450°F. Remove pork from marinade and discard marinade. Bake pork for 20 minutes or until an instant-read thermometer inserted diagonally in center registers 140°F. Let pork rest for 10 minutes. Slice into ½-inch slices. (You can do this a day in advance and refrigerate, tightly covered.)

5. In a large bowl combine spinach, cabbage, snow peas, cucumber, scallions, and bean sprouts. Toss salad with reserved dressing and divide salad onto 2 plates. Top each with pork and sprinkle with chopped peanuts and cilantro. Serve immediately.

Variation: Substitute boneless, skinless chicken breasts for pork.

Duet Dialogue

Silverskin is the thin, almost iridescent coating on lean cuts of meat like tenderloin. It's thin, but it's tough and must be trimmed away so the meat doesn't curl when it's cooked.

Asian Steak Salad

This is a colorful salad with green snow peas, red bell pepper, and other vegetables topped with grilled steak in a spicy dressing.

2 TB. rice vinegar

1 TB. soy sauce

1 TB. Dijon mustard

1 TB. grated fresh ginger

1 tsp. firmly packed dark brown sugar

½ tsp. Chinese chili sauce with garlic

⅓ cup olive oil

1 TB. Asian sesame oil

½ lb. flank steak or rib eye steak, trimmed of all visible fat, rinsed and patted dry with paper towels

¼ lb. snow peas, rinsed and stemmed

2 cups baby spinach leaves, rinsed and dried

1 cucumber, peeled, halved, seeded, and thinly sliced

1 red bell pepper, seeds and ribs removed, cut into thin strips

Active time: 20 minutes

Start to finish: 1½ hours, including 1 hour for marinating

Each serving has:

456 calories

278 calories from fat

31 g fat

7 g saturated fat

30 g protein

15 g carbohydrates

1. Combine rice vinegar, soy sauce, mustard, ginger, brown sugar, and chili sauce in a jar with a tight-fitting lid. Shake well. Add olive oil and sesame oil and shake well again.

2. Place steak in a heavy resealable plastic bag and pour in half of dressing. Marinate steak, turning bag occasionally, for 1 hour at room temperature.

3. While steak marinates, bring a large pot of salted water to a boil. Add snow peas and cook for 45 seconds. Drain and plunge snow peas into ice water to stop the cooking action. Drain again and set aside.

4. Preheat a grill or oven broiler. Remove steak from marinade and discard marinade. Broil steak for 3 minutes per side or to desired doneness. Allow steak to rest for 5 minutes.

5. Combine snow peas, spinach, cucumber, and red bell pepper in a bowl. Toss with remaining dressing and divide vegetables onto two plates. Slice steak thinly and place on top of vegetables. Serve immediately.

Double Trouble

One of the first rules of food safety is to never reuse a marinade used for poultry, meat, or seafood. While you may think that nothing could be wrong because the food was in the refrigerator, the marinade could have absorbed bacteria from the food.

Warm Lamb Salad with Mustard and Herb Dressing

Sharp mustard and aromatic rosemary are rubbed onto rosy lamb before it's roasted to top this salad dotted with sun-dried tomatoes.

Active time: 15 minutes

Start to finish: 40 minutes

Each serving has:

437 calories

285 calories from fat

32 g fat

7 g saturated fat

33 g protein

10 g carbohydrates

½ lb. boneless leg of lamb, rinsed and patted dry with paper towels

3 garlic cloves, peeled and minced

3 TB. Dijon mustard

2 tsp. chopped fresh rosemary or ½ tsp. dried

1 tsp. fresh thyme or ¼ tsp. dried

Salt and freshly ground black pepper to taste

2 TB. red wine vinegar

¼ cup extra-virgin olive oil

1 bunch arugula, rinsed and dried

1 cup sliced romaine, rinsed and dried

3 TB. sun-dried tomatoes packed in oil, drained and finely chopped

¼ cup freshly grated Parmesan cheese

Double Feature

Save the olive oil after you've drained sun-dried tomatoes. It's a great addition to salad dressings or drizzled over foods, and it's free!

---

1. Preheat oven to 450°F. Cover a baking sheet with foil and place lamb in the center. Combine 2 garlic cloves, 2 tablespoons mustard, rosemary, thyme, salt, and pepper in small bowl. Rub mixture onto all sides of lamb. Bake lamb for 15 to 20 minutes or until an instant-read thermometer registers 135°F for medium-rare. Remove lamb from the oven and allow it to rest for 10 minutes.

2. While lamb is roasting, combine remaining garlic clove, remaining mustard, and vinegar in a jar with a tight-fitting lid. Season to taste with salt and pepper and shake well. Add olive oil and shake well again.

3. Combine arugula, romaine, sun-dried tomatoes, and Parmesan cheese in a salad bowl. Drizzle with half of dressing, toss well, and divide salad onto two plates. Carve lamb against the grain into thin slices and arrange on top of salad. Drizzle with additional dressing and serve immediately.

Chapter 6

Between the Bread: Hot Sandwiches

In This Chapter

- ◆ Creative quesadillas
- ◆ Panini with panache
- ◆ International sandwiches

There's something about a hot sandwich that elevates everyone's favorite finger food into a more elegant meal. And you'll find recipes for these delicious combinations in this chapter.

All of these hot sandwiches are on the table in a matter of minutes. In fact, you might spend more time waiting in the supermarket deli line than making the sandwich.

Potential for Pressing

One of the greatest small appliances to come on the market in the past decade is the sloping double-sided grill. Boxing great George Forman's moniker is famous in this field, although many companies now manufacture these grills.

I love these grills for indoor cooking because they cook from both sides and cut down on cooking time. The slanted surface makes trimming fat easier because it rolls right down the ridges into a drip pan and away from your food.

Recently I've discovered how great they are for making sandwiches. While expensive panini presses are on the market, they're really superfluous unless you want every gadget in the aisle. But the double-sided grill is a great investment, not only for the recipes in this chapter but also for your general cooking. They're the perfect size for meals for two.

The Quesadilla Connection

Quesadillas—the word comes from the Spanish word *queso* which means cheese—used to be found only on Mexican menus and had a traditional filling of cheese and perhaps some strips of peppers.

But that's all changed today. The word "quesadilla" now means any hot sandwich made in a flour tortilla. While some recipes are fried, I prefer to bake them to cut back on the amount of fat. If you don't want to wait for the stove to preheat, then heat 2 tablespoons vegetable oil in a heavy 12-inch skillet over medium-high heat. Add the quesadillas and cook for 2 minutes on a side or until browned and the cheese has melted. Turn the quesadillas gently with a slotted spatula and blot them with paper towels before serving.

You can transform any of the hot sandwich recipes in this chapter into quesadillas. All you have to do is follow the procedure in a quesadilla recipe for layering the filling and baking them.

Panini Proliferation

If you hadn't heard of panini (or the singular in Italian, *panino*) until a few years ago, you're not alone. These grilled Italian sandwich snacks that traditionally have stripe marks on both sides from the grill have only become popular in this country during the past five years.

Panini (pronounced *pah-KNEE-knee*) are traditionally baked on small square loaves of Italian ciabatta (pronounced *cha-BAH-tah*) bread which has been sliced horizontally. There is no set filling for a panino, although cheese is frequently included but not required.

Italian Meat and Olive Quesadillas (*Muffuletta*)

New Orleans was the birthplace of the Muffuletta sandwich, of which this is a variation.

Vegetable oil spray

⅓ cup sliced salad olives

1 garlic clove, peeled and minced

2 tsp. olive oil

4 (8-in.) flour tortillas

⅛ lb. baked ham

⅛ lb. *mortadella*

⅛ lb. Genoa salami

4 slices provolone cheese

Active time: 5 minutes
Start to finish: 20 minutes
Each serving has:
736 calories
411 calories from fat
46 g fat
18 g saturated fat
36 g protein
45.5 g carbohydrates

1. Preheat the oven to 450°F. Cover a baking sheet with heavy duty aluminum foil and spray the foil with vegetable oil spray. Combine olives, garlic, and olive oil in a small bowl. Stir well and set aside.

2. Place tortillas on a counter. Layer baked ham, mortadella, Genoa salami, and provolone cheese on one half of each. Sprinkle olive salad over cheese. Fold blank side of tortillas over filling and press closed with the palm of your hand or a spatula. Arrange tortillas on the prepared baking sheet and spray tops with vegetable oil spray. (You can do this up to 6 hours in advance and refrigerate, covered with plastic wrap. Add 3 minutes to the baking time if chilled.)

3. Bake quesadillas for 10 minutes. Turn gently with a spatula and press them down if top has separated from filling. Bake for an additional 5 minutes or until crispy. Allow to sit for 3 minutes, cut each in half, and serve immediately.

Duet Dialogue

Mortadella (pronounced *mort-a-DELL-ah*) is a smoked pork sausage from Bologna, Italy, and is the product for which the slang "baloney" emerged. Authentic mortadella is not imported to the United States, so what we have is basically bologna with cubes of pork fat, pistachio nuts, and added garlic.

Cuban Quesadillas

Mustard, roast pork, ham, and Swiss cheese dotted with bits of dill pickle are the flavors you'll savor in this quesadilla.

Active time: 5 minutes	
Start to finish: 20 minutes	
Each serving has:	
635 calories	
268 calories from fat	
30 g fat	
15.5 g saturated fat	
51 g protein	
42.5 g carbohydrates	

Vegetable oil spray

4 (8-in.) flour tortillas

2 TB. *Dijon mustard*

⅓ lb. thinly sliced roast pork

⅓ lb. baked ham

⅓ cup thinly sliced dill pickles

1 cup grated Swiss cheese

1. Preheat the oven to 450°F. Cover a baking sheet with heavy duty aluminum foil and spray the foil with vegetable oil spray.

2. Place tortillas on a counter. Spread mustard on each. Layer roast pork, baked ham, and pickles on one half of each. Sprinkle Swiss cheese over filling. Fold blank side of tortilla over filling and press closed with the palm of your hand or a spatula. Arrange tortillas on the prepared baking sheet and spray tops with vegetable oil spray. (You can do this up to 6 hours in advance and refrigerate, covered with plastic wrap. Add 3 minutes to the baking time if chilled.)

3. Bake quesadillas for 10 minutes. Turn them gently with a spatula and press them down if top has separated from filling. Bake for an additional 5 minutes or until crispy. Allow to sit for 3 minutes, cut each in half, and serve immediately.

Variation: Substitute thinly sliced chicken or roast beef for roast pork.

Déjà Two

This quesadilla is a variation on the Cuban sandwich popular in Miami called the *medianoche*, which means "midnight." They are sold to patrons in the nightclubs of Little Havana to encourage them to stay later.

Spicy Chicken Quesadillas

Chicken strips baked with salsa are topped with tomatoes and spicy jalapeño Jack cheese in this dish.

½ **lb. boneless, skinless chicken breast**

½ **cup refrigerated salsa (found in the produce section of supermarkets)**

Salt and freshly ground black pepper to taste

¼ **cup mayonnaise**

2 TB. chopped fresh cilantro

2 tsp. chili powder

4 (8-in.) flour tortillas

Vegetable oil spray

2 ripe plum tomatoes, rinsed, cored, seeded, and thinly sliced

¼ **lb. (1 cup) grated jalapeño Jack cheese**

Active time: 15 minutes
Start to finish: 45 minutes
Each serving has:
786 calories
392 calories from fat
44 g fat
16 g saturated fat
56 g protein
41 g carbohydrates

1. Preheat the oven to 450°F and line a 9×13-inch baking pan with heavy duty aluminum foil. Rinse chicken, pat dry with paper towels, and trim off all visible fat. Place chicken between two sheets of plastic wrap and pound to an even thickness of ½-inch. Cut chicken into strips ½ inch wide.

2. Combine chicken and salsa in the pan and season to taste with salt and pepper. Arrange chicken in one layer. Bake chicken for 10 minutes. Remove the pan from the oven and turn chicken with a slotted spatula. Bake for an additional 5 minutes or until chicken is cooked through and no longer pink. Remove chicken from the pan with a slotted spoon. Drain liquid remaining in the pan and add vegetables from salsa remaining in the pan to chicken. Set aside.

3. Combine mayonnaise, cilantro, and chili powder in a small bowl. Stir well. Cover a baking sheet with heavy duty aluminum foil and spray the foil with vegetable oil spray.

4. Place tortillas on a counter. Layer chicken and tomatoes on one half of each. Sprinkle jalapeño Jack over filling. Fold blank side of tortilla over filling and press closed with the palm of your hand or a spatula. Arrange tortillas on the prepared baking sheet and spray tops with vegetable oil spray. (You can do this up to 6 hours in advance and refrigerate, covered with plastic wrap. Add 3 minutes to the baking time if chilled.)

5. Bake quesadillas for 10 minutes. Turn them gently with a spatula and press them down if top has separated from filling. Bake for an additional 5 minutes or until crispy. Allow to sit for 3 minutes, cut each in half, and serve immediately.

Variation: Use leftover roasted or grilled chicken for this recipe. Drain salsa and then combine vegetables from salsa with pre-cooked chicken before assembling quesadillas.

Double Trouble

The success of this recipe depends on using the fresh, refrigerated salsa found in produce sections and not jarred salsa. The refrigerated product is a convenience to avoid chopping and dicing vegetables, but it's the vegetables you need for this recipe.

Chicken, Mango, and Black Bean Quesadillas

Luscious fruit combined with spiced beans add flavor and texture to this quesadilla.

Active time: 15 minutes

Start to finish: 30 minutes

Each serving has:

929 calories

361 calories from fat

40 g fat

15 g saturated fat

62 g protein

87 g carbohydrates

Vegetable oil spray

2 TB. olive oil

1 small onion, peeled and diced

2 garlic cloves, peeled and minced

2 tsp. ground cumin

1 (15-oz.) can black beans, rinsed and drained

¼ cup water

Salt and cayenne to taste

¼ cup chopped fresh cilantro

4 (8-in.) flour tortillas

1 mango, peeled and chopped

1½ cups cooked diced chicken

¼ lb. (1 cup) Monterey Jack cheese, coarsely grated

1. Preheat the oven to 450°F. Cover a baking sheet with heavy-duty aluminum foil and spray the foil with vegetable oil spray. Set aside.

2. Heat olive oil in a medium skillet over medium heat. Add onion and garlic and cook, stirring frequently, for 3 minutes or until onion is translucent. Stir in cumin and cook for 30 seconds. Stir in beans and water and cook for 2 minutes or until water is almost evaporated. Season to taste with salt and cayenne and stir in cilantro.

3. Lay tortillas on the baking sheet and divide bean mixture, mango, and chicken on one half of each. Sprinkle Monterey Jack cheese over filling. Fold blank side of tortilla over filling and press closed with the palm of your hand or a spatula. Arrange tortillas on the prepared baking sheet and spray tops with vegetable oil spray. (You can do this up to 6 hours in advance and refrigerate, covered with plastic wrap. Add 3 minutes to the baking time if chilled.)

4. Bake quesadillas for 10 minutes. Turn them gently with a spatula and press them down if top has separated from filling. Bake for an additional 5 minutes or until crispy. Allow to sit for 3 minutes, cut each in half, and serve immediately.

Double Feature

Mangoes are difficult to dice because of their elliptical stone, so here's an easy way to cut them into cubes. Holding the mango horizontally, cut it in two lengthwise, slightly off-center, so the knife just misses the stone. Repeat on the other side so a thin layer of flesh remains around the stone. Slash the mango flesh in a lattice, cutting down to but not through the peel. Repeat with the other half of the mango. Then, holding the mango flesh upward, carefully push the center of the peel with your thumbs to turn it inside out, opening the cuts in the flesh. Cut the mango cubes from the peel.

Broccoli Rabe and Provolone Panini

Broccoli rabe is a more flavorful cousin of common broccoli, and it's topped with cream cheese in this crusty sandwich.

Active time: 10 minutes

Start to finish: 15 minutes

Each serving has:

640 calories

389 calories from fat

43 g fat

16 g saturated fat

29 g protein

35 g carbohydrates

½ lb. *broccoli rabe*, rinsed with tough ends discarded

3 TB. olive oil

1 garlic clove, peeled and minced

2 tsp. anchovy paste

4 slices Italian bread, ¼ inch thick and 8-inches wide

⅓ lb. sliced provolone cheese

1. Bring a large pot of salted water to a boil over high heat. Add broccoli rabe and boil for 3 minutes or until tender. Drain well, squeeze dry, and chop coarsely.

2. Heat 2 tablespoons olive oil in a heavy 10-inch skillet over medium heat. Add garlic and cook, stirring frequently, for 1 minute or until garlic is golden. Add anchovy paste and broccoli rabe and cook, stirring frequently, for 1 minute.

3. Preheat a two-sided grill, if using one. Brush one side of bread slices with remaining olive oil. Place slices, oiled sides down, on the counter or a plate. Divide half of cheese between 2 slices. Top with broccoli rabe mixture, remaining cheese, and remaining 2 bread slices, oiled sides up.

4. Grill sandwiches in a two-sided grill for 3 to 4 minutes or until bread is brown and cheese is melted. Alternately, fry sandwiches in a ridged grill pan, turning once, weighted down by a pan. Cut sandwiches in half and serve immediately.

Variation: Substitute cooked broccoli for broccoli rabe, and use fontina cheese in place of provolone.

Duet Dialogue

Broccoli rabe (pronounced *RAHB*) called by its Italian name of *rapini* in some supermarkets, is a vegetable related to both classic broccoli and the turnip family. It has leafy green stalks about 9 inches long that have clusters of small florets attached. Its flavor is both more pungent and more bitter than that of broccoli.

Grilled Chicken, Sun-Dried Tomato and Mozzarella Panini

Chicken marinated with herbs and garlic is the base for this sandwich that also contains flavorful sun-dried tomatoes all nestled under creamy, fresh mozzarella.

2 (6-oz.) boneless, skinless chicken breast halves

Salt and freshly ground black pepper to taste

⅓ cup olive oil

2 garlic cloves, peeled and minced

2 TB. chopped fresh rosemary or 2 tsp. dried

4 slices Italian bread, ¼ inch thick and 8 inches wide

¼ cup sun-dried tomatoes packed in olive oil, drained and chopped

¼ lb. fresh mozzarella, drained and sliced

Active time: 15 minutes

Start to finish: 40 minutes, including 15 minutes for marinating

Each serving has:

863 calories

416 calories from fat

46 g fat

12 g saturated fat

73 g protein

36 g carbohydrates

---

1. Rinse chicken and pat dry with paper towels. Place between two sheets of plastic wrap and pound to an even thickness of ¼ inch. Place chicken on a platter and season both sides to taste with salt and pepper. Combine ¼ cup olive oil, garlic, and 1 tablespoon rosemary in a small bowl. Rub mixture on both sides of chicken. Let chicken sit at room temperature for 15 minutes, covered with plastic wrap.

2. Preheat a grill or oven broiler. Grill or broil chicken for 4 minutes per side, turning it gently with tongs, or until chicken is cooked through and no longer pink. Set aside.

3. Preheat a two-sided grill, if using one. Brush one side of bread slices with remaining olive oil. Place slices, oiled side down, on the counter or a plate. Place 1 chicken breast on each of 2 bread slices and top each chicken breast with half of sun-dried tomatoes, half of mozzarella, and remaining 2 bread slices.

4. Grill sandwiches in a two-sided grill for 3 to 4 minutes or until bread is brown and cheese is melted. Alternately, fry sandwiches in a ridged grill pan, turning once, weighted down by a pan. Cut sandwiches in half and serve immediately.

Variation: Make this recipe with leftover roast chicken, or use a thin fish fillet, such as sole or tilapia.

 Déjà Two

Panini seem to have popped up in Italy about 60 years ago as snack food to be sold with glasses of wine in the afternoons. The name was coined in Milan at the Paninoteca Bar Quandronno.

French Ham and Grilled Cheese Sandwich (*Croque Monsieur*)

What could be more a definition of comfort food than a grilled cheese sandwich? And this one even has a fancy name!

Active time: 5 minutes

Start to finish: 8 minutes

Each serving has:

537 calories

304 calories from fat

34 g fat

19 g saturated fat

31 g protein

27 g carbohydrates

4 slices firm white sandwich bread, crusts trimmed (optional)

2 TB. unsalted butter, softened

¼ lb. Black Forest ham, thinly sliced

¼ lb. Gruyère cheese, thinly sliced

1. Preheat a two-sided grill, if using one. Spread both sides of bread with softened butter. Layer cheese on all four slices. Layer ham on two slices. Turn cheese side down on ham to enclose filling.

2. Grill sandwiches in a two-sided grill for 3 to 4 minutes or until bread is brown and cheese is melted. Alternately, fry sandwiches in a ridged grill pan, turning once, weighted down by a pan. Cut sandwiches in half and serve immediately.

Variation: Make sandwich with thinly sliced chicken instead of ham.

Déjà Two

The Croque Monsieur is a traditional French sandwich which is usually served in mid-morning. The female version, called the Croque Madame, is the same sandwich but with a fried egg on top, although in the United States it is often used incorrectly for a Croque Monsieur made with chicken instead of ham.

Tuna Melt with Olives

Sharp cheddar cheese tops a tuna salad enlivened with kalamata olives in this open-faced sandwich.

1 (6-oz.) can light tuna, drained and flaked

¼ cup mayonnaise

1 celery rib, rinsed, trimmed, and chopped

¼ cup kalamata or other brine-cured black olives, pitted and chopped

1 TB. chopped fresh parsley

2 tsp. freshly squeezed lemon juice

Freshly ground black pepper to taste

2 slices rye bread, lightly toasted

2 oz. (½ cup) grated sharp cheddar cheese

Active time: 10 minutes
Start to finish: 12 minutes
Each serving has:
520 calories
315 calories from fat
35 g fat
11 g saturated fat
32 g protein
18 g carbohydrates

1. Preheat an oven broiler and cover a baking sheet with heavy duty foil. Combine tuna, mayonnaise, celery, olives, parsley, lemon juice, and pepper in a medium mixing bowl. Stir well.

2. Place toast on baking sheet and divide tuna mixture between slices. Spread tuna evenly and top with grated cheese. Broil sandwiches 6 inches from broiling element for 2 minutes or until cheese is melted and bubbly. Serve immediately.

Double Trouble

Due to the high amount of salt in canned tuna, plus salt added to commercial mayonnaise, don't add salt to a tuna salad—at least before you taste it.

Grilled Reuben Sandwich

Creamy Russian dressing, pickled sauerkraut, and Swiss cheese are the toppings for corned beef in this New York deli classic.

Active time: 10 minutes

Start to finish: 13 minutes

Each serving has:

709 calories

417 calories from fat

46 g fat

20 g saturated fat

35 g protein

38 g carbohydrates

1 TB. unsalted butter, softened

4 slices rye bread or pumpernickel

¼ cup Russian or Thousand Island dressing

½ cup sauerkraut, drained, rinsed, and squeezed dry

¼ lb. thinly sliced Swiss cheese

⅓ lb. thinly sliced corned beef

1. Preheat a two-sided grill, if using one. Butter one side of each bread slice. Spread dressing on non-buttered sides. Layer sauerkraut, Swiss cheese, and corned beef on top of dressing. Enclose filling by topping it with other bread slices, buttered side up.

2. Grill sandwiches in a two-sided grill for 3 to 4 minutes or until bread is brown and cheese is melted. Alternately, fry sandwiches in a ridged grill pan, turning once, weighted down by a pan. Cut sandwiches in half and serve immediately.

Déjà Two

A few competing theories exist as to the parentage of the Reuben sandwich, but the most likely is that it comes from Reuben's Delicatessen in New York and was created by founder Arnold Ruben in 1914.

Part 3

Saucing to Success

Ask most two-person households what they don't like about cooking, and chances are a frequent response would be "leftovers." While the chapters in this part give you fresh food each time it's cooked, you're also getting a head start much of the time.

Fish and seafood cook far more quickly than their sauces, so why not make a triple batch of sauce and freeze most of it? That means the second and third time you make the dish, it's on the table in a matter of minutes and it's freshly cooked so there's no tired, leftover flavor or texture.

The reverse is true when it comes to hearty meat stews. What gets tired when stews are reheated are the vegetables. So you'll be cooking the meat and gravy part to the point of adding the vegetables. Then it's abracadabra time! You whisk two thirds away for future use. The same principle applies to pasta sauces, and you'll find a chapter with those dishes, too.

7

Poultry with Panache

In This Chapter

- ◆ Comfort classics
- ◆ Exotic Asian options
- ◆ Sunny Mediterranean flavors

For the past two decades, chicken consumption has been on the rise, with the figure in 2005 topping 86 pounds per capita. Almost 100 percent of American households eat chicken at least once a week, and about half that number of folks triple the figure.

So there's always room for new chicken recipes or new ways to look at old classics. And that's what you'll find when cooking the dishes in this chapter. Also, like all the chapters in this part, you'll cook three times the amount of sauce you need for one dinner so you'll have the chance to delight in these dishes within minutes the next time you want one.

Timing Is Everything

And notice that I've written these recipes for boneless, skinless chicken breasts or turkey cutlets. Feel free to use either interchangeably even though I don't list the other as a variation.

But what if you have a hankering for boneless thighs? Or maybe you want to cook a batch of drumsticks? There's no problem, but they'll have to cook longer.

For white meat cook chicken to 160°F, and for dark meat, to 180°F. Stick an instant-read thermometer into the thickest part of the chicken and leave it in for 20 seconds. Once the magic number is hit, it's *bon appetite!*

Turkey with Molé Sauce

This ancient Mexican sauce is richly flavored with tomatoes and spices, and then thickened with peanut butter and cocoa.

Active time: 15 minutes

Start to finish: 45 minutes

Each serving has:

419 calories

150 calories from fat

17 g fat

2.5 g saturated fat

47 g protein

25 g carbohydrates

¾ lb. turkey cutlets

5 TB. olive oil

3 large onions, peeled and chopped

6 garlic cloves, peeled and minced

3 TB. chili powder

1 TB. ground cumin

3 cups chicken stock

1 (14.5-oz.) can tomatoes, drained

¼ cup peanut butter

¼ cup raisins

2 TB. granulated sugar

2 TB. unsweetened cocoa powder

Salt and cayenne to taste

1. Rinse turkey cutlets and pat dry with paper towels. Set aside. Heat 3 tablespoons oil in a heavy saucepan over medium-high heat. Add onions and garlic and cook, stirring frequently, for 3 minutes or until onions are translucent. Stir in chili powder and cumin and cook, stirring constantly, for 1 minute.

2. Add stock, tomatoes, peanut butter, raisins, sugar, and cocoa powder. Stir well and bring to a boil over high heat. Reduce the heat to low and simmer sauce for 20 minutes or until lightly thickened. Season to taste with salt and cayenne. Remove ⅔ of sauce and divide it into two 1-quart resealable plastic bags for future use. (Sauce can be frozen for up to 3 months.)

3. While sauce is simmering, heat remaining 2 tablespoons oil in a skillet over medium-high heat. Sprinkle turkey with salt and cayenne and add turkey to the skillet. Cook for 2 minutes per side or until opaque. Add remaining sauce to the skillet and return to a boil. Simmer, uncovered, for 5 to 7 minutes or until turkey is cooked through and no longer pink. Serve immediately.

4. When using remaining sauce, bring it to a simmer and then cook turkey as instructed above.

Variation: Substitute boneless pork chops ½ inch thick and cook the same amount of time.

 **Déjà Two**

Molé is one of the oldest sauces in North America, dating back to the Aztec Indians of Mexico centuries before Columbus landed in America. Its most salient feature is the inclusion of some sort of bitter chocolate, which adds richness to the dark, reddish-brown sauce without adding sweetness.

Chicken with Tomatillo Sauce

Tomatillos are tart green tomatoes with a slightly lemony flavor that are blended with chilies and cilantro for this sauce.

2 (6-oz.) boneless, skinless chicken breast halves

3 lb. *tomatillos*

4 garlic cloves, peeled

1 jalapeño chili, seeds and ribs removed

1 cup chicken stock

2 TB. fresh cilantro, chopped

1 TB. granulated sugar

Salt and freshly ground black pepper to taste

2 TB. vegetable oil

Active time: 15 minutes

Start to finish: 40 minutes

Each serving has:

394 calories

166 calories from fat

18.5 g fat

3 g saturated fat

42 g protein

16 g carbohydrates

1. Rinse chicken and pat dry with paper towels. Cut into 1-inch cubes and set aside. Discard papery husks from tomatillos and rinse. Core tomatillos and cut into 1-inch cubes.

2. Combine tomatillos, garlic, jalapeño, and stock in a food processor fitted with a steel blade or in a blender. Purée until smooth. Pour mixture into a saucepan and add cilantro and sugar. Bring to a boil over medium-high heat, reduce the heat to low, and simmer sauce, uncovered, for 15 minutes, stirring occasionally. Season to taste with salt and pepper. Remove ⅔ of sauce and divide into two 1-quart resealable plastic bags for future use. (Sauce can be frozen for up to 3 months.)

3. While sauce is simmering, heat oil in a skillet over medium-high heat. Sprinkle chicken with salt and pepper and add to the skillet. Cook for 2 minutes or until chicken is opaque. Add remaining sauce to the skillet and return to a boil. Simmer, uncovered, for 5 to 7 minutes or until chicken is cooked through and no longer pink. Serve immediately.

4. When using remaining sauce, bring it to a simmer and then cook chicken as instructed above.

Variation: Substitute boneless pork chops ½-inch thick and cook the same amount of time.

Duet Dialogue

Tomatillos (pronounced *tohm-aah-TEE-os*) are green tomatoes often thought to be a cousin of our tomatoes because of their similar appearance, but are actually a member of the gooseberry family. Tomatillos, popular in Mexican and Southwestern cooking, are covered in a thin, parchment-like husk that you must pull off and discard before cooking. You can use these raw in salsa, but their distinctive tangy flavor with hints of lemon and herbs is released when they are cooked. Choose firm tomatillos with tight-fitting husks, and rinse them well before dicing or cooking.

Chicken Catalan

Vegetables and slivers of ham punctuate this hearty tomato sauce laced with sherry in this easy dish.

2 (6-oz.) boneless, skinless chicken breast halves

1 (½-lb.) ham steak

⅓ cup olive oil

2 large onions, peeled, halved, and sliced

6 garlic cloves, peeled and minced

2 red bell peppers, seeds and ribs removed, thinly sliced

2 TB. *paprika*

2 tsp. fresh thyme or ½ tsp. dried

1½ cups chicken stock

¾ cup dry sherry

1 (14.5-oz.) can diced tomatoes, undrained

Red pepper flakes to taste

Salt and freshly ground black pepper to taste

Active time: 20 minutes
Start to finish: 45 minutes
Each serving has:
659 calories
223 calories from fat
25 g fat
5 g saturated fat
64 g protein
18 g carbohydrates

1. Rinse chicken and pat dry with paper towels. Place between two sheets of plastic wrap and pound to an even thickness of ½ inch. Set aside. Trim ham of all visible fat and cut into strips ½ inch wide and 2 inches long. Set aside.

2. Heat ¼ cup olive oil in a heavy saucepan over medium-high heat. Add ham, onions, garlic, and red bell peppers. Cook, stirring frequently, for 3 minutes or until onions are translucent. Stir in paprika and thyme and cook for 1 minute, stirring constantly.

3. Add stock, sherry, tomatoes, and red pepper flakes. Bring to a boil and simmer sauce, uncovered, for 20 minutes, stirring occasionally. Season to taste with salt and pepper. Remove ⅔ of sauce and divide into two 1-quart resealable plastic bags for future use. (Sauce can be frozen for up to 3 months.)

4. While sauce is simmering, heat remaining olive oil in a skillet over medium-high heat. Sprinkle chicken with salt and pepper and add to the skillet. Cook for 2 minutes per side or until opaque. Add remaining sauce to the skillet and return to a boil. Simmer, uncovered, for 5 to 7 minutes or until chicken is cooked through and no longer pink. Serve immediately.

5. When using remaining sauce, bring it to a simmer and then cook chicken as instructed above.

Variation: Substitute boneless pork chops ½ inch thick and cook the same amount of time.

Duet Dialogue

Paprika is a powder made by grinding aromatic sweet red pepper pods several times. The color can vary from deep red to bright orange, and the flavor can range from mild to pungent and hot. Hungarian cuisine is characterized by paprika as a flavoring, and Hungarian paprika is considered the best of all paprika products.

Chicken Niçoise

All the sunny flavors of the Mediterranean—from onion and garlic to oranges and fennel—are part of the sauce for these chicken breasts.

Active time: 20 minutes

Start to finish: 45 minutes

Each serving has:

418 calories

182 calories from fat

20 g fat

3 g saturated fat

42 g protein

13 g carbohydrates

2 (6-oz.) boneless, skinless chicken breast halves

⅓ cup olive oil

1 large onion, peeled, halved, and thinly sliced

1 fennel bulb, rinsed, trimmed, and thinly sliced

4 garlic cloves, peeled and minced

1 large red bell pepper, seeds and ribs removed, thinly sliced

1½ cups chicken stock

½ cup dry white wine

Juice and zest of 1 orange

3 ripe plum tomatoes, rinsed, cored, and diced

¼ cup chopped fresh basil or 1 TB. dried

2 TB. chopped fresh oregano or 1 tsp. dried

1 TB. fresh thyme or 1 tsp. dried

1 bay leaf

Salt and freshly ground black pepper to taste

Double Feature

When using both the zest and juice of a citrus fruit, it's easier to grate the zest while the fruit is whole. Because it's still firm, it's easy to grate just the colored portion without getting the white pith.

1. Rinse chicken and pat dry with paper towels. Place between two sheets of plastic wrap and pound to an even thickness of ½ inch. Set aside. Heat ¼ cup olive oil in a heavy saucepan over medium-high heat. Add onion, fennel, garlic, and red bell pepper. Cook, stirring frequently, for 3 minutes or until onions are translucent.

2. Add stock, wine, orange juice, orange zest, tomatoes, basil, oregano, thyme, and bay leaf. Bring to a boil and simmer sauce, uncovered, for 20 minutes, stirring occasionally. Season to taste with salt and pepper. Remove and discard bay leaf. Remove ⅔ of sauce and divide into two 1-quart resealable plastic bags for future use. (Sauce can be frozen for up to 3 months.)

3. While sauce is simmering, heat remaining olive oil in a skillet over medium-high heat. Sprinkle chicken with salt and pepper and add to the skillet. Cook for 2 minutes per side or until opaque. Add remaining sauce to the skillet and return to a boil. Simmer, uncovered, for 5 to 7 minutes or until chicken is cooked through and no longer pink. Serve immediately.

4. When using remaining sauce, bring it to a simmer and then cook chicken as instructed above.

Variation: Substitute thick fillets of halibut, cod, or swordfish and cook the same amount of time.

Sweet and Spicy Chinese Chicken

Pineapple and squares of bell peppers and onion are additions to this updated variation on sweet and sour chicken.

2 (6-oz.) boneless, skinless chicken breast halves

2 TB. Asian sesame oil

¼ cup vegetable oil

4 garlic cloves, peeled and minced

2 TB. grated fresh ginger

3 scallions, rinsed, trimmed, and sliced

1 large jalapeño chili, seeds and ribs removed, finely chopped

1 large onion, peeled and cut into 1-inch squares

1 red bell pepper, seeds and ribs removed, cut into 1-inch squares

1 orange bell pepper, seeds and ribs removed, cut into 1-inch squares

2 cups chicken stock

1 (5.5-oz.) can unsweetened pineapple juice

¼ cup cider vinegar

¼ cup granulated sugar

2 TB. plum wine or medium sherry

2 TB. soy sauce

1½ cups fresh pineapple, cut into 1-inch cubes

Salt and freshly ground black pepper to taste

2 tsp. cornstarch

2 TB. cold water

Active time: 15 minutes
Start to finish: 35 minutes
Each serving has:
517 calories
241 calories from fat
27 g fat
4 g saturated fat
42 g protein
26 g carbohydrates

1. Rinse chicken and pat dry with paper towels. Cut into 1-inch cubes and set aside. Heat sesame oil and 2 tablespoons vegetable oil in a large deep skillet over medium-high heat. Add garlic, ginger, scallions, and jalapeño. Cook, stirring constantly, for 30 seconds or until fragrant. Add onion, red bell pepper, and orange bell pepper. Cook, stirring frequently, for 3 minutes or until onion is translucent.

2. Add stock, pineapple juice, vinegar, sugar, plum wine, and soy sauce. Bring to a boil and simmer for 10 minutes, stirring occasionally. Add pineapple and cook for an additional 5 minutes. Season to taste with salt and pepper. Remove ⅔ of sauce and divide into two 1-quart resealable plastic bags for future use. (Sauce can be frozen for up to 3 months.)

3. While sauce is simmering, heat remaining 2 TB. oil in a skillet over medium-high heat. Sprinkle chicken with salt and pepper and add to the skillet. Cook, stirring constantly, for 2 minutes or until opaque. Add remaining sauce to the skillet and

return to a boil. Simmer, uncovered, for 5 to 7 minutes or until chicken is cooked through and no longer pink. Combine cornstarch and water in a small bowl and stir well. Add mixture to chicken and simmer for 1 minute or until sauce slightly thickens. Serve immediately.

4. When using remaining sauce, bring it to a simmer and then cook chicken as instructed above.

Variation: Substitute shrimp or 1-inch cubes of firm-fleshed white fish. Reduce cooking time for either food to 3 to 5 minutes.

 **Double Feature**

Here's the foolproof way to cut a fresh pineapple. First cut off the top and bottom so it sits firmly on the cutting board. Then cut it into quarters. At this point use a small paring knife to cut out the woody core, and then cut between the peel and the fruit to release the fruit.

Lemongrass Chicken Curry

This Thai version of curry is made with tangy lemongrass and creamy coconut milk thickened with ground peanuts.

Active time: 25 minutes
Start to finish: 40 minutes
Each serving has:
435 calories
208 calories from fat
23 g fat
4.5 g saturated fat
44 g protein
15 g carbohydrates

2 (6-oz.) boneless, skinless chicken breast halves

1 small onion, peeled and diced

3 garlic cloves, peeled

1 (½-in.) slice peeled fresh ginger

⅓ cup roasted peanuts

1½ cups chicken stock

3 TB. vegetable oil

3 TB. curry powder

½ tsp. Chinese five-spice powder

2 (14-oz.) cans light coconut milk

¼ cup thinly sliced lemongrass

2 TB. soy sauce

3 carrots, peeled and cut into ½-inch slices

5 ripe plum tomatoes, rinsed, cored, seeded, and diced

Salt and freshly ground black pepper to taste

1. Rinse chicken and pat dry with paper towels. Cut into 1-inch cubes and set aside. Combine onion, garlic, ginger, peanuts, and ¼ cup stock in a food processor fitted with a steel blade or in a blender. Purée until smooth, scraping the sides as necessary. Set aside.

2. Heat 1 tablespoon oil in a saucepan over medium-high heat. Add curry powder and five-spice powder and cook, stirring constantly, for 1 minute. Add purée and cook for 2 minutes, stirring constantly. Add coconut milk, remaining 1¼ cups stock, lemongrass, soy sauce, and carrots. Bring to a boil, reduce the heat to medium, and simmer sauce for 15 minutes, stirring occasionally. Add tomatoes and simmer for an additional 15 minutes. Remove ⅔ of sauce and divide into two 1-quart resealable plastic bags for future use. (Sauce can be frozen for up to 3 months.)

3. While sauce is simmering, heat remaining 2 tablespoons oil in a skillet over medium-high heat. Sprinkle chicken with salt and pepper and add to the skillet. Cook for 2 minutes or until opaque. Add remaining sauce to the skillet and return to a boil. Simmer, uncovered, for 5 to 7 minutes or until chicken is cooked through and no longer pink. Serve immediately.

4. When using remaining sauce, bring it to a simmer and then cook chicken as instructed above.

Variation: Substitute shrimp or 1-inch cubes of firm-fleshed white fish. Reduce cooking time for either food to 3 to 5 minutes.

Double Feature

Fresh lemongrass is sold by the grayish green stalk that looks like a fibrous, woody scallion. Cut the lower bulb 5 to 8 inches from the stalk, discarding the fibrous upper part. Trim off the outer layers as you would peel an onion; then bruise the stem by slamming it with the blunt side of a knife to release the flavor.

Chicken Cacciatore

Woodsy porcini mushrooms add an elegant flavor to this dish of chicken cooked in an herbed tomato sauce.

Active time: 20 minutes
Start to finish: 45 minutes
Each serving has:
602 calories
296 calories from fat
33 g fat
5 g saturated fat
60 g protein
26 g carbohydrates

2 (6-oz.) boneless, skinless chicken breast halves

1 oz. dried porcini mushrooms

1 cup boiling chicken stock

½ lb. white mushrooms

⅓ cup olive oil

¼ lb. prosciutto, finely chopped

1 large onion, peeled and chopped

4 garlic cloves, peeled and minced

2 carrots, peeled and diced

2 celery ribs, rinsed, trimmed, and diced

2 (14.5-oz.) cans diced tomatoes, undrained

½ cup dry white wine

3 TB. chopped fresh parsley

1 tsp. Italian seasoning

1 bay leaf

Salt and freshly ground black pepper to taste

1. Rinse chicken and pat dry with paper towels. Place between two sheets of plastic wrap and pound to an even thickness of ½-inch. Set aside. Place dried mushrooms in a small bowl and pour boiling chicken stock over them. Allow mushrooms to sit in liquid for 10 minutes; then drain, reserving stock. Remove and discard stems, and finely chop mushrooms. Strain stock through a paper coffee filter or a paper towel. Reserve mushrooms and liquid. Wipe white mushrooms with a damp paper towel. Discard stems and slice mushrooms.

2. Heat 3 tablespoons olive oil in a heavy saucepan over medium-high heat. Add prosciutto, onion, and garlic. Cook, stirring frequently, for 3 minutes or until onion is translucent. Add white mushrooms, carrots, and celery and cook for 2 minutes, stirring frequently.

3. Add chopped porcini, stock, tomatoes, wine, parsley, Italian seasoning, and bay leaf. Bring to a boil and cook over low heat, uncovered, for 20 minutes or until carrots are tender. Remove and discard bay leaf. Remove ⅔ of sauce and divide into two 1-quart resealable plastic bags for future use. (Sauce can be frozen for up to 3 months.)

Déjà Two

Cacciatore is Italian for "hunter's style." A number of dishes from chicken to beef to veal use cacciatore as a handle, but all it means is that the dish is cooked with tomatoes. The rest of the ingredients are up to the cook.

4. While sauce is simmering, heat remaining oil in a skillet over medium-high heat. Sprinkle chicken with salt and pepper and add to the skillet. Cook for 2 minutes per side or until opaque. Add remaining sauce to the skillet and return to a boil. Simmer, uncovered, for 5 to 7 minutes or until chicken is cooked through and no longer pink. Serve immediately.

5. When using remaining sauce, bring it to a simmer and then cook chicken as instructed above.

Variation: Substitute boneless pork chops, cut ½-inch thick.

Cuban-Style Chicken

Heady rum is added to a sweet and sour sauce for a stew made with tomatoes and carrots in this authentic recipe.

2 (6-oz.) boneless, skinless chicken breast halves

5 TB. olive oil

2 large onions, peeled and thinly sliced

3 garlic cloves, peeled and minced

3 TB. grated fresh ginger

1 (14.5-oz.) can chicken stock

½ cup cider vinegar

½ cup dark rum

¼ cup firmly packed dark brown sugar

2 carrots, peeled and cut into ½-inch slices

4 ripe plum tomatoes, rinsed, cored, seeded, and diced

2 (15-oz.) cans black beans, drained and rinsed

Salt and freshly ground black pepper to taste

2 tsp. cornstarch

2 TB. cold water

Active time: 20 minutes
Start to finish: 45 minutes
Each serving has:
589 calories
205 calories from fat
23 g fat
3 g saturated fat
47 g protein
42 g carbohydrates

1. Rinse chicken and pat dry with paper towels. Place between two sheets of plastic wrap and pound to an even thickness of ½ inch. Set aside.

2. Heat 3 tablespoons oil in a heavy saucepan over medium- high heat. Add onion, garlic, and ginger. Cook and stir for 3 minutes or until onion is translucent. Add stock, vinegar, rum, brown sugar, and carrots. Bring to a boil, reduce the heat to low, and simmer for 15 minutes, stirring occasionally. Add

Double Trouble

The reason for adding cornstarch to the individual portions is that it has a tendency to lose its ability to thicken once it's cooled or frozen. It's best to add it to the freshly cooked meal.

tomatoes and beans and simmer for an additional 15 minutes. Remove ⅔ sauce and divide into two 1-quart resealable plastic bags for future use. (Sauce can be frozen for up to 3 months.)

3. While sauce is simmering, heat remaining 2 tablespoons oil in a skillet over medium-high heat. Sprinkle chicken with salt and pepper and add to the skillet. Cook for 2 minutes per side or until opaque. Add remaining sauce to the skillet and return to a boil. Simmer, uncovered, for 5 to 7 minutes or until chicken is cooked through and no longer pink. Combine cornstarch and water in a small bowl and stir well. Add mixture to chicken and simmer for 1 minute or until sauce slightly thickens. Season to taste with salt and pepper and serve immediately.

4. When using remaining sauce, bring it to a simmer and then cook chicken as instructed above.

Variation: Substitute boneless pork chops, cut ½-inch thick.

Chicken with Madeira Sauce

Dried fruit and apple cider balance the flavor of the wine for this dish inspired by Portuguese cuisine.

Active time: 20 minutes

Start to finish: 45 minutes

Each serving has:

513 calories

188 calories from fat

21 g fat

5.5 g saturated fat

41 g protein

28 g carbohydrates

2 (6-oz.) boneless, skinless chicken breast halves

2 TB. unsalted butter

1 large onion, peeled and diced

2 garlic cloves, peeled and minced

3 carrots, peeled and sliced

3 celery ribs, rinsed, trimmed, and sliced

1 cup apple cider

1 cup Madeira

¾ cup raisins

½ cup dried apricots, diced

½ tsp. ground cinnamon

½ tsp. dried thyme

2 TB. vegetable oil

Salt and freshly ground black pepper to taste

2 tsp. cornstarch

2 TB. cold water

1. Rinse chicken, pat dry with paper towels, cut into 1-inch cubes, and set aside.

2. Heat butter in a saucepan over medium-high heat. Add onion, garlic, carrots, and celery. Cook, stirring frequently, for

3 minutes or until onion is translucent. Add cider, Madeira, raisins, dried apricots, cinnamon, and thyme. Bring to a boil, reduce the heat to low, and simmer sauce for 20 minutes, stirring occasionally. Remove ⅔ of sauce and divide into two 1-quart resealable plastic bags for future use. (Sauce can be frozen for up to 3 months.)

3. While sauce is simmering, heat oil in a skillet over medium-high heat. Sprinkle chicken with salt and pepper and add to the skillet. Cook for 2 minutes per side or until opaque. Add remaining sauce to the skillet and return to a boil. Simmer, uncovered, for 5 to 7 minutes or until chicken is cooked through and no longer pink. Combine cornstarch and water in a small bowl and stir well. Add mixture to chicken and simmer for 1 minute or until sauce slightly thickens. Season to taste with salt and pepper and serve immediately.

4. When using remaining sauce, bring it to a simmer and then cook chicken as instructed above.

Variation: Substitute ham steaks, cut ½-inch thick.

Double Feature

Madeira is a wonderfully aromatic and flavorful wine from Portugal, but it's not as commonly used in cooking as other wines. Dry marsala or dry sherry are good substitutions.

Chapter 8

Sensational Seafood

In This Chapter

- ◆ Saucy shrimp
- ◆ Fish stews
- ◆ Fillets with international flavors

One of the great features about fish and seafood is that it cooks so quickly. You can have it on the table in far less time than even a pounded chicken breast. It's the sauces and stew bases that take the time to prepare when cooking fish.

That's where the recipes in this chapter come into play. It will take some time now to complete the whole dish, but on its next two outings you'll be eating in minutes. All you have to do is thaw a package of the base, and then *voilà!* Dinner is served.

Sizing Up the Situation

Shrimp are sorted by "count," which refers to the size and number that comprise 1 pound, and the smaller the number of shrimp in a pound, the higher the price will be. The general size categories into which shrimp fall are as follows:

- *Colossal* counts up as less than 10 per pound. These are also sometimes referred to as U8s.

- *Jumbo* is the term for shrimp that count up at 11 to 15 per pound. These yield the highest proportion of meat to shell.

- An *extra large* label means 16 to 20 per pound. These are frequently called "cocktail shrimp" because they look impressive in a shrimp cocktail.

- *Large*, which represents 21 to 30 shrimp per pound, is the most common size for shrimp found in the supermarket, both cooked and raw.

- *Small* shrimp, 36 to 45 per pound, and *miniature* shrimp, more than 45 per pound, are usually sold as "salad shrimp." Unless they are cooked and peeled, stay away from these because the labor involved in preparing them for cooking or eating is monumental.

Regardless of the color of the shell, raw shrimp are termed "green shrimp." Raw shrimp should smell of the sea with no hint of ammonia. Cooked, shelled shrimp should look plump and succulent. Before storing fresh, uncooked shrimp, rinse them under cold, running water and drain thoroughly. Tightly cover and refrigerate for up to 2 days. Cooked shrimp can be refrigerated for up to 3 days. Freeze shrimp for up to 3 months.

You'll find similar information on a variety of fin fish in Chapter 16.

The Dilemma of Deveining

To devein a shrimp means to remove the gray-black vein (the intestinal tract) from the back of a shrimp. You can do this with the tip of a sharp knife or a special tool called a deveiner.

On small and medium shrimp, deveining is more for cosmetic purposes. However, because the intestinal vein of large shrimp contains grit, you should always remove it. For these recipes, devein the shrimp before cooking and discard all peel, which is actually the shrimp's paperlike shell.

If you're cooking shrimp for a shrimp cocktail, it's better to peel and devein them after cooking because they will not shrink as much during the cooking process and will present a more pleasing shape.

Shrimp Creole

The "holy trinity" of celery, scallions, and bell peppers form the base of the tomato sauce in which tender shrimp are cooked.

3 TB. olive oil

1 bunch scallions, rinsed, trimmed, and sliced

2 celery ribs, rinsed and sliced

1 red bell pepper, seeds and ribs removed, diced

3 garlic cloves, peeled and minced

1 TB. dried oregano

1 TB. dried paprika

1 tsp. dried thyme

2 (8-oz.) cans tomato sauce

1 (8-oz.) bottle clam juice

2 bay leaves

½ lb. extra large (16 to 20 per lb.) raw shrimp, peeled and deveined

Salt and cayenne to taste

Active time: 20 minutes

Start to finish: 40 minutes

Each serving has:

243 calories

84 calories from fat

9 g fat

1 g saturated fat

25 g protein

15 g carbohydrates

1. Heat olive oil in a heavy 2-quart saucepan over medium heat. Add scallions, celery, red bell pepper, and garlic. Cook, stirring frequently, for 3 minutes or until scallions are translucent. Stir in oregano, paprika, and thyme. Cook, stirring constantly, for 1 minute. Stir in tomato sauce, clam juice, and bay leaves. Bring to a boil, stirring occasionally.

2. Reduce the heat to low and simmer sauce, uncovered, for 15 minutes. Remove and discard bay leaves. Remove ⅔ of sauce and divide it into two 1-quart resealable plastic bags for future use. (Sauce can be frozen for up to 3 months.)

3. Add shrimp to remaining sauce. Bring to a boil, cover pan, and simmer for 2 minutes. Turn off the heat, but do not uncover the pan; allow shrimp to sit for 5 minutes to complete cooking. Season to taste with salt and cayenne and serve immediately.

4. When using remaining sauce, bring it to a simmer and then cook shrimp as instructed above.

Variation: Use bay scallops, sea scallops cut into quarters, or 1-inch cubes of firm-fleshed white fish like cod or halibut in place of shrimp.

 Double Feature

Like all seafood, shrimp cooks very quickly. Do not overcook it, or it will be tough instead of tender. Use the method given above for all seafood. Allow it to simmer for no more than 2 minutes, and then turn off the heat and allow it to sit for an additional 5 minutes.

Shrimp Siciliana with Dried Currants, Pine Nuts, and Capers

Crunchy nuts, salty capers, and sweet dried currants make this a distinctive tomato sauce for shrimp.

Active time: 25 minutes

Start to finish: 40 minutes

Each serving has:

392 calories

186 calories from fat

21 g fat

2 g saturated fat

27 g protein

22 g carbohydrates

3 TB. olive oil

1 large onion, peeled and diced

4 garlic cloves, peeled and minced

1 (8-oz.) can tomato sauce

1 (14.5-oz.) can diced tomatoes, undrained

¾ cup dry white wine

2 TB. chopped fresh parsley

2 TB. chopped fresh oregano or 2 tsp. dried

2 tsp. fresh thyme or ½ tsp. dried

1 bay leaf

½ cup dried currants

¼ cup capers, drained and rinsed

¼ cup *pine nuts*

½ lb. extra large (16 to 20 per lb.) raw shrimp, peeled and deveined

Salt and freshly ground black pepper to taste

1. Heat olive oil in the pan over medium-high heat. Add onions and garlic and cook, stirring frequently, for 3 minutes or until onions are translucent. Stir in tomato sauce, tomatoes, wine, parsley, oregano, thyme, bay leaf, currants, and capers. Bring to a boil, stirring occasionally.

2. Reduce the heat to low and simmer sauce, uncovered, for 15 minutes, stirring occasionally. Remove and discard bay leaves. Remove ⅔ of sauce and divide it into two 1-quart resealable plastic bags for future use. (Sauce can be frozen for up to 3 months.)

3. While sauce is simmering, place pine nuts in a heavy small skillet over medium heat. Toast nuts, swirling the pan, for 3 minutes or until lightly browned. Remove nuts from the pan and set aside.

4. Add shrimp to remaining sauce. Bring to a boil, cover pan, and simmer for 2 minutes. Turn off the heat, but do not uncover the pan; allow shrimp to sit for 5 minutes to complete cooking. Season to taste with salt and pepper. Sprinkle with pine nuts and serve immediately.

5. When using remaining sauce, bring it to a simmer and cook shrimp as instructed above. Pine nuts should be toasted just prior to cooking the dish.

Variation: Use bay scallops, sea scallops cut into quarters, or ¾-inch cubes of firm-fleshed white fish in place of shrimp.

> ### Duet Dialogue
>
> **Pine nuts** also called *piñon* in Spanish and *pignoli* in Italian, are the nuts located inside the pine cones of various species of evergreen. To remove them, you must heat the pine cones and then pull out the nuts, which are in thin shells, by hand. This labor-intensive method is what makes them so expensive.

Mexican Red Snapper

This dish from the Veracruz region includes some chili flavors, as well as vegetables and green olives.

2 TB. olive oil

2 onions, peeled and thinly sliced

4 garlic cloves, peeled and minced

1 jalapeño chili, seeds and ribs removed, finely chopped

1 TB. chili powder

2 tsp. dried oregano, preferably Mexican

1 (14.5-oz.) can diced tomatoes, undrained

1½ cups fish stock or bottled clam juice

2 TB. freshly squeezed lemon juice

2 TB. tomato paste

1 tsp. grated lemon zest

½ cup sliced green olives

2 (6-oz.) red snapper or other firm-fleshed white fish fillets, rinsed

Salt and freshly ground black pepper to taste

Active time: 20 minutes
Start to finish: 35 minutes
Each serving has:
309 calories
123 calories from fat
14 g fat
2 g saturated fat
37 g protein
11 g carbohydrates

1. Heat oil in a medium skillet over medium-high heat. Add onion, garlic, and jalapeño. Cook, stirring frequently, for 3 minutes or until onion is translucent. Stir in chili powder and oregano. Cook for 1 minute, stirring constantly.

Double Feature

A chili pepper's seeds and ribs contain almost all of the capsaicin, the chemical compound that delivers the peppers' punch. Since small chilies have proportionately more seeds and ribs to flesh, a general rule is the smaller the chili, the hotter the pepper.

2. Add tomatoes, stock, lemon juice, tomato paste, lemon zest, and olives. Stir well. Bring to a boil, reduce the heat to low, and simmer sauce, uncovered, for 15 to 20 minutes or until vegetables are tender, stirring occasionally. Remove ⅔ of vegetable mixture and divide it into two 1-quart resealable plastic bags for future use. (Sauce can be frozen for up to 3 months.)

3. Add snapper to skillet, spooning vegetables and sauce on top of fillets. Cover the skillet and cook snapper for 5 minutes. Turn fillets gently with a slotted spatula and cook for an additional 3 to 5 minutes or until snapper flakes easily. Season to taste with salt and pepper. Serve immediately.

4. When using remaining sauce, bring it to a simmer and cook snapper as instructed above.

Variation: Use any firm-fleshed white fish fillet in place of snapper or ½ pound of peeled and deveined shrimp or bay scallops. If using shrimp or scallops, reduce cooking time to 2 minutes and allow the pan to sit covered for 5 minutes.

Sweet and Sour Cod

Fragrant ginger and sesame oil add nuances of flavor to this easy-to-prepare Chinese dish.

Active time: 12 minutes

Start to finish: 30 minutes

Each serving has:

288 calories

82 calories from fat

9 g fat

1 g saturated fat

32 g protein

19 g carbohydrates

¼ lb. fresh shiitake mushrooms

2 TB. Asian sesame oil

1 large red onion, peeled, halved, and sliced

3 scallions, rinsed, trimmed, and thinly sliced

4 garlic cloves, peeled and minced

2 TB. grated fresh ginger

½ tsp. red pepper flakes or more to taste

2 cups seafood stock or bottled clam juice

2 TB. balsamic vinegar

2 TB. soy sauce

2 TB. firmly packed dark brown sugar

2 celery stalks, trimmed and sliced

2 carrots, peeled and thinly sliced

⅔ lb. cod, rinsed and cut into 1-inch cubes

2 oz. snow peas, rinsed and stringed

1 cup bean sprouts, rinsed

2 tsp. cornstarch

2 TB. cold water

Salt to taste

1. Wipe mushrooms with a damp paper towel. Discard stems and slice mushrooms. Heat oil in a medium skillet over medium-high heat. Add onion, scallions, garlic, ginger, and red pepper flakes. Cook, stirring frequently, for 3 minutes or until onion is translucent. Stir in stock, vinegar, soy sauce, and brown sugar. Add celery, carrots, and mushrooms. Cook sauce for 15 to 20 minutes or until vegetables are crisp tender.

2. Remove ⅔ of sauce and divide it into two 1-quart resealable plastic bags for future use. (Sauce can be frozen for up to 3 months.)

3. Add fish, snow peas, and bean sprouts to remaining sauce. Bring to a boil, cover the pan, and simmer for 2 minutes. Combine cornstarch and water in a small bowl. Add mixture to sauce and stir well. Simmer sauce for 2 minutes or until sauce lightly thickens. Season to taste with salt. Serve immediately.

4. When using remaining sauce, bring it to a simmer and then cook cod and additional vegetables as instructed above.

Variation: Use any firm-fleshed white fish fillet in place of cod or ½ pound peeled and deveined shrimp or bay scallops. If using shrimp or scallops, reduce the cooking time to 2 minutes and allow the pan to sit covered for 5 minutes.

Double Trouble

Mixing cornstarch with cold water is essential to gaining a smooth sauce that is lightly thickened. Although this step might seem unnecessary, adding cornstarch directly into a boiling liquid forms instant lumps that you can not stir away.

Nantucket Seafood Stew with Linguiça

Sausage, fish stock, vegetables, and herbs form the base for this stew encountered when I lived on Nantucket.

Active time: 20 minutes

Start to finish: 40 minutes

Each serving has:

529 calories

286 calories from fat

32 g fat

1 g saturated fat

32 g protein

24 g carbohydrates

3 TB. olive oil

1 medium onion, peeled and diced

1 carrot, peeled and diced

1 celery rib, rinsed, trimmed, and diced

3 garlic cloves, peeled and minced

1 lb. mild *linguiça sausage*, diced

3 large tomatoes, rinsed, cored, seeded, and chopped

2 oranges, zest grated and juiced

½ cup dry white wine

3 cups fish stock or bottled clam juice

3 TB. chopped fresh parsley

2 tsp. fresh thyme or ½ teaspoon dried

1 bay leaf

3 TB. chopped fresh basil or 1 tsp. dried

Salt and freshly ground black pepper to taste

¼ lb. cod or any firm-fleshed white fillet, rinsed and cut into 1-inch cubes

¼ lb. bay scallops or sea scallops cut into quarters, rinsed

Duet Dialogue

Linguiça is a highly-spiced Portuguese sausage that's flavored with both garlic and paprika. Chorizo is the best sausage to substitute if linguiça is not available.

1. Heat olive oil in a heavy 2-quart saucepan over medium-high heat. Add onion, carrot, celery, and garlic. Cook, stirring frequently, for 3 minutes or until onion is translucent. Add linguiça and cook 3 minutes.

2. Add tomatoes, orange zest, orange juice, wine, stock, parsley, thyme, and bay leaf. Bring to a boil over high heat, reduce the heat to medium, and boil for 10 minutes or until liquid has reduced by ⅓, stirring occasionally. Add basil. Bring back to a boil and season to taste with salt and pepper. Remove and discard bay leaf. Remove ⅔ of stew base and divide it into two 1-quart resealable plastic bags for future use. (Stew base can be frozen for up to 3 months.)

3. Add cod and scallops to remaining soup. Bring to a boil, cover the pan, and simmer for 2 minutes. Turn off the heat, leave cover on the pan, and allow fish to sit for 5 minutes to complete the cooking. Serve immediately.

4. When using remaining soup, bring it to a simmer and then cook fish and scallops as instructed above.

Seafood Gumbo

What makes a true gumbo is both a dark brown roux and fresh okra, and this Creole classic has both.

½ cup vegetable oil

¾ cup all-purpose flour

2 TB. unsalted butter

1 large onion, peeled and diced

1 large green bell pepper, seeds and ribs removed, diced

2 celery ribs, trimmed and diced

5 garlic cloves, peeled and minced

4 cups fish stock or bottled clam juice

1 TB. fresh thyme or 1 tsp. dried

2 bay leaves

1 lb. okra, stems and tips trimmed, thinly sliced

1 (14.5-oz.) can diced tomatoes, undrained

½ to 1 tsp. hot red pepper sauce

Salt and freshly ground black pepper to taste

¼ lb. large (21 to 30 per lb.) shrimp, peeled and deveined

¼ lb. lump crabmeat, picked over to discard shell fragments

3 TB. chopped fresh parsley

| Active time: 20 minutes |
| Start to finish: 1¼ hours |
| Each serving has: |
| 459 calories |
| 249 calories from fat |
| 28 g fat |
| 7 g saturated fat |
| 30 g protein |
| 25 g carbohydrates |

1. Preheat the oven to 450°F. Combine oil and flour in an oven-proof Dutch oven and place in the oven. Bake *roux*, stirring occasionally, for 20 to 30 minutes or until walnut brown.

2. While roux is baking, melt butter in a large skillet over medium-high heat. Add onion, green bell pepper, celery, and garlic. Cook, stirring constantly, for 3 minutes or until onion is translucent. Set aside.

3. Remove roux from the oven and place it on the stove over medium heat. Add stock and whisk constantly until mixture comes to a boil and thickens.

4. Add vegetable mixture, thyme, bay leaves, okra, and tomatoes to the Dutch oven. Season to taste with hot red pepper sauce, salt, and pepper. Bring to a boil, cover, and cook over low heat for 35 to 40 minutes or until okra is very tender. Remove and discard bay leaves. Season to taste with salt and pepper. Remove ⅔ of mixture and divide it into two 1-quart resealable plastic bags for future use. (Gumbo base can be frozen for up to 3 months.)

5. Add shrimp, crabmeat, and parsley. Bring to a boil, cover the pan, and simmer for 2 minutes. Turn off the heat, leave cover on the pan, and allow seafood to sit for 5 minutes to complete the cooking. Serve immediately.

6. When using remaining gumbo, bring it to a simmer and then cook shrimp as instructed above.

Variation: Use any combination of seafood, including bay scallops or firm-fleshed fish fillets in place of shrimp or crab. To make chicken gumbo, use ½ pound chicken breast, cut into ½-inch cubes, and change stock to chicken stock. Cook chicken for 5 minutes or until cooked through and no longer pink.

Duet Dialogue

Roux (pronounced *ROO,* like in kangaroo) is French for a mixture of fat and flour used as a thickening agent for soups and sauces. The first step in all roux preparation is to cook the flour so the dish doesn't taste like library paste. For white sauces, cook this over low heat and use butter for fat. Many Creole and Cajun dishes, such as gumbo, use a fuller-flavored brown roux made with oil or drippings and cooked to a deep brown. The dark roux gives dishes an almost nutty flavor.

Seared Scallops with Creamed Leeks and Bacon

Silky sweet leeks are cooked in cream and then punctuated with crispy bacon as a base for quickly seared scallops.

8 leeks, white parts only

2 TB. unsalted butter

2 garlic cloves, peeled and minced

2 cups heavy cream

½ lb. bacon, cut into 1-inch pieces

Salt and freshly ground pepper to taste

½ lb. fresh bay scallops or sea scallops cut into quarters, rinsed, and patted dry with paper towels

Active time: 20 minutes
Start to finish: 35 minutes
Each serving has:
748 calories
537 calories from fat
60 g fat
30 g saturated fat
33 g protein
21 g carbohydrates

1. Trim leeks and slice thinly. Place slices in a colander and run under cold running water to remove all dirt.

2. Melt butter in a large skillet over low heat. Add leeks and garlic, cover, and cook, stirring occasionally, for 10 minutes. Add cream, increase the heat to medium, and cook, stirring occasionally, until mixture is reduced in volume by ⅔.

3. While sauce is cooking, fry bacon in a large skillet until crisp. Remove bacon with a slotted spoon and set aside. Discard all but 2 tablespoons bacon fat. When sauce is reduced, add bacon to it. Season to taste with salt and pepper. Remove ⅔ of mixture and divide it into two 1-quart resealable plastic bags for future use. (Leeks can be frozen for up to 3 months.)

4. Heat reserved bacon fat in a skillet over high heat, and when it begins to smoke, add scallops. Cook, stirring frequently, for 2 minutes. Season scallops to taste with salt and pepper. To serve, divide leek mixture onto 2 plates and top with scallops.

5. When using remaining sauce, heat it to a simmer and cook scallops in vegetable oil if bacon fat is not available.

Variation: Substitute jumbo (11 to 15 per lb.) shrimp or 1½-inch cubes of a firm-fleshed white fish, such as cod or halibut, for scallops.

Double Feature _____

You'll find two types of scallops on the market: tiny bay scallops, about the size of the top joint on your finger, and large sea scallops, about four times the size of bays. It's more important to have fresh, rather than frozen, scallops because scallops tend to turn tough after they're frozen. If you can only find fresh sea scallops, cut them into quarters for a recipe calling for bay scallops. In general, bay scallops are best for a fast sauté, and sea scallops are better for grilling and broiling.

Roast Cod with Tomatoes and Fennel

Vegetables cooked in wine and orange juice become the base for cod in this healthful dish.

Active time: 15 minutes

Start to finish: 55 minutes

Each serving has:

374 calories

99 calories from fat

11 g fat

2 g saturated fat

34.5 g protein

23 g carbohydrates

¼ **cup olive oil**

1 large onion, peeled and thinly sliced

3 garlic cloves, peeled and minced

2 fennel bulbs, trimmed, cored, and thinly sliced

1 (28-oz.) can diced tomatoes, undrained

2 cups fish stock or bottled clam juice

1 cup dry white wine

½ **cup orange juice**

¼ **cup *Pernod***

1 TB. grated orange zest

2 bay leaves

Salt and freshly ground black pepper to taste

2 (6-oz.) thick cod fillets, rinsed

1. Preheat the oven to 425°F. Heat olive oil in a large saucepan over medium heat. Add onion and garlic and cook, stirring frequently, for 3 minutes or until onion is translucent. Add fennel and cook for 2 minutes, stirring frequently. Add tomatoes, stock, wine, orange juice, Pernod, orange zest, and bay leaves to the saucepan. Bring to a boil, reduce the heat to low, and simmer, uncovered, stirring occasionally, for 10 minutes. Season to taste with salt and pepper.

2. Transfer vegetable mixture to a 9×13-inch baking pan. Cover the pan with aluminum foil and bake for 20 minutes. Remove the pan from the oven and stir well. Remove and discard bay leaves. Remove ⅔ of vegetable mixture and divide it into two 1-quart resealable plastic bags for future use. (Vegetables can be frozen for up to 3 months.)

3. Sprinkle cod with salt and pepper and place on top of remaining vegetables. Bake, uncovered, for about 10 to 15 minutes or until cod is opaque. Serve immediately.

4. When using remaining vegetables, reheat them covered with aluminum foil in a 425°F oven until simmering, and then cook cod as instructed above.

Variation: Bake any firm-fleshed white fish, such as halibut, snapper, or swordfish, for the same duration as cod. If using jumbo shrimp (11 to 15 per pound) or sea scallops, bake for 8 to 10 minutes.

Duet Dialogue

Pernod (pronounced *pear-NOH*) is a light green, licorice-flavored liqueur popular in France. It's usually mixed with water, at which time it turns milky white. Ouzo, a Greek concoction, is similar in flavor.

Swordfish *Tagine* with Dried Fruit and Garbanzo Beans

This Moroccan fish stew is made with vegetables, beans, and aromatic seasonings like coriander and ginger.

3 TB. olive oil

2 large onions, peeled and sliced

4 garlic cloves, peeled and minced

2 cups fish stock or bottled clam juice

1 (12-oz.) can apple juice

3 large carrots, peeled and cut into ½-inch slices

4 celery ribs, rinsed, trimmed, and cut into ½-inch slices

1 tsp. ground ginger

1 tsp. ground cumin

1 tsp. ground coriander

½ tsp. ground cinnamon

1 cup pitted prunes, halved

½ cup dried apricots, chopped

¼ cup dried currants

2 (15-oz.) cans garbanzo beans, drained and rinsed

⅔ lb. swordfish, rinsed and cut into 1-inch cubes

Salt and freshly ground black pepper to taste

Active time: 20 minutes

Start to finish: 55 minutes

Each serving has:

604 calories

141 calories from fat

16 g fat

3 g saturated fat

41 g protein

77 g carbohydrates

Duet Dialogue

Tagine (pronounced *tah-JEAN*) is the generic term used for Moroccan stews that can feature fish, meats, or poultry and are flavored with spices like cumin and coriander. They are traditionally cooked in a domed terra cotta pot, also called a "tagine," and are usually served with couscous.

1. Heat olive oil in a large saucepan over medium-high heat. Add onion and garlic. Cook, stirring frequently, for 3 minutes or until onion is translucent. Add stock, apple juice, carrots, celery, ginger, cumin, coriander, cinnamon, prunes, dried apricots, and currants to the pan. Bring to a boil and cook mixture, uncovered, over medium heat for 20 to 30 minutes or until vegetables are tender, stirring occasionally.

2. Add garbanzo beans to the pan and simmer for 5 minutes. Remove ⅔ of mixture and divide it into two 1-quart resealable plastic bags for future use. (Tagine base can be frozen for up to 3 months.)

3. Add swordfish to remaining mixture. Bring to a boil, cover pan, and simmer for 2 minutes. Turn off the heat, leave the pan covered, and allow fish to sit for 5 minutes to complete cooking. Season with salt and pepper.

4. When using remaining tagine base, bring it to a simmer and cook fish as instructed above.

Variation: Substitute jumbo (11 to 15 per pound) shrimp or 1½-inch cubes of a firm-fleshed white fish, such as cod or halibut, for swordfish.

Chapter 9

The Meat of the Matter

In This Chapter

- ◆ Vibrant beef stews
- ◆ Lusty lamb stews
- ◆ Delicate pork and veal stews

Meat stews are quintessential comfort food because they fill the house with wonderful scents as they slowly bake. And they're a full meal in a pot—complete with healthful vegetables.

You'll find delicious stew recipes in this chapter, drawn from a United Nations of cuisines. What we consider a stew in the United States is a sandpot in China or a ragout in France. Stews are popular worldwide, and the tantalizing flavors from these dishes validate that claim.

Speedy Stews

As with all recipes in this part of the book, you'll be able to enjoy a dish three times from one recipe preparation. But the difference in this chapter is that you're adding all the meat for the dish's three appearances to the initial cooking. The process is the reverse of the poultry recipes in Chapter 7 and the seafood recipes in Chapter 8. Those recipes instructed you to prepare the sauce as a triple batch but add the appropriate protein for one meal only.

The reason for this change in the game plan is simple—meats take time to cook and freeze beautifully while vegetables are rendered limp and lifeless after freezing. That's why leftover stews are never as appealing as one hot from the oven. After freezing, potatoes can be mealy while bright green peas or green beans are rendered a drab olive hue.

Even with this change, the portions you're saving for later will easily fit into a 1-quart resealable plastic bag. The vegetables—and not the meat—take up volume in these dishes, which also makes them most healthful.

An easy way to thaw stew is to place it in the refrigerator the day or two before you want to eat it, or you can always use a microwave oven. But do not thaw food at room temperature. That's a cardinal rule for food safety. (You can find more tips on food safety in Chapter 1.)

Of course, if you're having folks over for dinner, feel free to triple the extra ingredients needed to finish the dish, and you will have dinner for six.

The Benefits of Braising

Every culture has less-tender cuts of meat—which are also usually less expensive—that are simmered in aromatic liquid for many hours until they're tender.

That's what braising is all about—tenderness. And the amount of time it takes to reach the descriptive state of "fork tender" depends on each individual piece of meat. No hard-and-fast rules exist.

Braising is a low-heat method because the meat is the same temperature as the simmering liquid, 212°F. This simmering converts the collagen of the meat's connective tissue to gelatin, which makes the meat tender. There's no fear of the outside drying out, as in high-heat dry roasting, because the food is covered with a liquid that produces a moist heat. That's also why it takes almost as long to cook a stew, with meat cut in small pieces, as it does to braise a large roast. The only difference is the time the meat takes to reach the same temperature as the liquid.

The tougher the piece of meat, the more connective tissue it has, so the more tender it will become while braising. Conversely, if an innately tender cut of meat, such as a tenderloin or rib roast, is braised, it will become tough because there is no collagen to convert.

Beef in Red Wine (*Boeuf Bourgignon*)

Mushrooms, onions, and potatoes are cooked in an herbed wine sauce for this classic French stew.

½ lb. white mushrooms

2 lb. lean stewing beef

½ cup all-purpose flour

Salt and freshly ground black pepper to taste

½ lb. bacon, cut into 1-inch pieces

2 cups dry red wine

1 (14.5-oz.) can beef stock

¼ cup brandy

2 TB. tomato paste

1 large onion, peeled and diced

1 carrot, peeled and sliced

4 garlic cloves, peeled and minced

¼ cup chopped fresh parsley

1 TB. herbes de Provence

1 bay leaf

½ lb. baby potatoes, scrubbed and halved

2 carrots, peeled and cut into 1-inch pieces

2 TB. unsalted butter

1 TB. olive oil

½ cup frozen pearl onions

½ cup frozen peas

Active time: 30 minutes
Start to finish: 3 hours
Each serving has:
880 calories
395 calories from fat
44 g fat
16 g saturated fat
57 g protein
47 g carbohydrates

1. Preheat the oven to 350°F. Wipe mushrooms with a damp paper towel. Trim stems and cut in half if small or into quarters if large and set aside.

2. Rinse beef and pat dry on paper towels. Trim off all visible fat and cut beef into 1-inch cubes. Season flour with salt and pepper. Dust food with seasoned flour, shaking off any excess, and set aside.

3. Place bacon in an ovenproof Dutch oven over medium-high heat. Cook bacon for 5 to 7 minutes or until crisp. Remove bacon from the pan with a slotted spoon and set aside. Add beef cubes to the pan and turn beef with tongs to brown on all sides. Do this in batches if necessary.

4. Discard bacon grease and return bacon and beef to the Dutch oven. Add wine, stock, brandy, tomato paste, onion, carrot, garlic, parsley, Herbes de Provence, and bay leaf.

Double Trouble

It's important when cooking with wine or any liquid containing acid—even canned tomatoes—to use a nonreactive pan. That means stainless steel, tin-lined copper, or enameled iron. An aluminum pan will give food a metallic taste.

5. Bring to a boil, cover the pan, place it in the oven, and bake for 2 hours. Meat will not be tender at this point. Remove and discard bay leaf and season to taste with salt and pepper. Remove ⅔ of stew and divide it into two 1-quart resealable plastic bags for future use. (Stew can be frozen for up to 3 months.) For future meals, bring one portion to a simmer and then continue with the recipe as follows.

6. Add potatoes and carrots to remaining stew and bring to a boil on top of the stove. Return stew to the oven and bake for an additional 45 minutes. While stew is baking, heat butter and olive oil in a skillet over medium-high heat. Add mushrooms and cook, stirring frequently, for 5 to 7 minutes or until mushrooms are browned and liquid has evaporated.

7. Add mushrooms, onions, and peas to stew and bake an additional 15 minutes. Season to taste with salt and pepper and serve immediately.

Chinese Beef Stew

Every cuisine has stews; in Chinese cooking they're called sand-pots. This one is flavored with ginger, garlic, and sesame and has crispy snow peas as a garnish.

2 lb. lean stewing beef

2 TB. Asian sesame oil

3 scallions, trimmed and thinly sliced

2 TB. grated fresh ginger

4 garlic cloves, peeled and minced

1 (14.5-oz.) can beef stock

½ cup dry sherry

3 TB. soy sauce

2 TB. Chinese *oyster sauce*

1 TB. firmly packed dark brown sugar

1 TB. Chinese chili oil or ¼ tsp. red pepper flakes

1 tsp. Chinese five-spice powder

Salt and freshly ground black pepper to taste

½ lb. white mushrooms, wiped with a damp paper towel, trimmed, and sliced

10 baby carrots, peeled and halved lengthwise

¼ lb. asparagus, rinsed, trimmed, and cut into ½-inch slices

2 oz. snow peas, rinsed and stringed

2 tsp. cornstarch

2 TB. cold water

Active time: 20 minutes
Start to finish: 2¾ hours
Each serving has:
331 calories
151 calories from fat
17 g fat
6 g saturated fat
35.5 g protein
7 g carbohydrates

1. Preheat the oven to 350° F. Rinse beef and pat dry with paper towels. Trim off all visible fat and cut beef into 1-inch cubes.

2. Heat sesame oil in an ovenproof Dutch oven over medium-high heat. Add beef cubes to the pan and turn beef with tongs to brown on all sides. Do this in batches if necessary. Remove beef from the pan with a slotted spoon and set aside. Add scallions, ginger, and garlic to the pan. Cook, stirring constantly, for 1 minute.

3. Return beef to the pan and stir in stock, sherry, soy sauce, oyster sauce, brown sugar, chili oil, and five-spice powder. Bring to a boil, cover the pan, place it in the oven, and bake for 2¼ hours. Meat will not be tender at this point. Season to taste with salt and pepper. Remove ⅔ of stew and divide it into two 1-quart heavy resealable plastic bags for future use. (Stew can be frozen for up to 3 months.) For future meals bring one

Duet Dialogue

Oyster sauce, another seasoning staple of the Chinese pantry, is made from oysters, brine, and soy sauce, which is cooked until it's deep brown, thick, and concentrated. This sauce gives dishes a rich flavor that's not at all "fishy," and it's not as salty as soy sauce.

portion of frozen stew to a simmer and then continue with the recipe as follows.

4. Add mushrooms and carrots to remaining stew. Bring to a boil on top of the stove, return the pan to the oven, and bake for 20 minutes. Add asparagus and bake for an additional 10 minutes. Add snow peas and bake for 5 minutes more.

5. Combine cornstarch and water in a small bowl. Remove stew from the oven and place it on the stove over medium-high heat. Add cornstarch mixture and simmer for 2 minutes until stew thickens. Serve immediately.

Variation: Substitute cubes of pork loin for beef. Reduce the initial cooking time to 1 hour and then finish the recipe as instructed.

Greek-Style Beef Stew with Vegetables and Feta

Aromatic cinnamon and cloves, a touch of brown sugar and vinegar, and dried fruit give this stew a sweet and sour profile.

Active time: 20 minutes
Start to finish: 3 hours
Each serving has:
982 calories
554 calories from fat
61.5 g fat
13 g saturated fat
49 g protein
55 g carbohydrates

1 Italian eggplant

Salt to taste

1 medium zucchini

1 small red bell pepper

2 lb. lean stewing beef

Freshly ground black pepper to taste

½ cup olive oil

1 medium onion, peeled and chopped

3 garlic cloves, peeled and minced

1½ cups dry red wine

1 cup beef stock

3 TB. balsamic vinegar

3 TB. firmly packed light brown sugar

1 (6-oz.) can tomato paste

1 tsp. dried oregano

1 tsp. ground cumin

½ tsp. ground cloves

2 bay leaves

2 (2-inch) cinnamon sticks

½ cup dried currants

2 tsp. grated orange zest

¼ cup pine nuts

½ cup feta cheese, crumbled

1. Preheat the oven to 350°F. Rinse eggplant, discard cap, and cut into ½-inch cubes. Place eggplant in a colander and sprinkle liberally with salt. Place a plate on top of eggplant cubes and weight the plate with cans. Place the colander in the sink or on a plate and allow eggplant to drain for 30 minutes. Rinse eggplant cubes and squeeze hard to remove water. Wring out remaining water with a cloth tea towel.

2. Rinse and trim zucchini and cut into ½-inch cubes. Rinse red bell pepper, remove seeds and ribs, and slice thinly. Rinse beef and pat dry with paper towels. Trim off all visible fat and cut beef into 1-inch cubes. Season cubes with salt and pepper. Heat ¼ cup olive oil in an ovenproof Dutch oven over medium-high heat. Add beef cubes to the pan and turn beef with tongs to brown on all sides. Do this in batches if necessary. Remove beef from the pan with a slotted spoon and set aside.

3. Add onion and garlic and cook, stirring frequently, for 3 minutes or until onion is translucent. Add beef cubes, wine, stock, vinegar, brown sugar, and tomato paste. Stir together until smooth. Add oregano, cumin, cloves, bay leaves, cinnamon sticks, currants, and orange zest. Season to taste with salt and pepper.

4. Bring to a boil, cover the pan, place it in the oven, and bake for 2 hours. Meat will not be tender at this point. Remove and discard cinnamon sticks and bay leaves. Season to taste with salt and pepper. Remove ⅔ of stew and divide it into two 1-quart heavy resealable plastic bags for future use. (Stew can be frozen for up to 3 months.) For future meals, bring one portion to a simmer and then continue with the recipe as follows.

5. While beef is baking, heat remaining olive oil in a large skillet over medium heat. Add eggplant, zucchini, and red bell pepper. Cook, stirring frequently, for 3 to 5 minutes or until eggplant has begun to soften. Add vegetables to remaining stew and bake for 30 minutes. While stew is cooking, place pine nuts on a baking sheet and toast nuts in the oven for 5 to 7 minutes or until browned.

6. Remove stew from the oven and season to taste with salt and pepper. Serve immediately, sprinkled with feta and pine nuts.

Variation: Substitute cubes of boneless leg of lamb for beef. Decrease the initial baking time to 1¾ hours.

Double Feature

Using cinnamon sticks rather than ground cinnamon in dishes creates a more subtle cinnamon flavor. If you only have ground cinnamon, substitute ¼ teaspoon for each 2-inch cinnamon stick specified.

Beef Stew with Spiced Chutney Sauce

This stew is a fusion of Western and Asian flavors, and it contains curry, as well as crunchy water chestnuts.

Active time: 25 minutes

Start to finish: 3 hours

Each serving has:

519 calories

187 calories from fat

21 g fat

5 g saturated fat

39.5 g protein

46 g carbohydrates

2 lb. lean stewing beef

Salt and freshly ground black pepper to taste

¼ cup vegetable oil

1 onion, peeled and diced

3 garlic cloves, peeled and minced

2 tsp. curry powder

½ tsp. ground ginger

½ cup jarred mango *chutney*

⅓ cup raisins

1 (14.5-oz.) can beef stock

1 (8-oz.) can sliced water chestnuts, drained and rinsed

2 carrots, peeled and thinly sliced

2 celery ribs, rinsed, trimmed, and thinly sliced

1 cup broccoli florets, rinsed

2 oz. snow peas, rinsed and stringed

2 tsp. cornstarch

1 TB. cold water

2 scallions, rinsed, trimmed, and thinly sliced

Duet Dialogue

Chutney, from the Hindi word *chatni*, is a spicy Indian condiment containing some sort of fruit or vegetable, vinegar, and spices. It's always used as an accompaniment to curried dishes, but you can also use it with many foods to add a fat-free flavor accent.

1. Preheat the oven to 350°F. Sprinkle beef cubes with salt and pepper. Heat oil in an ovenproof Dutch oven over medium-high heat. Add beef cubes to the pan and turn beef with tongs to brown on all sides. Do this in batches if necessary. Remove beef cubes from the pan with a slotted spoon and set aside.

2. Add onion and garlic to the Dutch oven and cook, stirring frequently, for 3 minutes or until onion is translucent. Stir in curry powder and ginger and cook, stirring constantly, for 1 minute. Stir in chutney, raisins, stock, and water chestnuts.

3. Return beef to the pan, bring to a boil, cover the pan, place it in the oven, and bake for 2 hours. Meat will not be tender at this point. Season to taste with salt and pepper. Remove ⅔ of stew and divide it into two 1-quart heavy resealable plastic bags for future use. (Stew can be frozen for up to 3 months.) For future meals, bring one portion to a simmer and then continue with the recipe as follows.

4. Remove the Dutch oven from the oven and stir in carrots and celery. Cover and bake for 20 minutes. Add broccoli and bake for 10 minutes; then stir in snow peas and bake for an additional 10 minutes or until snow peas are crisp tender.

5. Combine cornstarch and water in a small bowl. Remove stew from the oven and place it over medium heat. Stir in cornstarch mixture, bring stew to a boil, and simmer for 1 minute or until stew thickens. Sprinkle dish with scallions and serve immediately.

Variation: Substitute cubes of boneless leg of lamb for beef. Decrease the initial baking time to 1¾ hours.

New Mexican Pork and Hominy Stew (Pozole)

Hominy are whole grains of corn that are preserved, and this hearty peasant stew is flavored with mild chilies and also contains corn and yams.

2 scallions

2 lb. lean pork

Salt and freshly ground black pepper to taste

3 TB. vegetable oil

1 large onion, peeled and diced

3 garlic cloves, peeled and minced

2 tsp. ground cumin

2 tsp. dried oregano, preferably Mexican

1 (14.5-oz.) can chicken stock

1 (14.5-oz.) can diced tomatoes, undrained

1 (4-oz.) can diced mild green chilies, drained

2 (15-oz.) cans yellow hominy, drained and well rinsed

1 medium yam, peeled and cut into ½-inch dice

½ cup frozen corn

2 oz. fresh green beans, rinsed, stemmed, and cut into 1-inch lengths or ⅔ cup frozen green beans, thawed

2 TB. fresh cilantro, chopped

Sour cream

Lime wedges

Active time: 20 minutes
Start to finish: 1⅓ hours
Each serving has:
311 calories
120 calories from fat
13 g fat
4 g saturated fat
20 g protein
29 g carbohydrates

1. Preheat the oven to 350°F. Rinse and trim scallions, discarding all but 2 inches of green tops. Slice scallions thinly and set aside.

2. Rinse pork and pat dry with paper towels. Trim all visible fat. Cut pork into 1-inch cubes and sprinkle with salt and pepper. Heat oil in an ovenproof Dutch oven over medium-high heat. Add pork cubes in a single layer and cook, turning pieces with tongs, until browned on all sides. Remove pork cubes with tongs and set aside.

3. Add onion and garlic to the Dutch oven and cook, stirring frequently, for 3 minutes or until onion is translucent. Stir in cumin and oregano and cook, stirring constantly, for 1 minute. Add pork cubes, stock, tomatoes, and green chilies.

4. Bring to a boil, cover the pan, place it in the oven, and bake for 45 minutes. Add hominy and bake for an additional 15 minutes. Meat will not be tender at this point. Season to taste with salt and pepper. Remove ⅔ of stew and divide it into two 1-quart heavy resealable plastic bags for future use. (Stew can be frozen for up to 3 months.) For future meals, bring one portion to a simmer and then continue with the recipe as follows.

5. Add yam to remaining stew and bake for 30 minutes. Add corn, green beans, and scallions and bake an additional 20 minutes or until pork is very tender. Season to taste with salt and pepper, sprinkle with cilantro, and serve immediately, passing bowls of sour cream and lime wedges.

Double Feature

Pork is much more delicate in flavor and lighter in color than beef or lamb, so use chicken stock rather than beef stock for pork dishes because beef stock would darken the delicate color and overpower the subtle flavor. Pork is rarely, if ever, made into a stock on its own, although you can use smoked ham bones to flavor stocks and soups.

Cuban Pork Stew

Summer squash and green beans add texture and color to this vibrant stew laced with rum.

2 lb. lean pork

½ cup all-purpose flour

Salt and freshly ground black pepper to taste

3 TB. vegetable oil

2 large onions, peeled and thinly sliced

3 garlic cloves, peeled and minced

3 TB. grated fresh ginger

1 (14.5-oz.) can chicken stock

⅓ cup cider vinegar

⅓ cup dark rum

⅓ cup firmly packed dark brown sugar

1 carrot, peeled and thinly sliced

1 celery rib, rinsed, trimmed, and thinly sliced

1 small summer squash, rinsed, trimmed, and thinly sliced

½ cup frozen green beans, thawed

Active time: 20 minutes
Start to finish: 1½ hours
Each serving has:
536 calories
226 calories from fat
25 g fat
7 g saturated fat
36.5 g protein
34 g carbohydrates

1. Preheat the oven to 350°F. Rinse pork and pat dry with paper towels. Trim all visible fat and cut pork into 1-inch cubes. Combine flour, salt, and pepper in a shallow bowl and mix well. Dust pork with seasoned flour, shaking off any excess.

2. Heat oil in an ovenproof Dutch oven over medium-high heat. Add pork cubes to the pan and turn pork with tongs to brown on all sides. Do this in batches if necessary. Remove pork from the pan with a slotted spoon and set aside. Add onion, garlic, and ginger. Cook, stirring frequently, for 3 minutes or until onion is translucent. Return pork to the pan and add stock, vinegar, rum, and brown sugar.

3. Bring to a boil, cover the pan, place it in the oven, and bake for 1 hour. Meat will not be tender at this point. Season to taste with salt and pepper. Remove ⅔ of stew and divide it into two 1-quart heavy resealable plastic bags for future use. (Stew can be frozen for up to 3 months.) For future meals, bring one portion to a simmer and then continue with the recipe as follows.

4. Add carrot and celery to remaining stew. Bring to a boil on top of the stove and then bake for 20 minutes. Add summer squash and green beans and bake for an additional 10 minutes. Season to taste with salt and pepper. Serve immediately.

Variation: Substitute cubes of turkey or veal for pork, and cook at the same rate.

Double Feature

Have you ever had brown sugar turn into a rock in the cupboard? Don't throw it out. Add a few slices of apple and close the bag securely. In a day or so, the sugar will have softened again. If you need to use some immediately, chip off some of the hard sugar and dissolve it in water.

Lamb Stew with Spring Vegetables (Navarin Printanier)

The lusty flavor of rosy lamb is balanced by the delicacy of fresh green vegetables in this classic French stew scented with rosemary.

Active time: 25 minutes

Start to finish: 2⅔ hours

Each serving has:

657 calories

197 calories from fat

22 g fat

5 g saturated fat

43 g protein

69 g carbohydrates

2 lb. boneless leg of lamb

½ cup all-purpose flour

2 TB. granulated sugar

Salt and freshly ground black pepper to taste

¼ cup olive oil

1 (14.5-oz.) can beef stock

1 (14.5-oz.) can diced tomatoes, undrained

1 cup dry red wine

2 TB. tomato paste

3 garlic cloves, peeled and minced

3 TB. chopped fresh rosemary or 1 TB. dried

1 TB. fresh thyme or 1 tsp. dried

1 bay leaf

10 baby carrots

¼ lb. red-skinned potatoes, scrubbed and cut into ½-inch dice

4 white boiling onions, peeled

½ cup frozen green peas

½ cup frozen green beans

2 TB. chopped fresh parsley

 Déjà Two

While it's never enjoyed the same popularity in the United States, lamb is the most popular meat by far in Mediterranean and Middle Eastern countries. Paintings of domesticated sheep are found in Egyptian tomb paintings dating from 2800 B.C.E., and the roasting of baby lamb has been part of Greek culture since the same era.

1. Preheat the oven to 350°F. Rinse lamb and pat dry with paper towels. Trim all visible fat and cut lamb into 1-inch cubes. Combine flour, sugar, salt, and pepper in a shallow bowl and mix well. Dust lamb with seasoned flour, shaking off any excess.

2. Heat olive oil in an ovenproof Dutch oven over medium-high heat. Add lamb cubes to the pan and turn lamb with tongs to brown on all sides. Do this in batches if necessary. Remove lamb with a slotted spoon and set aside. Discard oil from the Dutch oven and add stock, tomatoes, wine, tomato paste, garlic, rosemary, thyme, and bay leaf. Stir well and return lamb to the pan.

3. Bring to a boil, cover the pan, place it in the oven, and bake for 1½ hours. Remove and discard bay leaf and season to taste with salt and pepper. Meat will not be tender at this point. Remove ⅔ of stew and divide it into two 1-quart heavy resealable plastic bags for future use. (Stew can be frozen for up to 3 months.)

For future meals, bring one portion of frozen stew to a simmer and then continue with the recipe as follows.

4. Add carrots, potatoes, and onions to stew. Bring to a boil on top of the stove and then return the pan to the oven and bake for 45 minutes. Stir in peas and green beans and bake for an additional 10 minutes. Season to taste with salt and pepper, sprinkle with parsley, and serve immediately.

Moroccan Spiced Lamb Stew with Dried Fruit

Combining dried fruits with meats is a central theme to Moroccan cooking, and they're joined with tender vegetables and crunchy almonds in this stew.

2 lb. boneless leg of lamb	¼ tsp. ground cinnamon
½ cup all-purpose flour	¾ cup pitted prunes, diced
Salt and freshly ground black pepper to taste	½ cup dried apricots, diced
¼ cup olive oil	1 carrot, peeled and thinly sliced
1 large onion, peeled and chopped	1 sweet potato, peeled, halved, and thinly sliced
2 garlic cloves, peeled and minced	½ red bell pepper, seeds and ribs removed, thinly sliced
1 (14.5-oz.) can beef stock	1 yellow squash, rinsed, trimmed, and thinly sliced
1 cup dry red wine	¼ cup slivered blanched almonds
1 tsp. ground ginger	

> **Active time:** 20 minutes
> **Start to finish:** 2½ hours
> **Each serving has:**
> 576 calories
> 229 calories from fat
> 25 g fat
> 5 g saturated fat
> 40 g protein
> 51 g carbohydrates

1. Preheat the oven to 350° F. Rinse lamb and pat dry with paper towels. Trim all visible fat and cut lamb into 1-inch cubes. Combine flour, salt, and pepper in a shallow bowl and mix well. Dust lamb with seasoned flour, shaking off any excess.

2. Heat oil in an ovenproof Dutch oven over medium-high heat and add lamb cubes to the pan. Turn lamb with tongs to brown

Double Feature

In addition to looking more appealing, toasted nuts have a crispier texture and a more pleasing flavor because toasting releases the nuts' fragrant and aromatic oils.

on all sides, Do this in batches if necessary. Remove lamb cubes with a slotted spoon and set aside.

3. Add onion and garlic and cook, stirring frequently, for 3 minutes or until onion is translucent. Add lamb cubes, stock, wine, ginger, cinnamon, prunes, and dried apricots. Bring to a boil, cover the pan, place it in the oven, and bake for 1½ hours. Meat will not be tender at this point. Season to taste with salt and pepper. Remove ⅔ of stew and divide it into two 1-quart heavy resealable plastic bags for future use. (Stew can be frozen for up to 3 months.) For future meals, bring one portion to a simmer and then continue with the recipe as follows.

4. Add carrot, sweet potato, and red pepper. Bake for an additional 30 minutes or until sweet potato and lamb are tender. Add yellow squash and cook for an additional 10 minutes.

5. While stew is baking, place almonds on a baking sheet and toast for 5 to 7 minutes or until lightly browned. Remove from the oven and set aside. Remove stew from the oven and season to taste with salt and pepper. To serve, sprinkle each portion with almonds and serve immediately.

Variation: Use beef in place of lamb, and increase the initial baking time to 2 hours.

Veal Marengo

The delicacy of tender veal is highlighted by the herbed white wine and tomato sauce in which the meat is cooked.

¼ lb. white mushrooms

2 lb. veal stew meat

1 orange

½ cup all-purpose flour

Salt and freshly ground black pepper to taste

¼ cup olive oil

1 large onion, peeled and diced

3 garlic cloves, peeled and minced

1 (14.5-oz.) can diced tomatoes

1 (14.5-oz.) can chicken stock

¾ cup dry white wine

1 TB. fresh thyme or 1 tsp. dried

1 bay leaf

1 TB. unsalted butter

1 TB. olive oil

½ cup frozen pearl onions, thawed

½ cup frozen peas, thawed

> **Active time:** 20 minutes
> **Start to finish:** 1¼ hours
> **Each serving has:**
> 581 calories
> 303 calories from fat
> 34 g fat
> 10 g saturated fat
> 38 g protein
> 28 g carbohydrates

1. Preheat the oven to 350°F. Wipe mushrooms with a damp paper towel. Discard stems, slice mushrooms, and set aside.

2. Rinse veal and pat dry with paper towels. Trim all visible fat and cut veal into 1-inch cubes. Rinse orange, grate off zest, and squeeze for juice. Set aside. Season flour with salt and pepper. Dust veal with seasoned flour, shaking off any excess.

3. Heat oil in an ovenproof Dutch oven over medium-high heat and add veal cubes to the pan. Turn veal with tongs to brown on all sides. Do this in batches if necessary. Remove veal from the pan with a slotted spoon and set aside. Add onion and garlic to the skillet. Cook, stirring frequently, for 3 minutes or until onion is translucent. Add orange zest, orange juice, tomatoes, chicken stock, wine, thyme, and bay leaf. Stir well and return veal to the pan.

4. Bring to a boil, cover the pan, place it in the oven, and bake for 1 hour. Meat will not be tender at this point. Remove and discard bay leaf and season to taste with salt and pepper. Remove ⅔ of stew and divide it into two 1-quart heavy resealable plastic bags for future use. (Stew can be frozen for up to 3 months.) For future meals, bring one portion to a simmer and then continue with the recipe as follows.

Déjà Two

This dish was invented to celebrate a victory. When Napoleon's troops won the Battle of Marengo on June 14, 1800, his cook, Dunand, created this stew in the camp kitchen. It was originally made with chicken, but soon became a veal classic.

5. While stew is baking, heat butter and olive oil in a skillet over medium-high heat. Add mushrooms and cook, stirring frequently, for 5 to 7 minutes or until mushrooms are browned and liquid has evaporated.

6. Add mushrooms, onions, and peas to stew and bake an additional 15 minutes. Season to taste with salt and pepper and serve immediately.

Chapter 10

Pasta Perfect

In This Chapter

- ◆ Pastas sauced by delicate vegetables
- ◆ Italian pastas with meats and seafood
- ◆ Pastas with international flavors

With a few boxes of dried pasta in the house you know you'll never go hungry. And with a few batches of these sauces in your freezer, "emergency meals" will take on a new elegance.

The pasta sauces that I feature in this chapter can be frozen for up to three months and all take well to reheating. And their flavors vary from delicate to fiery and from authentic Italian to *nouvelle* Fusion Cuisine.

Pasta Power

Good-quality dried pasta is made with a high percentage of high-gluten semolina, the inner part of the grain of hard durum wheat. The gluten gives the pasta resilience and allows it to cook while remaining somewhat firm, thus reaching the state of *al dente*.

> **Duet Dialogue**
>
> **Al dente** (pronounced *al-DENT-ay*) is the Italian for "against the teeth" and refers to pasta (or other ingredients such as rice) that is neither soft nor hard, but just slightly firm against the teeth. This, according to many pasta aficionados, is the perfect way to cook pasta.

Pasta is merely flour and water, so it is high in carbohydrates. The higher the semolina content of pasta, the more protein it contains. The protein in pasta is an incomplete protein, like that of rice, which can be completed by mixing it with foods such as beans.

Eggless pasta contains no fat, and using spinach or tomato flour adds other nutrients. Each ounce of pasta is approximately 100 calories.

The Dried Dilemma

As a general rule, pasta imported from Italy is superior to American factory-made products due to its higher semolina content. Try to purchase pasta that you can see through a cellophane window in the box. The pasta should be smooth and shiny, not crumbly.

After you open the box, store pasta in a sealed plastic bag, and it will stay fresh for at least 6 months. You can still use pasta if it's stale; just add a few minutes to the cooking time.

Traditional dried Italian pastas are named according to their shape. For example, fusilli are twists, and fiochetti are bows. You could fill an entire kitchen with boxes of different-shaped pasta if you wanted a complete selection. Not many people have such a pantry luxury, however; so instead, use the cooking times and sizes in the following table to determine alternatives you might have on hand when making a recipe.

Pasta Name	Cooking Time
Farfalle, fiochetti, fusilli, orecchiette, penne, rigatoni, ziti	10 to 12 minutes
Anelli, cavatappi, macaroni, manicotti, mostaccioli, orzo, rotelle	8 to 10 minutes
Fettuccine, linguine, spaghetti, tagliatelli	6 to 9 minutes

Fusilli with Porcini Puttanesca Sauce

Olives, capers, and red pepper flakes in addition to woodsy wild mushrooms give this tomato sauce its texture and flavor.

½ cup dried porcini mushrooms, chopped

1 cup boiling water

3 TB. olive oil

1 large onion, peeled and chopped

4 garlic cloves, peeled and minced

2 (14.5-oz.) cans diced tomatoes, undrained

½ cup Niçcoise olives, pitted and chopped

2 TB. tomato paste

2 TB. capers, drained and rinsed

2 TB. anchovy paste (optional)

2 tsp. dried oregano

2 tsp. dried basil

¼ tsp. red pepper flakes or to taste

Salt to taste

6 oz. fusilli pasta

¼ cup freshly grated Parmesan cheese

Active time: 20 minutes

Start to finish: 40 minutes

Each serving has:

530 calories

112 calories from fat

12 g fat

3 g saturated fat

19 g protein

89 g carbohydrates

1. Soak mushrooms in boiling water for 10 minutes, pushing them into water with the back of a spoon. Drain mushrooms, reserving soaking liquid. Strain soaking liquid through a sieve or coffee filter and set aside.

2. While mushrooms are soaking, heat olive oil in a heavy 2-quart saucepan over medium-high heat. Add onion and garlic and cook, stirring frequently, for 3 minutes or until onion is translucent. Add tomatoes, olives, tomato paste, capers, anchovy paste (if using), oregano, basil, and red pepper flakes. Bring to a boil over medium-high heat.

3. Add mushrooms and strained soaking liquid to the saucepan. Reduce the heat to low and simmer sauce, uncovered, for 20 minutes or until slightly thickened, stirring occasionally. Season to taste with salt. Remove ⅔ of sauce and divide it into two 1-quart resealable plastic bags for future use. (Sauce can be frozen for up to 3 months.)

 Double Feature

Any food that comes in a tube, like anchovy paste or tomato paste, can be hard to extract fully, even if you roll up the tube. One way to make sure you're getting all the product out is to use a rolling pin on the metal tube before turning the tube forward.

4. While sauce is simmering, bring a large pot of salted water to a boil. Add pasta and cook according to package directions. Drain pasta and add to remaining sauce. Serve immediately, passing Parmesan cheese separately.

5. When using divided sauce, bring it to a simmer, cook 6 ounces of pasta, and freshly grate Parmesan cheese.

Ziti with Onion Sauce

If you like the sweet flavor of caramelized onions, then this sauce is for you, and there are herbs to add interest, too.

Active time: 30 minutes

Start to finish: 65 minutes

Each serving has:

536 calories

89 calories from fat

10 g fat

3 g saturated fat

20 g protein

92 g carbohydrates

2 TB. olive oil	1 TB. fresh thyme or 1 tsp. dried
3 lb. yellow onions, peeled and thinly sliced	3 TB. chopped fresh parsley
1 TB. granulated sugar	2 TB. balsamic vinegar
4 garlic cloves, peeled and minced	Salt and freshly ground black pepper to taste
3 cups chicken stock	6 oz. ziti
4 TB. freshly grated Parmesan cheese	¼ cup freshly grated Parmesan cheese
2 TB. chopped fresh oregano or 2 tsp. dried	

Duet Dialogue

To **sweat** vegetables is to cook them over low heat covered in a small amount of fat. As the juices are released, steam is created, and this softens vegetables without browning them.

1. Heat oil in a heavy 4-quart saucepan over medium heat. Add onions, tossing to coat them well. Cover the pan and *sweat* onions, stirring occasionally, for 15 minutes.

2. Stir in sugar and garlic. Raise the heat to medium-high, and cook onions for 15 minutes or until brown, stirring frequently. Add stock, bring to a boil, and cook over medium heat, stirring occasionally, for 20 minutes or until mixture is reduced by half.

3. Stir in Parmesan cheese, oregano, thyme, parsley, and vinegar and season to taste with salt and pepper. Remove ⅔ of sauce and divide it into two 1-quart resealable plastic bags for future use. (Sauce can be frozen for up to 3 months.)

4. While sauce is simmering, bring a large pot of salted water to a boil. Add pasta and cook according to package directions. Drain pasta and add to remaining sauce. Serve immediately, passing Parmesan cheese separately.

5. When using divided sauce, bring it to a simmer, cook 6 ounces of pasta and freshly grate Parmesan cheese.

Penne alla Vodka

This is really an herbed creamy tomato sauce; the vodka just accentuates the other flavors.

2 TB. olive oil

1 large onion, peeled and diced

2 celery ribs, rinsed, trimmed, and chopped

3 garlic cloves, peeled and minced

¼ cup vodka

1 (8-oz.) can tomato sauce

1 (14.5-oz.) can diced tomatoes, undrained

1½ cups heavy cream

2 TB. chopped fresh oregano or 2 tsp. dried

2 TB. fresh thyme or 2 tsp. dried

6 oz. penne pasta

¼ cup freshly grated Parmesan cheese

Active time: 15 minutes

Start to finish: 45 minutes

Each serving has:

666 calories

279 calories from fat

31 g fat

16 g saturated fat

18 g protein

75 g carbohydrates

1. Heat olive oil in a saucepan over medium heat. Add onion, celery, and garlic and cook, stirring frequently, for 3 minutes or until onion is translucent. Add vodka and cook for about 3 minutes or until liquid has almost evaporated. Stir in tomato sauce, tomatoes, cream, oregano, and thyme.

2. Bring to a boil, reduce the heat to low, and simmer, stirring occasionally, for 30 minutes. Remove ⅔ of sauce and divide it into two 1-quart resealable plastic bags for future use. (Sauce can be frozen for up to 3 months.)

4. While sauce is simmering, bring a large pot of salted water to a boil. Add pasta and cook according to package directions. Drain pasta and add to remaining sauce. Serve immediately, passing Parmesan cheese separately.

5. When using divided sauce, bring it to a simmer, cook 6 ounces of pasta and freshly grate Parmesan cheese.

 **Double Feature** _____

If you want to cut back on saturated fat in a recipe like this one that lists heavy cream as an ingredient, you can use whole milk; however, the sauce will not be as thick. If you want a thicker sauce, mix 1 tablespoon cornstarch with 2 tablespoons cold water, and add this mixture in 1 teaspoon measures into the sauce until it reaches a thicker consistency.

Soba Noodles with Creamy Asian Wild Mushroom Sauce

This sauce comes from the world of Fusion Cooking; it blends Asian ingredients like dried shiitake mushrooms and oyster sauce with Western cream.

Active time: 20 minutes

Start to finish: 35 minutes

Each serving has:

685 calories

297 calories from fat

33 g fat

15 g saturated fat

17 g protein

85.5 g carbohydrates

1 cup dried shiitake mushrooms

1 cup boiling water

½ lb. fresh shiitake mushrooms

2 TB. Asian sesame oil

2 TB. vegetable oil

4 scallions, rinsed, trimmed, and thinly sliced

4 TB. grated fresh ginger

4 garlic cloves, peeled and minced

½ cup dry sherry

1½ cups heavy cream

⅓ cup Chinese oyster sauce

2 TB. soy sauce

Salt and freshly ground black pepper to taste

6 oz. soba noodles

1. Soak dried mushrooms in boiling water for 10 minutes, pushing them into water with the back of a spoon. Drain mushrooms, reserving soaking liquid. Strain soaking liquid through a sieve or coffee filter and set aside. Discard mushroom stems and slice mushrooms. Set aside. Wipe fresh mushrooms with a damp paper towel. Discard stems and slice mushrooms. Set aside.

2. Heat sesame oil and vegetable oil in a heavy 2-quart sauce-pan over medium-high heat. Add scallions, ginger, and garlic. Cook, stirring constantly, for 30 seconds or until garlic is fragrant. Add mushrooms and cook for 3 minutes, stirring frequently, until mushrooms begin to soften. Raise the heat to high, add sherry, and cook for 2 minutes.

3. Add dried mushrooms and soaking liquid to the pan along with cream, oyster sauce, and soy sauce. Bring to a boil, reduce the heat to low, and simmer sauce uncovered for 15 minutes. Season to taste with salt and pepper. Remove ⅔ of sauce and divide it into two 1-quart resealable plastic bags for future use. (Sauce can be frozen for up to 3 months.)

4. While sauce is simmering, bring a large pot of salted water to a boil. Add pasta and cook according to package directions. Drain pasta and add to remaining sauce. Serve immediately.

5. When using divided sauce, bring it to a simmer and cook 6 ounces of pasta.

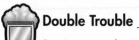

Double Trouble

Don't try to reheat pasta, including soba noodles, in a saucepan because it will become tough. Cooked pasta is best reheated in a micro-wave oven, covered, on full power for 1 minute. Check the temperature, and if necessary continue to reheat at 30-second intervals.

Linguine with White Clam Sauce

This sauce is an Italian classic with herbs and garlic enlivening a sauce based on white wine.

2 pt. fresh minced clams

¼ cup olive oil

2 large shallots, peeled and minced

6 garlic cloves, peeled and minced

1 (8-oz.) bottle clam juice

¾ cup dry white wine

¼ cup chopped fresh parsley

¼ cup chopped fresh basil

½ tsp. red pepper flakes or to taste

4 ripe plum tomatoes, rinsed, cored, seeded, and diced

Salt and freshly ground black pepper to taste

6 oz. linguine

¼ cup freshly grated Parmesan cheese

Active time: 15 minutes

Start to finish: 40 min-utes

Each serving has:

580 calories

122 calories from fat

13.5 g fat

3 g saturated fat

27 g protein

81 g carbohydrates

1. Place clams in a colander over a mixing bowl. Press with the back of a spoon to extract as much liquid as possible. Refrigerate clams if not proceeding immediately and reserve juice.

> **Double Feature**
>
> Always add foods like clams to dishes at the end of cooking time because they cook so quickly; however, don't season a sauce until after the clams are cooked because they will give off liquid into the food.

2. Heat olive oil in a heavy 2-quart saucepan over medium-high heat. Add shallots and garlic and cook, stirring frequently, for 3 minutes, until shallots are translucent. Add reserved clam juice from mixing bowl, bottled clam juice, wine, parsley, basil, and red pepper flakes. Bring to a boil, stirring occasionally. Simmer sauce uncovered for 20 minutes, stirring occasionally, or until sauce is reduced by half.

3. Add tomatoes and clams to sauce. Bring to a boil and simmer for 5 minutes. Season to taste with salt and pepper. Remove ⅔ of sauce and divide it into two 1-quart resealable plastic bags for future use. (Sauce can be frozen for up to 3 months.)

4. While sauce is simmering, bring a large pot of salted water to a boil. Add pasta and cook according to package directions. Drain pasta and add to remaining sauce. Serve immediately, passing Parmesan cheese separately.

5. When using divided sauce, bring it to a simmer, cook 6 ounces of pasta, and freshly grate Parmesan cheese.

Variation: Use red wine in place of white to create Red Clam Sauce.

Linguine with Thai Seafood Sauce

Creamy coconut milk balances the fiery flavors in this sauce for scallops and shrimp.

> **Active time:** 15 minutes
> **Start to finish:** 30 minutes
> **Each serving has:**
> 670 calories
> 240 calories from fat
> 27 g fat
> 16 g saturated fat
> 35 g protein
> 74 g carbohydrates

3 TB. vegetable oil

¾ lb. sea scallops, rinsed, patted dry with paper towels, and quartered

¾ lb. extra large (16 to 20 per lb.) raw shrimp, peeled and deveined

1 jalapeño chili, seeds and ribs removed, finely chopped

3 scallions, rinsed, trimmed, and sliced

4 garlic cloves, peeled and minced

1 (14-oz.) can coconut milk

1 TB. Thai green *curry paste*

¼ cup seafood stock or water

2 TB. Asian fish sauce (*nam pla*)

1 TB. firmly packed light brown sugar

1 TB. freshly squeezed lime juice

Salt and freshly ground black pepper to taste

6 oz. linguine

2 TB. chopped fresh cilantro

1. Heat 1½ tablespoons oil in a heavy 2-quart saucepan over high heat. Add scallops and shrimp. Cook, stirring constantly, for 1 minute or until scallops are opaque. Pour mixture into a mixing bowl and set aside.

2. Add remaining 1½ tablespoons oil and reduce the heat to medium-high. Add jalapeño, scallions, and garlic. Cook for 30 seconds, stirring constantly.

3. Add coconut milk, curry paste, stock, fish sauce, brown sugar, and lime juice to the pan. Bring to a boil, reduce the heat to low, and simmer sauce, stirring occasionally, for 10 minutes. Add scallops and shrimp and simmer for 5 minutes. Season to taste with salt and pepper. Remove ⅔ of sauce and divide it into two 1-quart resealable plastic bags for future use. (Sauce can be frozen for up to 3 months.)

4. While sauce is simmering, bring a large pot of salted water to a boil. Add pasta and cook according to package directions. Drain pasta and add to remaining sauce. Serve immediately, sprinkled with cilantro.

5. When using divided sauce, bring it to a simmer and cook 6 ounces of pasta.

Variation: In place of scallops and shrimp, use 1-inch cubes of any white firm-fleshed fish, such as halibut or cod.

> **Duet Dialogue**
>
> **Curry paste** is used often in Thai cooking, and the green or red color is determined by the type of chilies included with the curry powder, vinegar, and other spices. The base of what makes it a paste is frequently clarified butter, called *ghee* in Indian cooking.

Rigatoni with Mushroom and Sausage Ragù

This is a hearty sauce made with red wine, garlic, and herbs.

Active time: 20 minutes

Start to finish: 65 minutes

Each serving has:

743 calories

272 calories from fat

30 g fat

8 g saturated fat

36 g protein

76 g carbohydrates

1 lb. white mushrooms

1 TB. olive oil

1½ lb. bulk sweet Italian sausage

1 large onion, peeled and finely chopped

3 garlic cloves, peeled and minced

1 red bell pepper, seeds and ribs removed, thinly sliced

1 cup dry red wine

1 (14.5-oz.) can crushed tomatoes in tomato purée

1 (8-oz.) can tomato sauce

¼ cup chopped fresh parsley

2 TB. chopped fresh oregano or 2 tsp. dried

1 TB. fresh thyme or 1 tsp. dried

1 bay leaf

Salt and freshly ground black pepper to taste

6 oz. rigatoni

¼ cup freshly grated Parmesan cheese

1. Wipe mushrooms with a damp paper towel. Discard stems and slice mushrooms. Set aside. Heat olive oil in a heavy 2-quart saucepan over medium-high heat. Add sausage, breaking up lumps with a fork. Cook sausage, stirring occasionally, for 3 minutes or until no longer pink. Remove sausage from the pan with a slotted spoon and set aside.

2. Discard all but 2 tablespoons fat from the pan. Add onion, garlic, red bell pepper, and mushrooms. Cook, stirring frequently, for 3 minutes or until onion is translucent. Add wine, tomatoes, tomato sauce, parsley, oregano, thyme, and bay leaf to the pan. Return sausage to the pan and bring mixture to a boil.

3. Simmer sauce uncovered over low heat for 45 minutes, stirring occasionally. Season to taste with salt and pepper. Remove ⅔ of sauce and divide it into two 1-quart resealable plastic bags for future use. (Sauce can be frozen for up to 3 months.)

4. While sauce is simmering, bring a large pot of salted water to a boil. Add pasta and cook according to package directions. Drain pasta and add to remaining sauce. Serve immediately, passing Parmesan cheese separately.

5. When using remaining sauce, bring it to a simmer, cook
   6 ounces of pasta, and freshly grate Parmesan cheese.

Variation: Use ground beef or poultry sausage in place of pork.

Déjà Two

The birthplace of pasta has always been a subject of culinary
controversy. Many experts claim that Marco Polo brought the
idea of noodles back with him to Italy from China. However, the
truth is that this food form existed in both places independently
long before Polo's expeditions. Archaeological evidence now
substantiates that noodles probably originated in central Asia
and date back to 1000 B.C.E.

Spaghetti with Bolognese Sauce

This classic tomato sauce contains various meats, as well as vegetables and fresh herbs.

¼ **cup olive oil**

¾ **lb. ground veal**

¾ **lb. ground pork**

**2 medium onions, peeled and
finely chopped**

**3 celery ribs, rinsed,
trimmed, and finely chopped**

**2 carrots, peeled and finely
chopped**

**4 garlic cloves, peeled and
minced**

**2 (14.5-oz.) cans diced toma-
toes, undrained**

½ **cup whole milk**

½ **cup dry white wine**

¼ **cup chopped fresh parsley**

**2 TB. chopped fresh oregano
or 2 tsp. dried**

**1 TB. fresh thyme or 1 tsp.
dried**

1 bay leaf

**Salt and freshly ground black
pepper to taste**

6 oz. spaghetti

¼ **cup freshly grated
Parmesan cheese**

Active time: 20 minutes

Start to finish: 1⅓ hours

Each serving has:

761 calories

269 calories from fat

30 g fat

10 g saturated fat

38 g protein

80 g carbohydrates

1. Heat 2 tablespoons olive oil in a heavy 2-quart saucepan over
   medium-high heat. Add veal and pork, breaking up lumps with
   a fork. Cook meats, stirring occasionally, for 3 minutes or until
   no longer pink. Remove meats from the pan with a slotted
   spoon and set aside. Discard grease from the pan.

2. Heat remaining 2 tablespoons olive oil in the pan over medium-high heat. Add onions, celery, carrots, and garlic. Cook, stirring frequently, for 3 minutes or until onions are translucent. Return meats to the pan and add tomatoes, milk, wine, parsley, oregano, thyme, and bay leaf.

3. Bring to a boil, reduce the heat to low, and simmer sauce uncovered for 1 hour or until thickened, stirring occasionally. Remove and discard bay leaf and season to taste with salt and pepper. Remove ⅔ of sauce and divide it into two 1-quart resealable plastic bags for future use. (Sauce can be frozen for up to 3 months.)

4. While sauce is simmering, bring a large pot of salted water to a boil. Add pasta and cook according to package directions. Drain pasta and add to remaining sauce. Serve immediately, passing Parmesan cheese separately.

5. When using divided sauce, bring it to a simmer, cook 6 ounces of pasta, and freshly grate Parmesan cheese.

Variation: Use ground beef or turkey in place of veal and pork.

Double Feature

Disposing of hot grease by pouring it down the sink is not a good idea because it can quickly clog the drain line, even if you run hot water along with the grease. On the other hand, it's really messy in a trash can. One solution is to wash out small yogurt containers and keep them under the sink. Pour the hot grease into a cup, and when the grease cools, place it in the yogurt container and throw it all away.

Rigatoni with Greek Lamb Sauce

This hearty tomato sauce, scented with cinnamon, is similar to the meat filling of *moussaka*.

1 (1-lb.) eggplant	**1 cup dry red wine**
Salt	**3 TB. chopped fresh parsley**
½ cup olive oil	**2 TB. chopped fresh oregano or 2 tsp. dried**
1½ lb. ground lamb	
1 large onion, peeled and diced	**½ tsp. ground cinnamon**
	Salt and freshly ground black pepper to taste
4 garlic cloves, peeled and minced	
	6 oz. rigatoni
2 (8-oz.) cans tomato sauce	**¼ crumbled feta cheese**

> **Active time:** 30 minutes
> **Start to finish:** 1½ hours
> **Each serving has:**
> 928 calories
> 448 calories from fat
> 50 g fat
> 16 g saturated fat
> 34.5 g protein
> 78 g carbohydrates

1. Rinse eggplant, discard stem end, and cut eggplant into ½-inch dice. Put eggplant into a colander and sprinkle liberally with salt. Place a plate on top of eggplant cubes and weight the plate with cans. Place the colander in the sink or on a plate and allow eggplant to drain for 30 minutes. Rinse eggplant cubes and squeeze hard to remove water. Wring out remaining water with cloth tea towel.

2. Heat 2 tablespoons olive oil in a heavy 2-quart saucepan over medium-high heat. Add lamb, breaking up lumps with a fork. Cook, stirring occasionally, for 3 minutes or until lamb is no longer red. Remove meat from the pan with a slotted spoon and set aside. Discard grease from the pan.

3. Heat 2 tablespoons olive oil in the pan over medium-high heat. Add onion and garlic and cook, stirring frequently, for 3 minutes or until onion is translucent. Return lamb to the pan and add tomato sauce, wine, parsley, oregano, and cinnamon. Bring to a boil, reduce the heat to low, and simmer sauce uncovered for 30 minutes, stirring occasionally.

4. While sauce is simmering, heat remaining ¼ cup olive oil in a large skillet over medium-high heat. Add eggplant and cook, stirring frequently, for 3 minutes or until eggplant begins to soften. Stir eggplant into sauce and simmer for an additional

15 minutes. Season to taste with salt and pepper. Remove ⅔ of sauce and divide it into two 1-quart resealable plastic bags for future use. (Sauce can be frozen for up to 3 months.)

5. While sauce is simmering, bring a large pot of salted water to a boil. Add pasta and cook according to package directions. Drain pasta, and add to sauce. Serve immediately, passing feta separately.

6. When using divided sauce, bring it to a simmer, cook 6-ounces of pasta, and crumble feta cheese.

Variation: Use ground beef or turkey in place of lamb.

Double Feature

Because about two thirds of an eggplant's weight is water and the flesh is also porous, eggplant seems to drink up oil when it is fried. For these reasons, most eggplant should be salted and pressed before cooking to compact the flesh so it won't absorb as much fat. Salting also extracts the bitter juices found in mature eggplants with well-developed seeds.

Chinese Noodles with Spicy Pork Sauce

Orange zest, fermented black beans, and chilies add zesty flavors and aromas to this thick Asian sauce.

1½ lb. lean ground pork

2 TB. cornstarch

¼ cup soy sauce

3 TB. vegetable oil

2 TB. Asian sesame oil

6 scallions, rinsed, trimmed, and sliced

3 TB. grated fresh ginger

6 garlic cloves, peeled and minced

2 jalapeño chilies, rinsed, seeds and ribs removed, finely chopped

1 (14.5-oz.) can chicken stock

2 TB. dry sherry

2 TB. rice vinegar

2 TB. firmly packed dark brown sugar

2 TB. *fermented black beans*, chopped

2 tsp. grated orange zest

1 red bell pepper, seeds and ribs removed, thinly sliced

2 celery ribs, rinsed, trimmed, and thinly sliced

Salt and freshly ground black pepper to taste

6 oz. Chinese egg noodles or spaghetti

½ cup fresh bean sprouts, rinsed

Active time: 20 minutes
Start to finish: 65 minutes
Each serving has:
671 calories
178 calories from fat
20 g fat
4 g saturated fat
46 g protein
77 g carbohydrates

1. Place pork in a mixing bowl. Combine cornstarch with 2 tablespoons soy sauce and stir well. Pour mixture over pork and work it into pork with your fingers. Set aside.

2. Heat 1 tablespoon vegetable oil and all sesame oil in a heavy 2-quart saucepan over medium-high heat. Add scallions, ginger, garlic, and jalapeño and cook, stirring frequently, for 3 minutes or until scallions are translucent. Add pork and cook, breaking up lumps with a fork, for 5 minutes or until pork is no longer pink. Add stock, sherry, vinegar, brown sugar, fermented black beans, and orange zest to the pan. Stir well and bring to a boil. Reduce the heat to low and simmer sauce for 25 minutes, stirring occasionally.

Duet Dialogue

Fermented black beans are small black soybeans with a pungent flavor that have been preserved in salt before being packed. Prior to cooking, they should be chopped and soaked in some sort of liquid to soften them and release their flavor. Because they are salted as a preservative, if refrigerated once opened, they will last for up to 2 years.

3. While sauce is simmering, heat remaining 2 tablespoons vegetable oil in a large skillet over medium-high heat. Add red bell pepper and celery. Cook, stirring frequently, for 3 minutes or until peppers begin to soften. Add vegetables to sauce and simmer for an additional 15 minutes. Season to taste with salt and pepper. Remove ⅔ of sauce and divide it into two 1-quart resealable plastic bags for future use. (Sauce can be frozen for up to 3 months.)

4. While sauce is simmering, bring a large pot of salted water to a boil. Add noodles and cook according to package directions. Drain noodles and add to remaining sauce. Stir in bean sprouts and cook for 1 minute. Serve immediately.

5. When using divided sauce, bring it to a simmer and cook 6 ounces of pasta. Add ½ cup fresh bean sprouts to each additional batch of sauce.

Variation: Use ground turkey or veal in place of pork.

Part 4

Fast Food: Stir-Fries and Sautés for All Seasons

You'll be taking an around-the-world tour cooking the recipes in this part. The uniting factor is that all the dishes are ready in less time than it would take to have a pizza delivered.

Stir-fried dishes and sautéed foods are first cousins, and both use healthful, low-fat cooking methods. We think of stir-fries with Asian food, so one chapter contains recipes from those cuisines. The sunny and vibrant foods from countries bordering the Mediterranean Sea are represented in another chapter, and then there's a potpourri of dishes drawn from countries as varied in their food tastes as Mexico and Sweden.

This part ends with a chapter devoted to vegetarian fare. Many of these vibrantly flavored dishes are made with healthful tofu, and others are international mixes of vegetables and grains.

Chapter 11

Asian Accents

In This Chapter

- ◆ Subtle seasoning
- ◆ Fruity flavors
- ◆ Crunchy textures

When we think about Asian food, a common mental image is a platter of colorful bite-size morsels fresh from the wok. All those dishes—common to Chinese, Vietnamese, and Thai cooking—are produced quickly by stir-frying, and those are the recipes you'll find in this chapter.

The popularity of Asian foods continues to grow. Back in the Neanderthal era of my youth, Chinese was all you could find, and that was subtle Cantonese with some totally nonauthentic dishes, like chop suey, thrown in for good measure. But all that has changed, and now the fiery flavors of authentic Thai and Szechwan complete the spectrum.

While the cooking time for Asian stir-fries is short, the preparation time can be long if many ingredients need to be cut into small pieces. That's why these dishes are perfect for two servings! For small quantities there's only so much chopping one can do.

Stir-Fry Strategy

The ancient Chinese invented stir-frying as one of their more than 50 methods of food preparation. However, many recipes are now utilizing this technique for many non-Asian dishes because it's quick, requires little fat, and leaves food with the crisp-tender texture we enjoy today. Advanced planning, speed, and control are the keys to a successful stir-fry.

Because the final cooking is a quick process, the food must be sitting in bowls or dishes placed within arm's reach and ready to be cooked. Cut all pieces of the same ingredient the same size, have your seasonings at hand, and make sure that any vegetables requiring partial cooking—such as blanching broccoli—has been completed.

> **Double Trouble**
>
> Never place too much food in the wok or skillet at one time. You must be able to sear the food on all sides, without its steaming from being buried under a layer of food.

The game plan is that when the dish comes to the table all ingredients are properly cooked, so you have two options: either cut food that takes longer to cook into smaller pieces and cook everything at the same time or start with the longer-cooking food and keep adding ingredients in their decreasing need of time. Both strategies produce good results.

While it's possible to adapt many recipes to stir-frying, always use oil rather than butter. The dairy solids in butter burn at a very low temperature, 250°F, so it can only be added as a flavoring agent once food is cooked. Oil, on the other hand, does not begin to smoke until more than 400°F, so it is the better choice. Because there is no consensus as to what oil to use, I lump them together as vegetable oil in the ingredient lists. Peanut, corn, soy, or canola all work well. Olive oil will give the dish a pronounced flavor, but it smokes at too low a temperature to be effective in sealing the food.

Place the wok or skillet over a high flame and heat it very hot. Listen for the sound of sizzles; if a few drops of water evaporate immediately, the pan is ready. Add the required amount of oil to the pan and swirl it around gently to coat all sides.

Add the food and keep it moving in the pan. If stir-frying in a wok, use a wire mesh spoon designed for the job. If stir-frying in a skillet, use a spoon that will reach to all places on the bottom and with which you can keep food moving. In some recipes, liquid is added and the pan is covered for a brief time. In other recipes, it's fry and eat.

Chicken with Plum Sauce

This dish is a great balance of sweet and savory—tangy plum sauce along with garlic and ginger.

2 (6-oz.) boneless, skinless chicken breast halves

1 TB. cornstarch

1 TB. dry sherry

1 TB. soy sauce

2 tsp. rice vinegar

3 scallions

½ cup chicken stock

3 TB. plum sauce

½ tsp. Chinese five-spice powder

2 TB. vegetable oil

2 garlic cloves, peeled and minced

1 TB. grated fresh ginger

1 celery rib, rinsed, trimmed, and thinly sliced on the diagonal

½ red bell pepper, seeds and ribs removed, thinly sliced

Salt and freshly ground black pepper to taste

Active time: 20 minutes

Start to finish: 20 minutes

Each serving has:

423 calories

150 calories from fat

17 g fat

3 g saturated fat

42 g protein

24 g carbohydrates

---

1. Rinse chicken and pat dry with paper towels. Trim off visible fat, and cut into ½-inch cubes. Place chicken in a mixing bowl, and sprinkle with cornstarch. Toss to coat evenly and add sherry, soy sauce, and vinegar, tossing again to coat evenly.

2. Rinse and trim scallions. Cut scallions into 1-inch lengths and then slice lengthwise into thin strips. Set aside. Combine stock, plum sauce, and five-spice powder in a small bowl. Stir well and set aside.

3. Heat vegetable oil in a heavy wok or skillet over high heat, swirling to coat the pan. Add scallions, garlic, and ginger and stir-fry for 30 seconds or until fragrant, stirring constantly. Add chicken and cook for 1 minute, stirring constantly. Add celery and red pepper and stir-fry vegetables for 2 minutes more, stirring constantly.

4. Add sauce mixture and cook, stirring constantly, for 2 minutes or until chicken is cooked through and no longer pink and sauce thickens. Season to taste with salt and pepper and serve immediately.

Variation: Substitute boneless pork chops, trimmed of all fat and cut into ½-inch cubes.

Double Trouble

Rice vinegar is different from others on the shelf, like balsamic and cider. Some of it is plain, and other brands are pre-seasoned; they're sometimes called sushi vinegar. Choose the unseasoned for cooking.

Sesame Citrus Chicken

Orange and lemon are the dominant flavors in this colorful stir-fry made with snow peas and bok choy.

Active time: 20 minutes

Start to finish: 20 minutes

Each serving has:

597 calories

223 calories from fat

25 g fat

4 g saturated fat

55 g protein

47 g carbohydrates

2 (6-oz.) boneless, skinless chicken breast halves

3 cups water

1 TB. cornstarch

1 TB. cold water

⅓ cup freshly squeezed orange juice

2 TB. freshly squeezed lemon juice

2 TB. granulated sugar

2 TB. soy sauce

2 tsp. grated lemon zest

2 tsp. grated orange zest

2 TB. vegetable oil

1 TB. grated fresh ginger

2 cloves garlic, peeled and minced

1 TB. Asian sesame oil

2 baby bok choy, rinsed, trimmed, and cut into ½-inch slices

2 oz. snow peas, rinsed and stringed

Salt and freshly ground black pepper to taste

2 scallions, rinsed, trimmed, and thinly sliced

![Double Feature icon] **Double Feature**

A way to minimize the number of bowls you'll have to wash after cooking a stir-fried dish is to layer the vegetables starting with the one added last at the bottom of the bowl, separating the layers with plastic wrap. When it's time to add the next ingredient, just reach in, grab the sheet of plastic wrap, and toss it in.

1. Rinse chicken and pat dry with paper towels. Trim off visible fat, place between two sheets of plastic wrap, and pound to an even thickness of ¼ inch. Cut into strips 2 inches long and ¾ inch wide. Bring water to a boil in a saucepan over high heat. Immerse chicken strips in boiling water for 2 minutes. Remove chicken from the pan with a slotted spoon and set aside. Discard water. Combine cornstarch and cold water in a small bowl; stir well and set aside. Combine orange juice, lemon juice, sugar, soy sauce, lemon zest, and orange zest in another small bowl and set aside.

2. Heat vegetable oil in a wok or heavy skillet over high heat, swirling to coat the pan. Add ginger and garlic and stir-fry for 30 seconds or until fragrant. Add sesame oil and bok choy and stir-fry for 1 minute. Add chicken and stir in sauce mixture. Cook, stirring frequently, for 3 minutes or until chicken is cooked through and no longer pink.

3. Add snow peas and cook for 30 seconds. Stir in cornstarch mixture and cook, stirring constantly, for 1 minute or until sauce thickens. Season to taste with salt and pepper. Serve immediately, with scallions sprinkled on top.

Variation: Substitute boneless pork chops, trimmed of all fat and cut into ½-inch cubes.

Chicken with Green Beans and Peanuts

Peanuts add textural interest to this easy dish that joins tender chicken with crisp green beans.

2 (6-oz.) boneless, skinless chicken breast halves

4 TB. soy sauce

2 TB. honey

3 garlic cloves, peeled and minced

¼ tsp. red pepper flakes

½ cup chicken stock

2 TB. vegetable oil

2 scallions, rinsed, trimmed, and thinly sliced

1 TB. grated fresh ginger

¼ lb. fresh green beans, rinsed, trimmed, and cut into 1-inch lengths

¼ cup salted peanuts

Salt and freshly ground black pepper to taste

Active time: 20 minutes

Start to finish: 20 minutes

Each serving has:

535 calories

232 calories from fat

26 g fat

4 g saturated fat

49 g protein

30 g carbohydrates

1. Rinse chicken and pat dry with paper towels. Trim off visible fat and cut into ½-inch cubes. Combine 1 tablespoon soy sauce, 1 tablespoon honey, 1 garlic clove, and ⅛ teaspoon red pepper flakes in a mixing bowl. Stir well, add chicken, and mix well. Set aside. Combine remaining soy sauce, honey, red pepper flakes, and stock in a small bowl and set aside.

2. Heat vegetable oil in a heavy wok or skillet over high heat, swirling to coat the pan. Add scallions, remaining garlic, and ginger and stir-fry for 30 seconds or until fragrant. Add chicken and cook for 2 minutes, stirring constantly. Add green beans and stir-fry vegetables for 2 minutes more, stirring constantly.

3. Add peanuts and sauce mixture and cook, stirring constantly, for 2 minutes or until chicken is cooked through and no longer pink. Season to taste with salt and pepper and serve immediately.

Variation: Substitute boneless pork chops, trimmed of all fat and cut into ½-inch cubes, and asparagus for green beans.

Double Feature

For two servings, the best size peanuts to buy are the 1-ounce snack packs found in convenience stores and many liquor stores.

Asian Shrimp and Stir-Fried Vegetables

This dish from Cantonese tradition is subtly seasoned and contains both dried and fresh mushrooms.

Active time: 25 minutes

Start to finish: 30 minutes

Each serving has:

358 calories

149 calories from fat

17 g fat

2.5 g saturated fat

27 g protein

22 g carbohydrates

---

2 oz. fresh shiitake mushrooms

½ lb. extra large (16 to 20 per lb.) raw shrimp, peeled and deveined

4 large dried shiitake mushrooms

1 cup boiling water

3 TB. dry sherry

1 TB. soy sauce

1 TB. freshly squeezed lime juice

1 tsp. granulated sugar

2 TB. cold water

2 tsp. cornstarch

1 TB. Asian sesame oil

1 TB. vegetable oil

1 TB. finely grated fresh ginger

1 garlic clove, peeled and minced

2 scallions, rinsed, trimmed, and cut into 1-inch lengths

1 celery rib, rinsed, trimmed, and sliced

½ red bell pepper, seeds and ribs removed, cut into *julienne*

2 oz. snow peas, rinsed and stringed

Salt and freshly ground black pepper to taste

1. Wipe mushrooms with a damp paper towel. Discard stems and slice mushrooms. Rinse shrimp and pat dry with paper towels. Soak shiitake in boiling water for 10 minutes, pushing them down with the back of a spoon. When soft, drain mushrooms, squeezing them to remove excess water. Stem mushrooms and chop coarsely. Set aside. Combine sherry, soy sauce, lime juice, and sugar in a small bowl. Stir well and set aside. Combine water and cornstarch in a small bowl. Stir well and set aside.

2. Heat sesame oil and vegetable oil in a heavy wok or skillet over high heat, swirling to coat the pan. Add ginger and garlic and stir-fry for 30 seconds or until fragrant, stirring constantly. Add shrimp and cook for 1 minute. Remove shrimp from the pan with a slotted spoon, and add scallions, celery, red bell pepper, and fresh and dried mushrooms.

3. Stir-fry vegetables for 2 minutes; then return shrimp to the pan and add snow peas and sauce mixture. Bring to a boil, simmer for 2 minutes, and then stir in cornstarch mixture. Simmer briefly or until sauce thickens. Serve immediately. Season with salt and pepper to taste.

Variation: Substitute bay scallops, ¼-inch cubes of firm-fleshed white fish, such as grouper or swordfish, or ½-inch cubes of boneless chicken breast.

 **Duet Dialogue** _____

Julienne (pronounced *julie-N*) is the French word for very thin sticks of vegetables that can cook very quickly. To cut a vegetable julienne style, first cut into long, thin slices, about ⅛-inch thick or smaller. Stack these layers, and cut into thin strips. Then cut the strips into any length, as determined by the recipe.

Cod with Tangerine-Chili Sauce

The combination of aromatic tangerine juice and zest with the fiery flavor of jalapeño make this a tantalizing treatment for delicate cod.

½ lb. cod fillet or any white firm-fleshed fish

3 TB. soy sauce

1 small jalapeño chili, seeded and finely chopped

1 TB. grated tangerine zest

3 TB. fresh tangerine juice

1 TB. water

1 tsp. rice vinegar

½ tsp. coarsely ground fresh black pepper

1 tsp. Asian sesame oil

½ tsp. granulated sugar

3 TB. vegetable oil

3 cloves garlic, peeled and minced

2 tsp. grated fresh ginger

2 oz. snow peas, rinsed and stringed

½ red bell pepper, seeds and ribs removed, thinly sliced

Salt and freshly ground black pepper to taste

Active time: 20 minutes

Start to finish: 20 minutes

Each serving has:

459 calories

231 calories from fat

26 g fat

4 g saturated fat

43 g protein

13 g carbohydrates

Déjà Two

Tangerines, along with tiny clementines, are members of the mandarin orange family. What differentiates mandarin oranges is the fact that their very thin skin slips off easily.

1. Rinse cod and pat dry with paper towels. Cut into strips 2 inches long and 1 inch wide, place in a mixing bowl, and toss with 1 tablespoon soy sauce. Combine jalapeño, tangerine zest, tangerine juice, remaining 2 tablespoons soy sauce, water, vinegar, black pepper, sesame oil, and sugar in a bowl. Stir well and set aside.

2. Heat vegetable oil in a heavy wok or skillet over high heat, swirling to coat the pan. Add garlic and ginger and stir-fry for 30 seconds or until fragrant. Add cod and cook for 2 minutes, stirring constantly. Add snow peas and red bell pepper and stir-fry vegetables for 2 minutes more, stirring constantly.

3. Add sauce mixture and cook, stirring constantly, for 2 minutes or until cod is cooked through and no longer pink. Season to taste with salt and pepper and serve immediately.

Variation: Substitute bay scallops, ¼-inch cubes of firm-fleshed white fish, such as grouper or swordfish, or ½-inch cubes of boneless chicken breast.

Spicy Pork in Garlic Sauce

Pork tenderloin is joined with vegetables in this quick stir-fry flavored with red pepper as well as garlic.

Active time: 25 minutes

Start to finish: 25 minutes

Each serving has:

421 calories

191 calories from fat

21 g fat

4 g saturated fat

28 g protein

25 g carbohydrates

½ lb. pork tenderloin

3 TB. soy sauce

3 TB. dry sherry

6 garlic cloves, peeled and minced

1 TB. grated fresh ginger

½ tsp. red pepper flakes or to taste

1 tsp. Asian sesame oil

2 tsp. cornstarch

¼ cup water

3 TB. hoisin sauce

2 TB. vegetable oil

1 small carrot, rinsed, trimmed, and cut into julienne

1 celery rib, rinsed, trimmed, and cut into julienne

3 scallions, rinsed, trimmed, and cut into julienne

1. Rinse pork and pat dry with paper towels. Trim off all visible fat and iridescent silverskin. Cut pork against the grain into slices ⅛ inch thick. Cut slices into julienne pieces and set aside. Combine 1 tablespoon soy sauce, 1 tablespoon sherry, garlic, ginger, red pepper flakes, sesame oil, and cornstarch in a mixing bowl. Stir well, add pork, and toss to coat evenly. Set aside.

2. Combine remaining soy sauce, remaining sherry, water, and hoisin sauce in a small bowl. Stir well and set aside.

3. Heat oil in a heavy wok or skillet over high heat, swirling to coat the pan. Add pork, carrot, and celery and stir-fry for 2 minutes or until pork slices separate and are no longer red. Add scallions and stir-fry 1 minute. Add sauce and stir-fry 2 minutes or until slightly thickened. Serve immediately.

Variation: Substitute thinly sliced chicken breast.

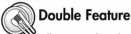

Double Feature

All meats slice better into thin slices if the meat is partially frozen. Rinse the meat, pat it dry, and wrap it in plastic wrap. Freeze it for 15 minutes for thin cuts, like pork tenderloin, to 1 hour for thick leg of lamb.

Sweet and Hot Pork

Aromatic Chinese five-spice powder adds complexity to this dish made with chutney for the sweet aspect.

½ lb. pork tenderloin

⅓ cup water

¼ cup mango chutney, such as Major Grey's

2 garlic cloves, peeled and minced

1 TB. grated fresh ginger

2 TB. soy sauce

1½ tsp. Chinese chili paste with garlic or to taste

½ tsp. Chinese five-spice powder

3 TB. vegetable oil

½ small red onion, peeled and thinly sliced

2 baby bok choy rinsed, trimmed, and thinly sliced

1 cup bean sprouts, rinsed

2 TB. fresh cilantro, chopped

Active time: 20 minutes

Start to finish: 20 minutes

Each serving has:

509 calories

241 calories from fat

27 g fat

5 g saturated fat

39 g protein

38 g carbohydrates

1. Rinse pork and pat dry with paper towels. Trim off all visible fat and iridescent silverskin. Cut pork against the grain into slices ⅛ inch thick. Cut slices into julienne pieces and set aside. Combine water and chutney in a blender or food processor fitted with a steel blade. Purée until smooth. Scrape mixture into a small bowl and add garlic, ginger, soy sauce, chili paste, and five-spice powder. Stir well and set aside.

Double Trouble

It's important to purée the chutney. If you don't, the sauce will not have the intensity of flavor, but you'll be chewing large chunks of mango.

2. Heat oil in a heavy wok or skillet over high heat, swirling to coat the pan. Add pork and onion, and stir-fry for 2 minutes or until slices separate and pork is no longer red.

3. Add bok choy and stir-fry 1 minute. Add sauce and stir-fry 2 minutes or until slightly thickened. Add bean sprouts and cilantro. Stir-fry for 30 seconds. Serve immediately.

Variation: Substitute thinly sliced chicken breast.

Pepper Steak

With the many colors of bell peppers and red onion, this is a visually stunning dish to bring to the table.

Active time: 25 minutes

Start to finish: 25 minutes

Each serving has:

616 calories

413 calories from fat

46 g fat

9 g saturated fat

30 g protein

23 g carbohydrates

½ lb. flank steak

3 TB. soy sauce

1 TB. dry sherry

1 TB. Asian sesame oil

¼ cup beef stock

1 TB. Chinese fermented black beans, finely chopped

2 tsp. cornstarch

1 tsp. granulated sugar

4 TB. vegetable oil

2 garlic cloves, peeled and minced

1 TB. grated fresh ginger

¼ tsp. red pepper flakes or to taste

1 small red onion, peeled, halved lengthwise, and thinly sliced

1 red bell pepper, seeds and ribs removed, thinly sliced

1 orange bell pepper, seeds and ribs removed, thinly sliced

2 TB. fresh cilantro, chopped

1. Rinse steak and pat dry with paper towels. Trim all visible fat. Cut steak into thirds lengthwise and then slice each piece thinly against the grain. Toss beef with 2 tablespoons soy sauce, sherry, and sesame oil. Combine remaining soy sauce, stock, black beans, cornstarch, and sugar in a small bowl. Stir well and set aside.

2. Heat 2 tablespoons vegetable oil in a heavy wok or skillet over high heat, swirling to coat the pan. Add beef and stir-fry for 2 minutes or until slices separate and are no longer red. Remove beef from the pan and set aside.

3. Wipe out wok with paper towels. Heat remaining oil over high heat, swirling to coat. Add garlic, ginger, and red pepper flakes and stir-fry for 15 seconds or until fragrant. Add onion, red and orange bell peppers, and stir-fry for 2 minutes. Add sauce and stir-fry for 2 minutes or until sauce thickens.

4. Return beef to the pan and stir-fry until heated through. Stir in cilantro and serve immediately.

Variation: Substitute boneless leg of lamb.

Double Feature

Cutting meats and chicken breasts against the grain is a key to success. While shreds are cut with the grain because they're like matchsticks, the thin slices cut against the grain are much more tender because the length of the muscle filaments is so small.

Lamb with Eggplant and Scallions

Tender eggplant and rich, rosy lamb are treated with Asian flair and flavors in this stir-fried dish.

½ lb. boneless leg of lamb

1 egg white

2 TB. soy sauce

2 tsp. cornstarch

2 Japanese eggplant

2 TB. rice vinegar

2 TB. hoisin sauce

1 TB. Chinese chili paste with garlic

1 tsp. Asian sesame oil

2 TB. beef stock or water

3 TB. vegetable oil

2 scallions, rinsed, trimmed, and cut into 1-inch pieces

Active time: 25 minutes
Start to finish: 25 minutes
Each serving has:
525 calories
280 calories from fat
31 g fat
6 g saturated fat
31 g protein
36 g carbohydrates

1. Rinse lamb and pat dry with paper towels. Trim all visible fat and gristle. Slice lamb into slices ½ inch thick and then into strips ½ inch wide. Combine egg white, soy sauce, and cornstarch in a mixing bowl. Whisk well and add lamb strips. Toss to coat lamb evenly and set aside.

2. Rinse and trim eggplants. Cut eggplants lengthwise into ½-inch strips and then cut strips into ½-inch sections. Set aside. Combine vinegar, hoisin sauce, chili paste, sesame oil, and stock in a small bowl. Stir well and set aside.

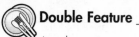
Double Feature

An alternative to serving stir-fried dishes over rice is to wrap them in Chinese pancakes or flour tortillas and roll them up like egg rolls. This is traditional for foods, such as Peking duck and mu shu preparations, but there's no reason any stir-fry couldn't be wrapped.

3. Heat 2 tablespoons oil in a heavy wok or skillet over high heat, swirling to coat the pan. Add eggplant and stir-fry for 3 minutes. Add scallions and stir-fry 1 minute. Remove vegetables from the pan and set aside.

4. Add remaining oil to the pan over high heat, again swirling to coat the pan. Add lamb and stir-fry for 2 minutes or until slices separate and lamb is no longer red. Add sauce to the pan and return eggplant mixture. Cook for 2 minutes or until sauce thickens. Serve immediately.

Variation: Substitute flank steak.

Mediterranean Madness

In This Chapter

- ◆ Chicken with bright flavors
- ◆ Sublime seafood
- ◆ Meats cooked in a flash

This part of the book is about redefining "fast food." In Chapter 11, you took a tour of Asia with the stir-fried dishes. So now it's time to turn your taste buds to the sunny shores of the Mediterranean Sea and those cuisines you'll encounter when cooking the recipes in this chapter.

All these foods are on the table in less time than you'd take to pick up take-out. You'll find the flavors of Spain, France, Italy, the Middle East, and more. So allow your taste buds to take this vacation.

Sauté Savvy

Sauté, another cooking term we've adopted from the French, literally means "to jump." What it means for the dishes in this chapter is quick cooking with just a little fat over moderate to high heat.

Stir-frying and sautéing are first cousins. The main difference is that stir-fried foods are cut into small pieces and stirred continually to keep them moving, while sautéed food can be larger and is left alone for longer periods of time. (Learn more about stir-frying in Chapter 11.)

Even though we're calling these dishes "sautés," you actually sauté all the time and don't even know it. All those times you cook onions or shallots (with or without garlic) at the beginning of cooking a dish, that's a sauté. The reason for this initial cooking is to soften the natural harshness of these ingredients before they're transferred to the finished dish.

And like a stir-fry, these dishes produce a meal in very little time and in one pan. Like broiling, sautéing is reserved for relatively thin and tender pieces of protein. It's not for "stewing meat" that needs both time and moisture to get tender. Nor is it suited to large pieces, because the outer portions would become dry—and possibly burnt—before the interiors cooked properly.

The Rules of the Game

Preparing food is the first step to a great sauté. The pieces of food must be of equal size and/or thickness so that they cook evenly, regardless whether they are diced onions or veal scallops. Sautéing is not recommended for any pieces of poultry or fish more than ½-inch thick because the centers would not likely be properly cooked before the outsides were dried. For meat, the thickness can be up to 1 inch since most people would want the center rare in the end.

Fat is used to lubricate the pan and keep the food from sticking. Since selected fat must be able to reach relatively high temperatures without breaking down or smoking, the best selections are cooking oil or a combination of oil and butter.

The purpose of sautéing is to cook foods quickly without steaming them. This means the food should have space around it so that steam does not form as juices are released. Also, putting too much food into the pan at one time will lower the temperature of the pan so that heat will not be transferred with the proper intensity.

Subbing with Success

I have listed variations for many recipes in this chapter, but you may want to improvise on your own, so here's a chart of which cuts of different meats you can sauté successfully:

Meat Choices for Sautéing

Meat	Thickness
Beef: Rib-eye or Delmonico steak, filet mignon, flank steak, New York strip, round steak, boneless sirloin	1 to 1½ inches
Lamb: Boneless rib chops, boneless loin chops or saddle	1 to 1½ inches
Pork: Pounded tenderloin, boneless loin chops, ham steaks, butterflied chops	½ inch
Veal: Scallops or cutlets from the leg, tenderloin or round steak	¼ to ½ inch

Tarragon Chicken with Spring Vegetables

A mélange of asparagus, zucchini, peas, and other delicate vegetables are combined with chicken in a cream sauce flavored with tarragon.

2 (6-oz.) boneless, skinless chicken breast halves

Salt and freshly ground black pepper to taste

1 large leek, white part only

¼ lb. asparagus

2 TB. unsalted butter

1 garlic clove, peeled and minced

½ cup chicken stock

⅓ cup dry white wine

⅓ cup heavy cream

2 TB. chopped fresh tarragon or 1 tsp. dried

1 carrot, peeled and thinly sliced

1 small zucchini, rinsed, trimmed, and sliced

⅓ cup frozen peas, thawed

> **Active time:** 15 minutes
> **Start to finish:** 25 minutes
> **Each serving has:**
> 556 calories
> 265 calories from fat
> 29.5 g fat
> 17.5 g saturated fat
> 46 g protein
> 21 g carbohydrates

1. Rinse chicken under cold water and pat dry with paper towels. Trim all visible fat and cut chicken into 1-inch cubes. Season to taste with salt and pepper. Trim leek, slice in half lengthwise, slice thinly, and rinse slices well in a colander. Set aside. Rinse asparagus and discard woody stems. Cut into 1-inch lengths.

Double Feature

While we don't use the green tops of leeks very often in cooking, if you're making a stock, save them and use them in place of an onion. They give stocks a rich color as well as an improved flavor.

2. Heat butter in a heavy 12-inch skillet over medium heat. Add chicken cubes and cook, stirring frequently, for 3 minutes or until chicken is opaque. Add leek and garlic and cook, stirring occasionally, for 3 minutes or until leek is translucent.

3. Stir stock, wine, cream, tarragon, and carrot into the skillet. Bring to a boil, reduce the heat to medium-low, and simmer for 5 minutes. Add zucchini and asparagus and simmer for an additional 5 minutes or until chicken is cooked through and no longer pink. Stir in peas and simmer 1 minute. Season to taste with salt and pepper and serve immediately.

Chicken Marsala with Mushrooms and Sage

This Italian classic is given more interest by the woodsy sage added as the herb in the richly flavored wine sauce.

Active time: 15 minutes

Start to finish: 25 minutes

Each serving has:

491 calories

212 calories from fat

24 g fat

3.5 g saturated fat

44 g protein

15 g carbohydrates

2 (6-oz.) boneless, skinless chicken breast halves

¼ lb. white mushrooms

3 TB. all-purpose flour

Salt and freshly ground black pepper to taste

3 TB. olive oil

1 shallot, peeled and diced

3 garlic cloves, peeled and minced

½ cup dry marsala wine

½ cup chicken stock

3 TB. chopped fresh parsley

1 TB. chopped fresh sage or 1 tsp. dried

1. Rinse chicken under cold water and pat dry with paper towels. Trim all visible fat and cut chicken into 1-inch cubes. Wipe mushrooms with a damp paper towel, discard stems, and slice thinly. Season flour to taste with salt and pepper. Dust chicken with seasoned flour, shaking off any excess.

2. Heat olive oil in a heavy 10-inch skillet over medium high heat. Add chicken pieces, and cook, stirring frequently, for 3 minutes or until chicken is opaque. Remove chicken from the pan with a slotted spoon and set aside.

3. Add shallot, garlic, and mushrooms to the skillet. Cook, stirring frequently, for 3 minutes or until shallot is translucent. Return chicken to the skillet and add marsala, stock, parsley, and sage. Bring to a boil, stirring occasionally.

4. Reduce the heat to medium and simmer mixture uncovered for 10 minutes or until chicken is cooked through and no longer pink. Season to taste with salt and pepper. Serve immediately.

Variation: Use veal scallops pounded to an even thickness of ½ inch in place of chicken. Cooking time will not change.

> ### Double Feature
>
> If you have stock left in a can and don't think you'll be using it soon, make ice cubes from it. Measure the capacity of your ice cube tray with a measuring tablespoon, and once the cubes are frozen, transfer them to a resealable plastic bag. If you need a few tablespoons of stock, you're all set.

Italian Chicken with Lemon and Capers (*Pollo Piccata*)

Chicken meals don't get any easier than this quick sauté of chicken in a lemony sauce enlivened with parsley and capers.

2 (6-oz.) boneless, skinless chicken breast halves

3 TB. all-purpose flour

Salt and freshly ground black pepper to taste

3 TB. olive oil

¾ cup chicken stock

¼ cup freshly squeezed lemon juice

3 TB. chopped fresh parsley

2 TB. capers

Active time: 10 minutes
Start to finish: 20 minutes
Each serving has:
424 calories
203 calories from fat
22.5 g fat
3 g saturated fat
42 g protein
12 g carbohydrates

1. Rinse chicken under cold water and pat dry with paper towels. Trim all visible fat, place chicken between two sheets of plastic wrap, and pound it to an even thickness of ½ inch. Season flour to taste with salt and pepper. Dust chicken with seasoned flour, shaking off any excess.

Double Feature

Want to get every drop of juice out of your lemons? Try rolling them on the counter a few times before you cut them in half. The rolling weakens the fibers so you can squeeze them with greater force.

2. Heat olive oil in a heavy 10-inch skillet over medium high heat. Add chicken and cook for 2 minutes per side, turning with a slotted spatula.

3. Add stock, lemon juice, parsley, and capers to the skillet. Bring to a boil, reduce the heat to low, cover the pan, and simmer chicken for 5 minutes. Turn chicken over and simmer for an additional 5 minutes or until chicken is cooked through and no longer pink. Season to taste with salt and pepper. Serve immediately.

Variation: Use veal scallops pounded to an even thickness of ¼ inch in place of chicken. Cook veal for 2 minutes per side.

Chicken Provençal

Red peppers, tomatoes, and black olives add all the sunny flavors of Provence to this easy dish.

Active time: 15 minutes

Start to finish: 25 minutes

Each serving has:

597 calories

228 calories from fat

25 g fat

4 g saturated fat

45 g protein

38.5 g carbohydrates

1 leek, white part only

2 (6-oz.) boneless, skinless chicken breast halves

3 TB. all-purpose flour

Salt and freshly ground black pepper to taste

1 orange

3 TB. olive oil

4 garlic cloves, peeled and minced

½ red bell pepper, seeds and ribs removed, thinly sliced

2 ripe plum tomatoes, rinsed, cored, and diced

¾ cup chicken stock

½ cup dry white wine

¼ cup pitted oil-cured black olives

2 TB. chopped fresh parsley

2 tsp. Herbes de Provence

1 bay leaf

1. Trim leek and slice thinly. Place slices in a colander, rinse well under cold running water, and set aside. Rinse chicken under cold water and pat dry with paper towels. Trim all visible fat, place chicken between two sheets of plastic wrap, and pound it to an even thickness of ½ inch. Season flour to taste with salt and pepper. Dust chicken with seasoned flour, shaking off any

excess. Rinse orange, grate off zest, and squeeze out juice. Set aside.

2. Heat olive oil in a heavy 10-inch skillet over medium-high heat. Add chicken and cook for 2 minutes per side, turning with a slotted spatula. Remove chicken breasts from the pan and set aside.

3. Add leek, garlic, and red bell pepper. Cook, stirring frequently, for 3 minutes or until leek is translucent. Add orange juice and zest, tomatoes, stock, wine, olives, parsley, herbes de Provence, and bay leaf. Bring to a boil and return chicken breasts to the pan, including any juices that may have accumulated.

4. Bring to a boil, reduce the heat to low, cover the pan, and simmer chicken for 5 minutes. Turn chicken over and simmer for an additional 5 minutes or until chicken is cooked through and no longer pink. Remove chicken from the pan and keep warm. Raise the heat to high and cook sauce for 3 minutes or until reduced by one fourth. Season to taste with salt and pepper and serve immediately.

Variation: Substitute swordfish steaks 1 inch thick which will cook in the same time as chicken. For fillets of cod or halibut, reduce total cooking time to 5 minutes after the initial sauté.

> **Double Trouble**
>
> Leeks are like the character Pigpen in "Peanuts," always dirty. So always trim and slice them before rinsing them. Dirt will hide all through a leek, so it's best to rinse it in a colander.

Shrimp Scampi

This Venetian version of scampi is incredibly elegant and tasty with garlic and herbs simmered in a quick white wine sauce.

Active time: 15 minutes

Start to finish: 15 minutes

Each serving has:

438 calories

304 calories from fat

34 g fat

14 g saturated fat

24 g protein

4.5 g carbohydrates

3 TB. unsalted butter

2 TB. olive oil

3 garlic cloves, peeled and minced

1 large shallot, peeled and minced

½ lb. extra large (16 to 20 per lb.) raw shrimp, peeled and deveined

¼ cup dry white wine

2 TB. chopped fresh parsley

½ tsp. Italian seasoning

Salt and red pepper flakes to taste

1. Heat butter and oil in a heavy 10-inch skillet over medium-high heat. When butter foam starts to subside, add garlic, shallot, and shrimp. Cook, stirring constantly, for 3 minutes or until shallot is translucent.

2. Add wine, parsley, and Italian seasoning. Stir well and season to taste with salt and red pepper flakes. Cook for 2 minutes. Serve immediately.

Variation: Substitute any firm-fleshed white fish, such as cod or halibut, cut into 1-inch cubes for shrimp.

Double Trouble

While butter gives food a delicious flavor, never use it alone when sautéing food. Because all fats burn at a certain temperature, the dairy solids in butter makes that temperature rather low. Because of this fact, some sort of oil is always added to the butter to raise the smoke point.

Spanish Garlic Shrimp

In Spain these shrimp made with garlic and paprika are eaten at tapas bars, but they're great on rice to soak up every bit of sauce.

⅓ cup olive oil

4 garlic cloves, peeled and minced

2 TB. sweet paprika, preferably Spanish

½ lb. extra large (16 to 20 per lb.) raw shrimp, peeled and deveined

Salt and freshly ground black pepper to taste

Active time: 12 minutes
Start to finish: 12 minutes
Each serving has:
434 calories
317 calories from fat
35 g fat
5 g saturated fat
24 g protein
7 g carbohydrates

1. Heat olive oil in a heavy 10-inch skillet over medium-high heat. Add garlic and cook, stirring constantly, for 30 seconds or until garlic is fragrant.

2. Add paprika and shrimp. Cook, stirring frequently, for 3 to 4 minutes or until shrimp are bright pink. Season to taste with salt and pepper. Serve immediately.

Variation: Substitute bay scallops or sea scallops cut into quarters for shrimp.

Déjà Two

It's a fair guess that Shakespeare was not a great fan of garlic. In *A Midsummer Night's Dream* as Bottom is preparing his play, he says: "And, most dear actors, eat no onions or garlic, for we are to utter sweet breath."

Tuna Steaks with Fennel and Peppers

The anise-flavored fennel and rosy bell peppers remain crisp, which is a lovely contrast to the tender tuna.

Active time: 15 minutes

Start to finish: 20 minutes

Each serving has:

409 calories

141 calories from fat

16 g fat

2 g saturated fat

43 g protein

20 g carbohydrates

2 (6-oz.) tuna steaks, about 1 inch thick

Salt and freshly ground black pepper to taste

1 small fennel bulb

2 TB. olive oil

1 small red onion, peeled and sliced

2 garlic cloves, peeled and minced

1 red bell pepper, seeds and ribs removed, thinly sliced

¼ cup dry white wine

¼ cup water

1 tsp. Herbes de Provence

1. Rinse tuna steaks and pat dry with paper towels. Season to taste with salt and pepper. Trim bottom off fennel and remove green stalks. Cut bulb in half lengthwise and cut each half into ¼-inch slices. Set aside.

2. Heat 1 tablespoon olive oil in a heavy 10-inch skillet over high heat. Add tuna steaks. Sear for 2 minutes per side or to desired doneness, turning tuna gently with a spatula. Remove tuna from the skillet and cover with aluminum foil. Set aside.

3. Add remaining 1 tablespoon oil to the skillet and reduce the heat to medium-high. Add fennel, onion, garlic, and red bell pepper. Cook, stirring frequently, for 3 minutes or until onion is translucent.

4. Add wine, water, and Herbes de Provence. Cover the skillet and cook, stirring occasionally, for 5 minutes or until vegetables are crisp-tender. Season to taste with salt and pepper. Serve immediately with vegetables on top of tuna.

Variation: Substitute swordfish steak for tuna, but cook for 4 minutes per side.

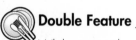 **Double Feature**

While we rarely use fennel stalks when we cook the bulb, don't send them to the compost heap. Use them in place of celery in cold salads. They'll give the same crunch with a more interesting licorice-like flavor.

Pork Scaloppine

Sautéed mushrooms match the delicacy of the breaded pork slices in this dish that's fast to the finish line.

1 (12-oz.) pork tenderloin	**1 tsp. Italian seasoning**
Salt and freshly ground black pepper to taste	**3 TB. olive oil**
	2 TB. unsalted butter
½ lb. white mushrooms	**¼ cup onion, peeled and chopped**
1 large egg	
1 cup Italian breadcrumbs	**3 TB. freshly squeezed lemon juice**
3 TB. freshly grated Parmesan cheese	**1 TB. chopped fresh parsley**

> **Active time:** 20 minutes
>
> **Start to finish:** 20 minutes
>
> **Each serving has:**
>
> 862 calories
>
> 461 calories from fat
>
> 51 g fat
>
> 16 g saturated fat
>
> 55 g protein
>
> 48 g carbohydrates

1. Preheat the oven to 150°F. Trim tenderloin by cutting off all visible fat and then scrape off iridescent silverskin. Cut tenderloin crosswise into 6 slices. Pound slices between two sheets of plastic wrap to an even thickness of ¼ inch and sprinkle with salt and pepper. Wipe mushrooms with a damp paper towel. Discard stems and slice mushrooms.

2. In a shallow bowl, beat egg with a fork. Combine bread crumbs, Parmesan cheese, and Italian seasoning in another shallow bowl. Dip meat slices into egg, let any excess drip off, and then dip meat into crumb mixture, pressing crumbs into meat on both sides.

3. Heat olive oil in a large heavy skillet over medium-high heat. Cook pork for 1½ minutes or until nicely browned. Turn gently with tongs and cook the second side. Transfer pork to a baking sheet, and place it in the oven to keep warm.

4. Wipe the skillet with paper towels. Heat butter over medium-high heat. Add onion and cook, stirring frequently, for 3 minutes or until onion is translucent. Add mushrooms and cook, stirring frequently, for 3 to 5 minutes or until mushrooms are lightly browned and most of their liquid has evaporated. Stir in lemon juice and parsley and season to taste with salt and pepper.

5. Remove pork from the oven. Spoon mushrooms over pork and serve immediately.

Variation: Substitute chicken breasts pounded to the same thickness of ¼ inch for pork. Cook chicken for 2 minutes per side or until cooked through and no longer pink.

Double Feature

It's important to remove the silverskin from tenderloins because it becomes tough gristle when the meats are cooked, and it also prevents them from being pounded properly.

Pan-Seared Filet Mignon with Barolo Sauce

Steak topped with a richly flavored red wine sauce is an easy and elegant way to enjoy beef.

Active time: 10 minutes

Start to finish: 15 minutes

Each serving has:

519 calories

295 calories from fat

33 g fat

12 g saturated fat

37 g protein

4.5 g carbohydrates

2 (6-oz.) filet mignons

Salt and freshly ground black pepper to taste

2 TB. olive oil

2 TB. unsalted butter

1 large shallot, peeled and chopped

2 garlic cloves, peeled and minced

¾ cup Barolo or other dry red wine

⅓ cup beef stock

1 TB. chopped fresh oregano or 1 tsp. dried

1 tsp. fresh thyme or ¼ tsp. dried

Double Feature

Meat is rare and ready to turn when drops of blood come to the surface and the meat begins to feel spongy. It is medium when drops of juice begin to appear and the meat resists when pressed, and it is well done when clear juices are visible.

1. Preheat the oven to 200° F. Rinse steaks and pat dry with paper towels. Trim off visible fat, season to taste with salt and pepper, and set aside. Heat oil in a heavy 10-inch skillet over high heat. Add steaks and sear on each side for 1 minute. Reduce the heat to medium-high and cook steaks for 2 to 3 minutes per side for rare or to desired doneness. Remove steaks from the pan with tongs and place them on a serving platter. Place steaks in the oven to keep warm.

2. Pour oil out of the pan and place the pan over medium heat. Heat butter and add shallots and garlic. Cook, stirring frequently, for 3 minutes or until shallot is translucent.

3. Raise the heat to medium-high, add wine, stock, oregano, and thyme. Cook, stirring occasionally, until sauce is reduced by half. Season to taste with salt and pepper and pour sauce over steaks. Serve immediately.

Middle Eastern Lamb and Eggplant Patties

Quickly cooked eggplant becomes a stuffing for these richly flavored lamb "burgers."

1 Italian eggplant	½ red bell pepper, seeds and ribs removed, finely chopped
Salt and freshly ground black pepper to taste	½ lb. lean ground lamb
5 TB. olive oil	2 TB. chopped fresh parsley
1 shallot, peeled and diced	2 TB. plain bread crumbs
2 garlic cloves, peeled and minced	2 TB. water
	1 tsp. ground coriander

Active time: 20 minutes

Start to finish: 50 minutes, including 30 minutes for salting eggplant

Each serving has:

732 calories

554 calories from fat

61.5 g fat

16 g saturated fat

23 g protein

25 g carbohydrates

---

1. Rinse and trim eggplant and cut into ¼-inch dice. Place eggplant in a colander and sprinkle liberally with salt. Place a plate on top of eggplant cubes and weight the plate with cans. Place the colander in the sink or on a plate and allow eggplant to drain for 30 minutes. Rinse cubes and squeeze hard to remove water. Wring out remaining water with cloth tea towel.

2. Heat 2 tablespoons olive oil in a heavy 12-inch skillet over medium heat. Add shallot, 1 garlic clove, and red bell pepper. Cook, stirring frequently, for 3 minutes or until shallot is translucent. Remove mixture from the pan with a slotted spoon and add 2 tablespoons olive oil. Add eggplant and cook for 5 minutes or until eggplant softens. Return other vegetables to the pan and cook for 3 minutes, stirring frequently. Season to taste with salt and pepper and set aside.

3. Combine remaining garlic, lamb, parsley, bread crumbs, water, and coriander in a mixing bowl. Season to taste with salt and pepper and mix well.

4. Divide meat mixture into 4 balls and flatten to an even thickness of ½ inch between two sheets of plastic wrap. Place half of eggplant filling in the center of 2 patties and press remaining patties on top, pressing edges together to seal.

5. Heat remaining 1 tablespoon olive oil in a heavy 10-inch skillet over medium-high heat. Cook patties for 4 to 5 minutes per side or until lamb is still slightly rare. Serve immediately.

Variation: Substitute ground beef or turkey for lamb. If using ground turkey, cook it through until it is no longer pink.

 Déjà Two

Coriander, a member of the parsley family, is one of few foods that are native to both the Mediterranean and Asia, although it's also used extensively in Latin American cooking. The leaves we know as "cilantro," and the seeds have a flavor that combines those of sage and caraway. Mention of coriander seeds are found in early Sanskrit writings.

Veal with Prosciutto and Sage (Vitello Saltimbocca)

Salty ham and woodsy sage pair beautifully with delicate veal scallops in this Italian dish.

Active time: 15 minutes

Start to finish: 18 minutes

Each serving has:

462 calories

320 calories from fat

35.5 g fat

10 g saturated fat

28 g protein

2 g carbohydrates

½ lb. veal scallops in 4 pieces

2 garlic cloves, peeled and pressed through a garlic press

Salt and freshly ground black pepper to taste

12 to 16 large fresh sage leaves

4 thin slices prosciutto

3 TB. olive oil

¼ cup dry white wine

¼ cup chicken stock

1 TB. unsalted butter

1. Rinse veal and pat dry with paper towels. Place veal between two sheets of plastic wrap, and pound to an even thickness of ¼ inch.

2. Rub veal with garlic and season to taste with salt and pepper. Arrange 2 or 3 sage leaves on top of each cutlet and cover sage with 1 slice of prosciutto. Use wooden toothpicks like straight pins to attach prosciutto to veal.

3. Heat olive oil in a heavy 12-inch skillet over high heat. Add 2 veal cutlets, prosciutto sides down, and cook for 45 seconds. Turn cutlets over with tongs and cook for an additional 20 seconds or until just cooked through. Transfer to a platter and keep warm, loosely covered with foil. Cook remaining cutlets in the same manner.

4. Pour off oil from the skillet, add wine and stock, and *deglaze* the skillet by boiling over high heat, stirring and scraping up brown bits, for 1 minute. Continue boiling until liquid is reduced to 3 tablespoons. Add butter and swirl the skillet until incorporated.

5. Remove and discard the wooden toothpicks from veal. Drizzle sauce over veal and serve immediately.

◆ Duet Dialogue

Deglaze is the cooking term for making a quick pan sauce. Once food has been sautéed and the excess grease is out of the pan, a liquid is added. And as you stir the liquid, all the nuggets of flavor stuck to the bottom become part of the sauce.

Chapter 13

International Intrigue

In This Chapter

- ◆ Mexican favorites
- ◆ Elegant European fare
- ◆ Dishes with fruits and nuts

The continuation of your tour of fast dishes from the world's cuisines takes you from lusty Latin flavors to delicate Scandinavian fare when cooking the recipes in this chapter.

Tender cuts of meat, like beef steaks and veal scallops, are perfect for quickly cooked dishes, as are chicken breasts and all aquatic species. Here you'll find a range of preparations for pieces large and small.

The Benefits of Boning

As in other chapters, in many of these recipes we will use boneless, skinless chicken breasts. Ready to use and available in all supermarkets with reasonable prices, the price per pound is still less if you bone them yourself. In addition, by boning the chicken yourself, you can always replenish your cache of bones and skin to use for making chicken stock. Boning isn't difficult; just make sure your knife is sharp before you start—it makes all the difference.

If possible, buy chicken breasts whole rather than split. Pull off the skin with your fingers, and then make an incision on both sides of the breast bone (just adjacent to the bone), cutting down until you feel the bone resisting the knife.

Treating one side at a time, place the blade of your boning knife against the carcass and scrape away the meat. You will then have two pieces—the large fillet and the small tenderloin.

To trim the fillet, cut away any fat. Some recipes will tell you to pound the breast to an even thickness so it will cook evenly and quickly. To do this, place the breast between two sheets of plastic wrap, and pound with the smooth side of a meat mallet or the bottom of a small, heavy skillet or saucepan.

To trim the tenderloin, secure the tip of the visible tendon with your free hand. Using a paring knife, scrape down the tendon, and the meat will push away. With this done, you are ready to prepare your chicken recipe.

Chicken Fajitas

Chicken is cooked with red onion and bell peppers and then rolled in flour tortillas in this popular Mexican dish.

2 (6-oz.) boneless, skinless chicken breast halves

3 TB. olive oil

1 small red onion, peeled and thinly sliced

1 small red bell pepper, seeds and ribs removed, and thinly sliced

1 jalapeño chili, seeds and ribs removed, and finely chopped

2 garlic cloves, peeled and minced

1 tomato, rinsed, cored, seeded, and diced

3 TB. freshly squeezed lime juice

1 tsp. ground *cumin*

2 TB. chopped fresh cilantro

Salt and freshly ground black pepper to taste

4 (6-in.) flour tortillas

Garnish (optional):

Sour cream

Salsa

Guacamole

Active time: 25 minutes

Start to finish: 25 minutes

Each serving has:

636 calories

252 calories from fat

28 g fat

5 g saturated fat

47 g protein

49 g carbohydrates

---

1. Rinse chicken and pat dry with paper towels. Trim off visible fat, and pound between two sheets of plastic wrap to an even thickness of ½-inch. Cut into strips 2-inches long and ¾-inch wide.

2. Heat 2 tablespoons olive oil in a heavy 12-inch skillet over medium-high heat. Add chicken and cook, stirring frequently, for 4 to 5 minutes or until chicken is cooked through and no longer pink. Remove chicken from the skillet with a slotted spoon, and set aside.

3. Add remaining 1 tablespoon olive oil to the skillet and heat over medium-high heat. Add onion, red bell pepper, jalapeño, and garlic. Cook, stirring frequently, for 4 to 6 minutes or until onion is soft. Add tomato and cook for 1 minute. Add lime juice, cumin, cilantro, and chicken. Cook for 2 minutes, stirring frequently. Season to taste with salt and pepper.

4. Roll up filling in tortillas, and serve with small bowls of sour cream, salsa, and guacamole, if desired. Serve immediately.

Variation: Substitute flank steak or pork loin cut to the same size as chicken strips for chicken. Cook beef to desired doneness, and cook pork for the same amount of time as chicken.

 **Duet Dialogue**

Cumin (pronounced *KOO-men*) is frequently found in markets under its Spanish name, *comino*. The seeds from which it's ground are the dried fruit from a plant in the parsley family, which is very aromatic. It's one of the major ingredients in commercial chili powder, so you can always substitute chili powder if necessary.

Chicken with Dried Fruit and Mustard Sauce

Sharp Dijon mustard is balanced by succulent dried fruits and sweet apple juice in this modification of an Austrian recipe.

Active time: 15 minutes

Start to finish: 30 minutes

Each serving has:

545 calories

149 calories from fat

17 g fat

3 g saturated fat

46 g protein

59 g carbohydrates

2 (6-oz.) boneless, skinless chicken breast halves

Salt and freshly ground black pepper to taste

2 TB. vegetable oil

1 small onion, peeled and minced

2 garlic cloves, peeled and minced

½ red bell pepper, seeds and ribs removed, and thinly sliced

1 (5.5-oz.) can apple juice

½ cup chicken stock

2 TB. *Dijon mustard*

¼ cup chopped dried apricots

¼ cup raisins, preferably golden raisins

¼ cup dried currants (or additional raisins)

1. Rinse chicken and pat dry with paper towels. Trim all visible fat, and cut into 1-inch cubes. Sprinkle chicken with salt and pepper.

2. Heat oil in a large, deep skillet over medium-high heat. Add chicken in a single layer and cook, stirring frequently, for 2 minutes or until chicken is opaque. Remove chicken and set aside.

3. Add onion and garlic to the skillet and cook, stirring frequently, for 3 minutes or until onion is translucent. Add red bell pepper and cook, stirring frequently, for 2 minutes. Add chicken, apple juice, stock, mustard, dried apricots, raisins, and currants. Bring to a boil, stirring occasionally. Reduce the heat to medium, and simmer for 10 minutes or until chicken is cooked through and no longer pink.

4. Season to taste with salt and pepper. Serve immediately.

Variation: Substitute pork loin cut into ½-inch slices for chicken. Cook it for 15 to 20 minutes or until tender.

Duet Dialogue

Dijon mustard, known for its clean, sharp flavor, was actually invented in Dijon, France. Made from a combination of brown and black mustard seeds, its essential ingredients are white wine and unfermented grape juice.

Normandy-Style Chicken with Apples

The cuisine of Normandy usually involves cream, apples, and the region's famed Calvados apple brandy, and you'll find them all in this dish.

2 (6-oz.) boneless, skinless chicken breast halves

1 Granny Smith apple

2 leeks, white part only

3 TB. unsalted butter

1 TB. granulated sugar

Salt and freshly ground black pepper to taste

2 tsp. fresh thyme or ½ tsp. dried

2 TB. Calvados or brandy

1 (5.5-oz.) can apple juice

½ cup heavy cream

Active time: 20 minutes

Start to finish: 30 minutes

Each serving has:

721 calories

367 calories from fat

41 g fat

25 g saturated fat

42 g protein

39 g carbohydrates

---

1. Rinse chicken and pat dry with paper towels. Trim all visible fat, and pound between two sheets of plastic wrap to an even thickness of ½-inch. Rinse and core apple. Cut apple into slices ½-inch thick. Slice leeks in half lengthwise and then thinly slice each half. Place leek slices into a colander and rinse well under cold running water. Set aside.

2. Heat 1½ tablespoons butter in a large heavy skillet over medium heat. Add apple slices and cook for 3 minutes. Turn apple slices gently with a spatula, sprinkle with sugar, and cook for an additional 3 to 5 minutes or until apple is tender. Remove apple slices with a spatula and keep warm.

3. Heat remaining 1½ tablespoons butter in the skillet over medium-high heat. Sprinkle chicken with salt and pepper and add to the skillet. Cook for 2 minutes per side, turning chicken gently with tongs. Add leeks, thyme, Calvados, apple juice, and cream. Bring to a boil, cover the skillet, and cook over low heat for 10 to 15 minutes or until chicken is cooked through and no longer pink.

4. Remove chicken with a slotted spatula and keep warm. Reduce sauce over medium heat for 3 minutes or until slightly thickened. Season to taste with salt and pepper. To serve, place chicken on plates with apple slices and spoon sauce on top of chicken. Serve immediately.

Variation: Substitute boneless pork chops for chicken. Cook it for 15 to 20 minutes or until tender.

> **Double Feature**
>
> An easy way to core apples or pears is with a melon baller. It also creates a nice round hole so the slices look even.

Spicy Southwest Shrimp

Shrimp are cooked with black beans, tomato, and spices in this vibrantly flavored dish.

Active time: 15 minutes

Start to finish: 17 minutes

Each serving has:

537 calories

205 calories from fat

23 g fat

4 g saturated fat

39 g protein

44 g carbohydrates

3 slices bacon, cut into ½-inch pieces

½ lb. extra large (16 to 20 per lb.) raw shrimp, peeled and deveined

1 small onion, peeled and diced

2 garlic cloves, peeled and minced

1 jalapeño chili, seeds and ribs removed, and finely chopped

1½ tsp. ground cumin

1 ripe plum tomato, rinsed, cored, seeded, and diced

1 (15-oz.) can pinto beans, drained and rinsed

½ cup seafood stock or bottled clam juice

2 TB. chopped fresh cilantro

1 tsp. fresh thyme or ¼ tsp. dried

Salt and freshly ground black pepper to taste

Freshly squeezed lime juice to taste

Duet Dialogue

To **sear** food is to cook it quickly over very high heat to seal in the juices and keep it moist for future cooking. Meats are seared before being braised which also adds a nice rich color to the resulting dish, and foods like shrimp are seared as a preliminary cooking step.

1. Place bacon in a large skillet over medium-high heat. Cook for 5 to 7 minutes or until crisp. Remove bacon from the pan with a slotted spoon, and drain on paper towels. Discard all but 2 tablespoons of bacon fat. Raise the heat to high and add shrimp. *Sear* shrimp for 1 minute, stirring constantly. Remove shrimp from the pan with a slotted spoon and set aside.

2. Add onion and garlic to the pan. Lower the heat to medium, and cook for 2 minutes, stirring constantly. Add jalapeño and cumin, and continue to cook for 1 minute. Add tomato, beans, and stock. Bring to a boil, reduce the heat to low, and simmer for 5 minutes.

3. Add shrimp, cilantro, and thyme to bean mixture. Lower the heat to medium and cook for about 3 minutes or until shrimp are cooked through. Season to taste with salt, pepper, and lime juice. Serve immediately.

Variation: Substitute chicken breast, cut into ½-inch cubes for shrimp and use chicken stock rather than seafood stock. Cook them for 5 minutes or until cooked through and no longer pink.

Caribbean Curried Shrimp

Creamy coconut milk is the base of this sauce that's dotted with black beans and green peas.

2 TB. olive oil

1 medium onion, peeled and diced

2 garlic cloves, peeled and minced

1 small jalapeño or Scotch bonnet chili, seeds and ribs removed, and finely chopped

2 TB. curry powder

1 ripe tomato, rinsed, cored, seeded, and diced

1 cup coconut milk

Salt and freshly ground black pepper to taste

1 (15-oz.) can black beans, drained and rinsed

½ cup frozen peas, thawed

½ lb. large (21 to 30 per pound) raw shrimp, peeled and deveined

Active time: 12 minutes
Start to finish: 20 minutes
Each serving has:
723 calories
408 calories from fat
45 g fat
28 g saturated fat
38 g protein
54 g carbohydrates

1. Heat oil in a saucepan over medium-high heat. Add onions, garlic, and jalapeño. Cook for 3 minutes or until onion is translucent. Reduce heat to low, add curry powder, and cook, stirring constantly, for 1 minute.

3. Add tomato and coconut milk, and season to taste with salt and pepper. Bring to a boil over medium heat, stirring occasionally.

4. Stir in black beans, peas, and shrimp. Cook, covered, over low heat, stirring occasionally, for 3 minutes or until shrimp are pink and cooked through. Serve immediately.

Variation: Substitute bay scallops or sea scallops cut into quarters for shrimp, and cook the same length of time.

 Double Trouble

Never confuse coconut milk, usually found in the Asian or Caribbean aisle of supermarkets, with sweetened coconut cream, which more often than not is shelved with drink bases, like Bloody Mary mix. Coconut milk gives dishes a creamy appearance but has no sugar.

Pan-Fried Flounder with Black Walnut Butter

Black walnuts have a flavor that's more distinctive than common walnuts, and the nuts create a crispy coating for the delicate fish.

Active time: 25 minutes

Start to finish: 25 minutes

Each serving has:

1077 calories

743 calories from fat

82.5 g fat

16 g saturated fat

58 g protein

40 g carbohydrates

2 (6- to 8-oz.) flounder fillets

2 cups black walnut pieces

½ cup yellow cornmeal

¼ cup all-purpose flour

Salt and freshly ground black pepper to taste

½ cup milk

1 large egg

¼ tsp. hot red pepper sauce

½ cup vegetable oil

3 TB. unsalted butter, sliced into thin slices

2 TB. freshly squeezed lemon juice

¼ cup chopped fresh parsley

1. Rinse flounder and pat dry with paper towels. Place 1 cup black walnut pieces in a food processor fitted with a steel blade. Chop finely using on and off pulsing action.

2. Combine ground nuts, cornmeal, flour, salt, and pepper in a shallow dish and mix well. Combine milk, egg, and red pepper sauce in a mixing bowl and whisk well.

3. Heat vegetable oil in a large skillet over medium-high heat. Dip fillets in milk mixture and then *dredge* fillets in black walnut flour, coating them evenly. Add fillets to the skillet and cook for 2 to 3 minutes per side or until browned, turning fillets gently with a slotted spatula. Remove fillets from the skillet and pat with paper towels. Keep warm.

4. Discard grease from the skillet, and wipe the skillet clean with paper towels. Return the skillet to the stove over medium heat. Add butter and remaining 1 cup black walnut pieces and cook, stirring frequently, for 2 minutes or until black walnuts are browned. Add lemon juice and parsley and cook for 1 minute. Season sauce to taste with salt and pepper.

5. To serve, place fillets on plates, and spoon sauce across center of each fillet. Serve immediately.

Duet Dialogue

Dredge is the culinary term for completely coating food with some sort of dry mixture before cooking it. The mixture can be as simple as seasoned flour for cubes of meat to be browned before braising or a flavorful mixture such as this one.

Indian-Style Sautéed Tuna

Richly flavored tuna is marinated in yogurt and then coated with spices before being quickly seared.

1 (6-oz.) container plain non-fat yogurt

2 (6- to 8-oz.) tuna steaks, at least 1-inch thick

2 TB. freshly squeezed lemon juice

3 garlic cloves, peeled and minced

2 tsp. grated fresh ginger

1 small jalapeño chili, seeds and ribs removed, finely chopped

¼ cup olive oil

1 ripe plum tomato, rinsed, cored, seeded, and chopped

1 small pickling cucumber, peeled and chopped

1 scallion, rinsed, trimmed, and chopped

Salt and freshly ground black pepper to taste

⅓ cup plain breadcrumbs

1 TB. ground cumin

1 tsp. turmeric

Active time: 15 minutes
Start to finish: 2¼ hours, including 2 hours for marinating tuna
Each serving has:
525 calories
197 calories from fat
22 g fat
3 g saturated fat
54 g protein
26 g carbohydrates

1. Place yogurt in a sieve suspended over a mixing bowl, and allow it to drain at room temperature for 2 hours.

2. Rinse tuna, and place it in a heavy resealable plastic bag along with lemon juice, 2 garlic cloves, ginger, jalapeño, and 2 tablespoons olive oil. Refrigerate and marinate tuna for 2 hours, turning the bag occasionally.

3. For sauce, combine drained yogurt, remaining garlic, tomato, cucumber, and scallion in a mixing bowl. Stir well and season to taste with salt and pepper. Refrigerate until ready to serve.

4. Combine breadcrumbs, cumin, and turmeric on a plate. Remove tuna from marinade and discard marinade. Sprinkle tuna with salt and pepper. Coat both sides of fish with breadcrumb mixture. Heat remaining 2 tablespoons olive oil in a large skillet over high heat. Add fish and cook for 2 minutes on each side for medium-rare. Serve immediately topped with yogurt sauce.

Variation: Substitute swordfish or salmon steaks for tuna. Cook according to the rule of 10 minutes total time per inch of thickness.

Double Feature

Draining the yogurt creates a thicker sauce. Drain yogurt for up to eight hours, and it will lose about half its volume. When recipes are made with thicker yogurt, sauces have a texture similar to that of sour cream.

Stir-Fried Beef with Tomato and Herbs

The steak is coated with herbs, and then aromatic basil, oregano, and rosemary are included in the dish, too.

Active time: 15 minutes

Start to finish: 20 minutes

Each serving has:

568 calories

289 calories from fat

32 g fat

9 g saturated fat

37 g protein

21.5 g carbohydrates

1 (12- to 14-oz.) strip sirloin steak

2 garlic cloves, peeled and minced

2 TB. chopped fresh parsley

2 tsp. fresh thyme or ½ tsp. dried

Salt and freshly ground black pepper to taste

3 TB. olive oil

1 small onion, peeled and sliced

2 ripe plum tomatoes, rinsed, cored, seeded, and diced

½ cup dry red wine

2 TB. chopped fresh basil or 1 tsp. dried

1 TB. chopped fresh oregano or ½ tsp. dried

1 TB. chopped fresh rosemary or ½ tsp. dried

1 TB. firmly packed dark brown sugar

1. Rinse steak and pat dry with paper towels. Trim all visible fat and gristle. Cut steak against the grain into ¼-inch slices. Combine garlic, parsley, thyme, salt, pepper, and 1 tablespoon olive oil in a small bowl and mix well. Toss meat with mixture.

2. Heat remaining 2 tablespoons olive oil in a large heavy skillet over medium-high heat. Add onion and cook, stirring frequently, for 3 minutes or until onion is translucent. Add beef and cook, stirring constantly, for 2 to 3 minutes for medium-rare and 3 to 4 minutes for medium. Remove beef and onions from the pan with a slotted spoon and set aside.

3. Add tomatoes to the skillet and cook for 1 minute. Add wine, basil, oregano, rosemary, and brown sugar to the skillet. Raise the heat to high, and cook mixture for 3 minutes or until reduced by half. Return beef and onions to the skillet, stir well, and season to taste with salt and pepper. Serve immediately.

Variation: Substitute boneless leg of lamb for beef and cook for the same amount of time.

 **Double Feature**

If you don't drink very much wine, for cooking buy small 375 ml. bottles instead of the standard 750 ml. And if you have some left over from a recipe, freeze it for future use (without the bottle) in a resealable plastic bag. Once thawed, it will be cloudy but perfectly fine for use in cooking.

Beef Stroganoff

Delicate mushrooms and tender steak are cooked in a sauce enriched with sour cream in this historic dish.

½ lb. crimini mushrooms	1 TB. tomato paste
½ lb. beef tenderloin	2 TB. olive oil
Salt and freshly ground black pepper to taste	2 large shallots, peeled and thinly sliced
3 TB. unsalted butter	3 TB. sour cream
1 TB. all-purpose flour	1 tsp. Dijon mustard
1 cup beef stock	1 TB. chopped fresh parsley

> **Active time:** 20 minutes
> **Start to finish:** 20 minutes
> **Each serving has:**
> 723 calories
> 581 calories from fat
> 64.5 g fat
> 27 g saturated fat
> 28.5 g protein
> 12 g carbohydrates

1. Wipe mushrooms with a damp paper towel. Discard stems and slice mushrooms. Rinse tenderloin and pat dry with paper towels. Trim all visible fat, and scrape off iridescent silverskin. Cut tenderloin into slices ½-inch thick, and pound between two sheets of plastic wrap to an even thickness of ¼-inch. Season to taste with salt and pepper and set aside.

2. Melt 1½ tablespoons butter in a heavy 1-quart saucepan over medium heat. Stir in flour, and cook, stirring constantly, for 1 minute. Add stock in a slow stream, whisking constantly, and bring to a boil. Whisk in tomato paste. Reduce the heat to low and simmer, whisking occasionally, for 3 minutes. Remove the pan from the heat, and cover to keep warm.

3. While sauce is simmering, heat 1 tablespoon olive oil in a heavy 12-inch skillet over medium-high heat. Add beef and cook, turning gently with tongs, until browned on both side but still pink inside, about 1 minute total time. Remove meat from the skillet.

4. Add remaining 1½ tablespoons butter and 1 tablespoon olive oil to the skillet and heat over medium-high heat. Add shallots and cook, stirring frequently, for 3 minutes or until shallots are translucent. Add mushrooms and cook, stirring occasionally, for 5 to 7 minutes or until liquid mushrooms give off has evaporated.

5. Return meat to the skillet, along with any juices that accumulated. Add sauce then whisk in sour cream, mustard, and parsley. Do not let sauce boil. Season to taste with salt and pepper and serve immediately.

 Déjà Two

> Beef Stroganoff was named for a nineteenth-century Russian diplomat, Count Paul Stroganoff. Many years ago, it was one of the dishes that became a hallmark of what Americans called "continental cuisine."

Dilled Swedish Meatballs

Dill is used in many Swedish dishes, including this one with meatballs made from ground pork in a cream sauce.

Active time: 25 minutes
Active time: 25 minutes
Start to finish: 30 minutes
Each serving has:
755 calories
580 calories from fat
64.5 g fat
26 g saturated fat
25 g protein
19 g carbohydrates

3 TB. unsalted butter

1 large shallot, peeled and finely chopped

1 garlic clove, peeled and minced

½ lb. ground pork

¼ cup plain bread crumbs

3 TB. milk

1 large egg yolk, lightly beaten

Pinch of ground allspice

Pinch of ground nutmeg

Salt and freshly ground black pepper to taste

3 TB. vegetable oil

2 TB. all-purpose flour

½ cup chicken stock

¼ cup heavy cream

2 TB. chopped fresh dill or 2 tsp. dried

1. Preheat the oven to 200°F. Heat 1 tablespoon butter in a small skillet over medium-high heat. Add shallot and garlic, and cook, stirring frequently, for 3 minutes or until shallot is translucent. Scrape mixture into a large mixing bowl.

2. Add ground pork, breadcrumbs, milk, egg yolk, allspice, nutmeg, salt, and pepper to the mixing bowl. Mix well with your hands or a wooden spoon. Form mixture into 1-inch balls.

3. Heat oil in a large skillet over medium-high heat. Add meatballs and cook for 5 to 7 minutes, turning gently with tongs, or until cooked through. Transfer meatballs to an ovenproof dish, and keep warm in the oven.

4. Pour grease out of the pan, and melt remaining 2 tablespoons butter over low heat. Stir in flour and cook, stirring constantly, for 1 minute. Whisk in stock, cream, and dill. Cook, whisking constantly, until sauce comes to a boil. Simmer 2 minutes, and season to taste with salt and pepper.

5. Ladle sauce over meatballs, and serve immediately. (You can do this a day in advance and refrigerate, tightly covered. Reheat meatballs in a 350°F oven covered for 10 to 15 minutes or until hot.)

Variation: Substitute ground turkey or chicken for pork.

Double Feature

Herb bunches are frequently larger than what's needed for a recipe for two servings, so here's a way to use it in the future. Rinse leafy herbs like dill, parsley, and cilantro, dry them with paper towels, and then wrap them in small bunches in plastic wrap, and freeze. The next time you need a few tablespoons, take a packet from the freezer and "chop" it with the blunt edge of a heavy knife.

Veal with Dried Fruit and Swiss Chard

Swiss chard is one of the delicate members of the greens family, so it pairs well with the subtle flavor of veal.

½ lb. veal scallops

Salt and freshly ground black pepper to taste

1 Granny Smith apple

2 TB. unsalted butter

1 large shallot, peeled and minced

1 garlic clove, peeled and minced

1 (5.5-oz.) can apple juice

¼ cup freshly squeezed orange juice

¼ cup cider vinegar

¼ cup chopped dried apricots

¼ cup chopped pitted prunes

2 TB. firmly packed dark brown sugar

1 tsp. grated orange zest

¼ tsp. ground cinnamon

¼ tsp. hot red pepper sauce, or more to taste

1 cup chopped *Swiss chard*, rinsed well

Active time: 15 minutes

Start to finish: 25 minutes

Each serving has:

542 calories

208 calories from fat

23 g fat

12 g saturated fat

24 g protein

62.5 g carbohydrates

1. Rinse veal and pat dry with paper towels. Place veal between two sheets of plastic wrap, and pound to an even thickness of ¼-inch. Sprinkle with salt and pepper and set aside. Peel and core apple. Cut apple into ½-inch dice.

2. Heat butter in a large skillet over medium-high heat. Add veal and cook for 2 minutes, browning it on both sides and turning it gently with tongs. Remove veal from the pan with a slotted spoon, and set aside.

Duet Dialogue

Swiss chard is a member of the beet family grown for its crinkly green leaves and silvery, celery-like stalks. The variety with dark green leaves and reddish stalks has a stronger flavor than those bunches with lighter leaves and stalks.

3. Add shallot and garlic to the skillet, and cook, stirring frequently, for 3 minutes or until shallot is translucent. Add apple, apple juice, orange juice, vinegar, dried apricots, prunes, brown sugar, orange zest, cinnamon, and red pepper sauce. Bring to a boil, stirring occasionally, and boil for 5 minutes or until reduced by a third. Add Swiss chard, and cook for 3 to 5 minutes or until Swiss chard is wilted.

4. Return veal to the skillet along with any accumulated juices, and cook for 1 minute. Season to taste with salt and pepper, and serve immediately.

Variation: Use pork or chicken instead of veal, and substitute collard greens or beet greens for Swiss chard.

Chapter 14

Vibrant and Vegetarian

In This Chapter

- ◆ Terrific tofu
- ◆ Vegan options
- ◆ Fast vegetarian pasta

Even devout carnivores are joining the ranks of the "occasional vegetarian." This growing group chooses to eat vegetarian meals on a regular but not exclusive basis. If you're one of these people, then the recipes in this chapter are for you. Or if you're a true vegetarian, here you'll find some hearty and delicious additions to your repertoire.

Many of these hearty recipes are made with tofu which adds protein without saturated fat. Some are made with pasta, and others are just a cornucopia of fresh produce. A nice facet of these recipes is that many of them can do double duty as side dishes, too.

The Joy of Soy

No wonder they call soy a wonder food! Lately, researchers are discovering more and more nutritional benefits from soy products. For example, soybeans are the only known plant source of *complete protein*. In addition, the

Food and Drug Administration (FDA) has approved a health claim stating that diets containing 25 grams soy protein a day may reduce the risk of heart disease.

While soy milk is growing in popularity as an alternative to cow's milk, the way we eat soybeans most often is as tofu. A custard-like substance, it's also called doufu in Chinese recipes or bean curd, which is the literal translation. Tofu has no innate flavor of its own, so it absorbs the flavor of the sauce in which it's cooked.

Making tofu is similar to making cheese. Both methods involve curds and whey. For tofu, the first step is creating soy milk by soaking, grinding, boiling, and straining dried soybeans. Then either salts or acids are added to the milk to create coagulation. Later, the curds are extracted from the whey, and packaged.

> **Duet Dialogue**
>
> **Complete protein** is the term used for a food that contains all the essential amino acids in the appropriate proportions that are part of the growth and maintenance of cells. Meats and some dairy products have complete protein, while grains and beans contain incomplete proteins. Blending incomplete proteins, such as rice and beans, produces complete protein. But in the plant world, soy alone has it all.

Types of Tofu

The texture of tofu depends on the amount of water that has been pressed out. You will find three different consistencies in the supermarket:

- Soft (or silken) tofu. This tofu has had no water removed and has the texture of a silky custard. While it's great added to smoothies or juices, it does not hold together when cooked.

- Firm tofu. Some whey has been pressed out, so this tofu has the texture of raw meat, although that texture will not change once it's cooked. It bounces back when pressed with your finger and can easily be picked up by chopsticks or a fork.

- Dry tofu. The most solid of all tofu, it has the texture of cooked meat and crumbles easily. This type of tofu is used in processed tofu products.

Looking at tofu packages can be confusing because the net weights vary although the package size stays uniform. The net weight is that of the product with the weight of the surrounding water subtracted from the total. Silken tofu packages weigh 1 pound, while the net weight of firm tofu can vary between 12 and 14 ounces, depending on the brand. Dry tofu can have a net weight as low as 8 ounces.

Handle with Care

While tofu is a vegetable product, it's as perishable as delicate seafood, so always check the "sell by" date before buying it. Tofu is packed in water, and this water should be changed daily once it's home and the package has been opened. With fresh water daily, tofu will last up to a week but may spoil within a few days otherwise.

Tofu can be frozen for up to three months. After it's thawed, the texture will change to become slightly chewy, but if you're blending silken tofu into a smoothie, this makes little difference.

Déjà Two _____

Like cheese and butter, the origins of tofu may never be proven conclusively. The most widely held theory is that Lord Liu An, a Chinese prince, invented it in 164 B.C.E. during the Han Dynasty. A second theory is that it was accidentally invented when sea salt was added to some boiled soybeans. With the spread of Buddhism, tofu spread to other parts of Asia and arrived in Japan in the eighth century.

Curried Tofu and Vegetables

Broccoli and cauliflower become crisp counterpoints to tofu in this vibrantly seasoned Indian dish.

Active time: 15 minutes

Start to finish: 20 minutes

Each serving has:

685 calories

457 calories from fat

51 g fat

27.5 g saturated fat

22.5 g protein

39.5 g carbohydrates

1 (12- to 14-oz.) pkg. firm tofu

2 TB. vegetable oil

1 small onion, peeled and sliced

1 carrot, peeled and grated

2 garlic cloves, peeled and minced

2 TB. curry powder

1 tsp. ground cumin

1 cup coconut milk

1 cup broccoli florets

1 cup cauliflower florets

¼ cup dried currants

Salt and freshly ground black pepper to taste

1. Drain tofu, cut into ¾-inch dice, and set aside. Heat oil in a medium saucepan over medium heat. Add onion, carrot, and garlic. Cook, stirring frequently, for 5 minutes or until onion is soft. Stir in curry powder and cumin. Cook, stirring constantly, for 1 minute.

2. Add coconut milk, raise the heat to medium-high, and bring to a boil. Add broccoli, cauliflower, tofu, and currants, and reduce the heat to medium-low. Simmer, uncovered, for 5 to 7 minutes or until vegetables are crisp-tender. Season to taste with salt and pepper. Serve immediately.

Variation: Substitute boneless chicken breast, cut into ½-inch cubes for tofu, and cook for the same length of time. Be sure to cook chicken through until longer pink.

Double Trouble

It's a good idea to toss out any dried herb or spice that's been opened for more than six months, but abbreviate the life of curry powder to two months. This ground blend, made up of about 20 herbs and spices, loses its flavor and aroma very quickly.

Thai Tofu with Zucchini and Basil

Coconut milk becomes a vivid red when mixed with fiery red curry paste, and the addition of aromatic basil is characteristic of Thai cooking.

1 (12- to 14-oz.) pkg. firm tofu

2 TB. vegetable oil

1 small red bell pepper, rinsed, seeds and ribs removed, and thinly sliced

1 medium zucchini, rinsed, trimmed, and thinly sliced

2 tsp. grated fresh ginger

2 garlic cloves, peeled and minced

1 cup coconut milk

2 TB. freshly squeezed lime juice

1 TB. soy sauce

1 tsp. Thai red curry paste

⅓ cup firmly packed fresh basil leaves, preferably Thai basil

Salt and freshly ground black pepper to taste

Active time: 10 minutes

Start to finish: 20 minutes

Each serving has:

609 calories

452 calories from fat

50 g fat

27.5 g saturated fat

22 g protein

22 g carbohydrates

1. Drain tofu, cut into ¾-inch dice and set aside. Heat oil in a heavy 12-inch skillet over medium high heat. Add red bell pepper, zucchini, ginger, and garlic. Cook, stirring frequently, for 4 minutes or until peppers begin to soften.

2. Add tofu, coconut milk, lime juice, soy sauce, and curry paste. Stir well to dissolve curry paste.

3. Bring to a boil, reduce the heat to medium, simmer, stirring occasionally, for 5 minutes or until sauce thickens. Stir in basil, and cook for 1 minute. Season to taste with salt and pepper and serve immediately.

Double Feature

You'll get far more life out of fresh basil if you treat it like a bouquet of flowers. Trim the stems when you get some and stand the basil upright in a glass of water. Refrigerate the glass and it will stay fresh for up to four days.

Pan-Fried Tofu Burgers with Wasabi Mayonnaise

Crunchy almonds add texture and Asian seasonings lend their flavor to these tofu patties served like a burger.

Active time: 10 minutes

Start to finish: 16 minutes

Each serving has:

852 calories

539 calories from fat

60 g fat

8 g saturated fat

31 g protein

46 g carbohydrates

1 (12 to 14-oz.) pkg. firm tofu ¼ cup blanched slivered almonds

2 TB. mayonnaise

½ tsp. *wasabi* paste

2 sesame seed buns

1 large egg, lightly beaten

3 scallions, rinsed, trimmed, and thinly sliced

1 garlic clove, peeled and minced

2 tsp. grated fresh ginger

1 TB. soy sauce

Salt and freshly ground black pepper to taste

½ cup panko bread crumbs

2 TB. Asian sesame oil

2 TB. vegetable oil

1 ripe plum tomato, rinsed, cored, and sliced

½ cup shredded romaine

Duet Dialogue

Wasabi (pronounced *wah-SAH-bee*) is a Japanese form of horseradish that's light green and has a sharp, fiery flavor. Sold both as paste and powder, the powder is mixed with water like dry mustard to make a paste. In a pinch you can use bottled Western horseradish.

1. Preheat the oven to 350°F. Drain tofu and cut into 1-inch thick slices. Wrap tofu in several layers of paper towels, and place it on a platter. Place a pan on top, and weight the pan with 5 pounds of food cans. Allow tofu to drain for 5 minutes. Place almonds on a baking sheet and bake for 5 to 7 minutes or until browned. Chop almonds coarsely, and set aside. Combine mayonnaise and wasabi paste in a small bowl, and stir well. Refrigerate until ready to use. Toast sesame buns and set aside.

2. Transfer tofu to a medium mixing bowl, and mash into small pieces with a fork. Add almonds, egg, scallions, garlic, ginger, and soy sauce. Season to taste with salt and pepper, and mix well. Form mixture into two patties ½-inch thick, and pat panko crumbs on both sides.

3. Heat sesame oil and vegetable oil in a heavy skillet over medium heat. Add patties and cook for 3 to 4 minutes per side or until browned. Turn burgers gently with a slotted spatula, and cook on the other side. Remove from the skillet and pat with paper towels.

4. Place burgers on bottom of bun, spread with mayonnaise, and top with tomato and lettuce. Serve immediately.

Southwest Tofu Burritos

Tofu is given Mexican flair for these rollups made with onion and bell peppers, too.

1 (12- to 14-oz.) pkg. firm tofu

2 TB. olive oil

1 small red bell pepper, seeds and ribs removed, and thinly sliced

½ small red onion, peeled and thinly sliced

2 garlic cloves, peeled and minced

1 TB. chili powder

1 tsp. ground cumin

¼ cup enchilada sauce or jarred salsa

2 TB. chopped fresh cilantro

Salt and freshly ground black pepper to taste

2 (10-in.) flour tortillas

2 ripe plum tomatoes, rinsed, cored, seeded, and sliced

½ cup shredded romaine

Active time: 10 minutes

Start to finish: 12 minutes

Each serving has:

625 calories

253 calories from fat

28 g fat

4 g saturated fat

26 g protein

65.5 g carbohydrates

1. Drain and crumble tofu and set aside. Heat olive oil in a heavy 12-inch skillet over medium-high heat. Add red bell pepper, onion, and garlic. Cook, stirring frequently, for 5 minutes or until onion is soft. Stir in chili powder and cumin, and cook, stirring constantly, for 1 minute.

2. Add enchilada sauce, tofu, and cilantro, reduce the heat to medium, and cook for 2 minutes or until tofu is warm. Season to taste with salt and pepper.

3. Place half tofu mixture on bottom half of each tortilla, leaving a 2-inch margin on sides. Top tofu with tomato and romaine. Tuck in sides of tortillas around filling and, beginning with filled edge, roll tortilla firmly but gently. Repeat with second tortilla. Serve immediately.

Variation: Substitute boneless chicken breast, cut into ¼-inch cubes for tofu and cook for 5 minutes. Make sure chicken is cooked through and no longer pink.

Double Trouble

Do not substitute tempeh for tofu. Tempeh is made from fermented soybeans, and its crumbly texture and savory flavor are assertive and will not absorb the seasonings in a dish.

Tofu and Vegetable Fried Rice

You can serve this rice and vegetable dish as an entrée or to six people as a side dish.

Active time: 15 minutes

Start to finish: 15 minutes

Each serving has:

741 calories

310 calories from fat

34.5 g fat

5 g saturated fat

36 g protein

71 g carbohydrates

1 (12- to 14.-oz.) pkg. firm tofu	1 garlic clove, peeled and minced
1 leek, white part only	1 baby bok choy, rinsed, trimmed, and thinly sliced
2 cups cold steamed white rice	½ cup fresh bean sprouts, rinsed
2 large eggs	¼ cup frozen peas, thawed
Salt and freshly ground black pepper to taste	2 tsp. dry sherry
3 TB. vegetable oil	¼ cup vegetable stock
2 scallions, rinsed, trimmed, and thinly sliced	1 TB. soy sauce

Double Feature

It seems there's always white rice left over when the rest of an Asian take-out is long gone. Freeze it, and you're half way to making fried rice some night.

1. Drain tofu, cut into ½-inch cubes and set aside. Trim leek, and slice thinly. Place slices in a colander and rinse well. To separate rice grains, place rice in a bowl. Rub grains between wet fingers until separated. Set aside. Whisk eggs in a mixing bowl, season to taste with salt and pepper and set aside.

2. Heat 1 tablespoon oil in a wok or heavy 12-inch skillet over medium heat, swirling to coat the bottom and sides. When oil is hot, add eggs and stir continuously until soft curds form, about 1 minute. Scrape eggs into a bowl, and set aside.

3. Add another tablespoon oil to the pan over medium-high heat, and swirl to coat. When hot, add tofu. Cook for 3 minutes or until tofu begins to brown. Add tofu to eggs.

4. Add remaining tablespoon oil, and swirl to coat. When hot, add scallions, garlic, and leek. Cook, stirring frequently, for 3 minutes or until leek is translucent. Add bok choy, and cook for 2 minutes. Add bean sprouts, peas, sherry, stock, and soy sauce and stir well.

5. Add rice and eggs to the skillet. Cook for 2 minutes or until rice is hot, stirring frequently. Serve immediately.

Pasta Primavera

If you're not in a tofu mood, try this easy pasta dish with a cornucopia of colorful vegetables.

¼ lb. white mushrooms

¼ lb. dried angel hair pasta

3 TB. olive oil

1 shallot, peeled and finely chopped

1 garlic clove, peeled and minced

1 small zucchini, rinsed, trimmed, and cut into ½-inch dice

½ red bell pepper, seeds and ribs removed, and thinly sliced

2 ripe plum tomatoes, rinsed, cored, seeded, and diced

½ cup vegetable stock

½ cup half-and-half

2 TB. finely chopped fresh basil or 1 tsp. dried

2 TB. chopped fresh parsley

½ tsp. Italian seasoning

½ cup broccoli florets

¼ cup frozen peas, thawed

Salt and red pepper flakes to taste

¼ cup freshly grated Parmesan cheese

Active time: 20 minutes
Start to finish: 25 minutes
Each serving has:
592 calories
281 calories from fat
31 g fat
9 g saturated fat
19.5 g protein
63 g carbohydrates

1. Wipe mushrooms with a damp paper towel. Discard stems and slice mushrooms. Bring a large pot of salted water to a boil. Add pasta, and cook according to package directions until al dente. Drain, toss with 1 tablespoon olive oil, and keep warm.

2. Heat remaining 2 tablespoons olive oil in a large skillet over medium-high heat. Add shallot and garlic and cook, stirring frequently, for 3 minutes or until shallot is translucent. Add zucchini, mushrooms, and red bell pepper. Cook for 3 minutes.

3. Add tomatoes, stock, half-and-half, basil, parsley, Italian seasoning, broccoli, and peas to the skillet. Bring to a boil over medium-high heat, and simmer, uncovered, for 3 minutes. Season to taste with salt and red pepper flakes, and simmer for an additional 2 minutes.

4. Add drained pasta to skillet, and toss with Parmesan cheese. Serve immediately.

Variation: Feel free to experiment with the vegetables in this dish. Asparagus, green beans, carrots, or cauliflower are all good additions or substitutions.

 Déjà Two

Primavera is the Italian word for "springtime," and although this dish sounds quintessentially Italian, it was born and bred in New York. Restaurateur Sirio Maccioni created it in the mid-1970s for his famed Le Cirque restaurant, and food writers popularized the dish nationally.

Angel Hair in Chipotle Sauce with Monterey Jack Cheese

Chipotle chilies are smoked jalapeños, and their distinctive flavor underpins this easy Mexican dish.

Active time: 12 minutes	
Start to finish: 20 minutes	
Each serving has:	
566 calories	
219 calories from fat	
24 g fat	
7 g saturated fat	
19 g protein	
69 g carbohydrates	

2 TB. olive oil

1 onion, peeled and finely chopped

2 garlic cloves, peeled and minced

¼ lb. angel hair or vermicelli pasta, broken into 2-inch lengths

1 tsp. dried oregano, preferably Mexican

1 tsp. ground cumin

1 (14.5-oz.) can diced tomatoes, undrained

1 (8-oz.) can tomato sauce

1 (6-oz.) can tomato juice

1 canned chipotle chili in adobo sauce, drained and finely chopped

Salt and freshly ground black pepper to taste

½ cup grated Monterey Jack cheese

2 TB. chopped fresh cilantro

Double Feature

Toasting pasta, as in this recipe, is a technique used in much of Mexico and Latin America. The toasting keeps the strands much more separate as they cook; however, they take longer to cook because the starch on the surface has hardened.

1. Heat oil in a large covered skillet over medium-high heat. Add onions and garlic, and cook, stirring frequently, for 3 minutes or until onion is translucent. Add angel hair, oregano, and cumin. Cook, stirring constantly, for 2 to 3 minutes or until angel hair is lightly browned.

2. Add tomatoes, tomato sauce, tomato juice, and chipotle chili, and bring to a boil over high heat, stirring occasionally. Reduce the heat to medium, and simmer for 8 to 10 minutes or until pasta is soft and very little liquid remains. Season to taste with salt and pepper, and stir in Monterey Jack. Sprinkle with cilantro, and serve immediately.

Hot and Sweet Asian Ratatouille

This version of the French dish contains the same mushrooms, squash, and eggplant; it's the ginger and sesame oil that give it Asian flair.

¼ lb. white mushrooms

1 TB. vegetable oil

1 TB. Asian sesame oil

1 small onion, peeled and diced

3 garlic cloves, peeled and minced

2 TB. grated fresh ginger

1 small zucchini, rinsed, trimmed, and cut into ½-inch slices

1 small yellow squash, rinsed, trimmed, and cut into ½-inch slices

2 Japanese eggplants, rinsed, trimmed, and cut into ½-inch slices

½ cup vegetable stock

¼ cup tomato sauce

2 TB. dry sherry

1 TB. black bean sauce

1 TB. hoisin sauce

1 TB. tamari

1 TB. red wine vinegar

½ tsp. Chinese chili paste with garlic

Salt and freshly ground black pepper to taste

Active time: 15 minutes
Start to finish: 30 minutes
Each serving has:
395 calories
155 calories from fat
17 g fat
2.5 g saturated fat
13 g protein
53 g carbohydrates

1. Wipe mushrooms with a damp paper towel. Discard stems and halve mushrooms if small or quarter if large. Heat vegetable oil and sesame oil in a Dutch oven over medium-high heat. Add onion, garlic, and ginger, and cook, stirring frequently, for 3 minutes or until onion is translucent. Add zucchini, yellow squash, mushrooms, and eggplant. Cook, stirring frequently, for 3 minutes or until squash begins to soften.

2. Add stock, tomato sauce, sherry, black bean sauce, hoisin sauce, tamari, vinegar, and chili paste. Bring to a boil, stirring occasionally. Cover, reduce the heat to low, and cook for 10 minutes. Uncover, increase the heat to medium, and simmer, stirring frequently, for 5 minutes or until vegetables are tender and sauce slightly thickens. Season to taste with salt and pepper. Serve immediately.

Double Feature

Zucchini is Italian in origin and retained its native name when it was integrated into American cooking. Choose small zucchini because they tend to have a sweeter flavor and the seeds are tender and less pronounced.

Sesame Stir-Fried Vegetables

This is a colorful and delicately flavored dish that is also a star as a side dish for four or six on other nights.

Active time: 15 minutes

Start to finish: 20 minutes

Each serving has:

401 calories

229 calories from fat

25 g fat

4 g saturated fat

22 g protein

31 g carbohydrates

Duet Dialogue

Tamari (pronounced *tah-MAR-ee*) like soy sauce, is made from soybeans, but its flavor is more mellow and less salty, and its texture is thicker than soy sauce.

¼ **cup sesame seeds**

¼ **lb. fresh shiitake mushrooms**

2 **baby bok choy**

⅓ **cup vegetable stock**

3 **TB.** *tamari*

1 **TB. dry sherry**

2 **TB. Asian sesame oil**

2 **garlic cloves, peeled and minced**

2 **scallions, rinsed, trimmed, and sliced**

1 **TB. grated fresh ginger**

2 **oz. snow peas, rinsed and stemmed**

Salt and freshly ground black pepper to taste

1. Place sesame seeds in a small dry skillet over medium heat. Toast seeds for 2 minutes or until browned, shaking the pan frequently. Set aside. Wipe mushrooms with a damp paper towel. Discard stems and slice thinly. Rinse and trim bok choy. Slice into ½-inch pieces on the diagonal. Combine stock, tamari, and sherry in a small bowl, stir well, and set aside.

2. Heat sesame oil in a heavy 10-inch skillet over medium-high heat. Add garlic, scallions, and ginger. Cook, stirring constantly, for 30 seconds or until fragrant. Add bok choy, snow peas, and mushrooms. Cook, stirring constantly, for 1 minute.

3. Add liquid mixture to the skillet, raise the heat to high, and cook for 2 minutes or until vegetables are crisp-tender. Season to taste with salt and pepper. Serve immediately.

Part  5

Anticipatory Aromas: Slow Roasts, Casseroles, and Braises

This part creates a yin yang with the rapid cooking in Part 4. These are dishes that bake in the oven or simmer on the stove and fill the house with the wonderful scent of food cooking before you sit down to eat it.

These chapters are divided by what type of food you're cooking. You'll find chapters devoted to poultry, fish and seafood, and meats all done with international flair. There's everything from classic French chicken in wine, the legendary *coq au vin*, to old-fashioned meatloaf.

And do keep in mind that slow is a relative term. No recipe requires more than 30 minutes of active preparation time, and then you can read a magazine or enjoy a glass of wine for the relatively short unattended cooking time.

Chapter 15

From the Coops

In This Chapter

- Favorites from around the world
- Oven-frying for less fat
- Rock Cornish hen creations

Chicken is to the cook what a blank canvas is to an artist, the starting place for any number of great masterpieces. Because great art and great chicken dishes aren't instantaneous, most of the recipes in this chapter take about an hour to complete, but you're only involved for a fraction of that time.

In most of these dishes I use whole pieces of chicken and simmer them in sauces drawn from many of the world's great cuisines. Some are classics like French *coq au vin*, but some are innovative treatments inspired by the foods of North Africa and Thailand.

Choosing Your Chicken

Always look for chicken marked USDA "Grade A," and choose packages that have no accumulation of liquid in the bottom. Accumulated liquid can be a sign that the chicken has been frozen and defrosted. This is especially important if you plan to freeze some of the chicken after you purchase it because more than one freezing and defrosting can really damage the flavor and texture of the bird.

Store chicken in the coldest part of your refrigerator (40°F or below), sealed as it comes from the market, and use it within 2 or 3 days. If you need to keep it longer, freeze it. Although freezing can reduce flavor, moisture, and tenderness, it does preserve effectively.

To freeze chicken, rinse it under cold running water, and pat the pieces dry with paper towels. Wrap each piece individually in plastic wrap, and then place the pieces in a heavy resealable plastic bag. Discard the giblet package, or remove the giblets and add them to a cache for chicken stock. Don't add chicken livers to stock, but you can use the necks and gizzards.

To defrost, place the frozen chicken on a plate in the refrigerator or thaw it in the microwave, following the manufacturer's instructions. To speed up thawing an uncooked chicken, place the package in cold water, changing the water frequently. After it's thawed, cook it as soon as possible, especially if you defrosted it in the microwave.

Better Birds

Only after World War II, when modern mass-production came into being, were chickens anything but "free-range." Nowadays, these birds, slightly larger than broiler fryers, are the elite of the coop.

As the name implies, free-range chickens have the freedom to roam outdoors, and most chefs agree that this develops a fuller flavor—at a much fuller price. Free-range whole chickens are frequently priced higher than the prime boneless, skinless breasts of commercial chickens.

While many free range chickens are fed a vegetarian diet that is usually free of antibiotics and growth hormones, free-range is not synonymous with organic. The organic label, as specified by the U.S. Department of Agriculture, ensures that birds are fed a diet of organic foods and are not given any supplemental antibiotics or hormones.

Chicken with Potatoes, Mushrooms, and Onions in Red Wine Sauce (Coq au Vin)

Every cuisine has its comfort foods, and this dish is a French classic, with herbs and vegetables simmered with the chicken in a red wine sauce.

½ lb. small white mushrooms

2 to 4 chicken pieces of your choice (breasts, thighs, legs), rinsed and patted dry with paper towels

Salt and freshly ground black pepper to taste

¼ cup all-purpose flour

4 slices bacon, cut into 1-inch pieces

1 TB. unsalted butter

2 garlic cloves, peeled and minced

1 cup dry red wine

½ cup chicken stock

2 TB. chopped fresh parsley

2 tsp. fresh thyme or ¾ tsp. dried

1 bay leaf

½ lb. small new potatoes, scrubbed and quartered

½ cup frozen pearl onions, thawed

Active time: 20 minutes
Start to finish: 60 minutes
Each serving has:
965 calories
578 calories from fat
64 g fat
22 g saturated fat
41 g protein
36 g carbohydrates

1. Preheat the oven to 350°F. Wipe mushrooms with a damp paper towel. Discard stems and cut mushrooms in half if larger than 1-inch in diameter. Sprinkle chicken with salt and pepper, dust with flour, shaking off any excess, and set aside.

2. Place bacon in an ovenproof Dutch oven over medium-high heat. Cook, stirring frequently, until bacon is crisp. Remove bacon with a slotted spoon and set aside.

3. Add chicken pieces to the Dutch oven in a single layer, and brown well on all sides turning gently with tongs. Remove chicken and discard all but 1 tablespoon fat. Add garlic and mushrooms to the Dutch oven, and cook, stirring frequently, for 3 to 5 minutes or until mushrooms are lightly browned. Add wine and bring to a boil over high heat. Cook for 2 minutes; then add stock, parsley, thyme, and bay leaf. Bring to a boil, and add bacon, chicken pieces, and potatoes.

 Double Feature

If you have to buy a package of bacon rather than the few slices you'll need, freeze it for future use. Roll a few slices up into a cylinder, and secure them with a toothpick. Freeze them in a heavy resealable plastic bag, and remove just the number you want at a later time.

4. Cover the Dutch oven, place it into the oven, and bake for 30 minutes or until potatoes are almost tender and chicken is tender and no longer pink. Add onions, season to taste with salt and pepper if necessary, and bake for an additional 10 minutes or until potatoes are tender. Remove and discard bay leaf, and serve immediately. (You can do this up to 2 days in advance and refrigerate, tightly covered. Reheat in a 350°F oven for 20 minutes or until hot.)

Variation: Use white wine instead of red. The dish will be just as delicious but a bit lighter in flavor.

Mexican Chicken with Rice and Peas (*Arroz con Pollo*)

This is a one-dish dinner in which the rice gains great flavor from the Mexican seasonings and tomatoes in which it's cooked.

Active time: 15 minutes

Start to finish: 45 minutes

Each serving has:

604 calories

226 calories from fat

25 g fat

4 g saturated fat

31.5 g protein

62 g carbohydrates

2 to 4 chicken pieces of your choice (breasts, thighs, legs), rinsed and patted dry with paper towels

Salt and freshly ground black pepper to taste

3 TB. olive oil

1 small onion, peeled and diced

2 garlic cloves, peeled and minced

½ cup long-grain rice

1 (14.5-oz.) can diced tomatoes, drained

2 TB. canned diced green chilies, drained

½ cup chicken stock

1 tsp. dried oregano, preferably Mexican

1 bay leaf

2 TB. chopped fresh cilantro

½ cup frozen peas, thawed

½ cup frozen corn, thawed

1. Sprinkle chicken with salt and pepper. Heat olive oil in a large, deep skillet over medium-high heat. Add chicken pieces to the skillet in a single layer, and brown well on all sides, turning gently with tongs. Remove chicken and set aside.

2. Add onion and garlic to the skillet, and cook, stirring frequently, for 3 minutes or until onion is translucent. Add rice and cook for 1 minute, stirring constantly.

3. Add tomatoes, chilies, stock, oregano, and bay leaf, and bring to a boil over high heat, stirring frequently. Add chicken pieces, cover, reduce the heat to medium-low, and cook for 25 to 35 minutes or until chicken is tender and no longer pink and almost all liquid has been absorbed.

4. Stir in cilantro, peas, and corn. Cover and cook for 2 to 3 minutes or until hot and remaining liquid is absorbed. Remove and discard bay leaf, season to taste with salt and pepper, and serve immediately. (You can do this up to 2 days in advance and refrigerate, tightly covered. Reheat in a 350°F oven for 20 minutes or until hot.)

Variation: Use boneless pork chops in place of chicken, or reduce quantity of chicken and add a few links of Mexican chorizo sausage.

Double Trouble

Be very careful when choosing a can of chilies to put into your shopping cart. More than one cook has had to call out for pizza after discovering too late that the innocuous can held fiery jalapeño peppers rather than mild green chilies.

Baked Chicken and Broccoli Risotto

Simmering the broccoli stalks in the stock adds additional flavor to this dish that's easy to make in the oven.

2 (6-oz.) boneless, skinless chicken breast halves

2 broccoli stalks

1 (14.5-oz.) can chicken stock

3 sprigs fresh parsley

1 sprig fresh thyme or ½ tsp. dried

1 bay leaf

Salt and freshly ground black pepper to taste

2 TB. unsalted butter

1 small onion, peeled and chopped

2 garlic cloves, peeled and minced

¾ cup Arborio rice

¼ cup dry white wine

⅓ cup freshly grated Parmesan cheese

Active time: 20 minutes

Start to finish: 45 minutes

Each serving has:

694 calories

167 calories from fat

18.5 g fat

11 g saturated fat

56 g protein

69 g carbohydrates

1. Preheat the oven to 400°F. Grease a 9×9-inch baking pan. Rinse chicken and pat dry with paper towels. Trim all visible fat, and cut chicken into 1-inch cubes. Set aside.

📖 **Duet Dialogue**

Risotto (pro-nounced *re-SOH-toh*) is a traditional Italian rice dish that dates back to the Renaissance. The key ingredient is Arborio rice, which is a short, fat-grained Italian rice with a high starch content. Stirring it into stock creates a creamy matrix when this starch is released.

2. Remove and slice bottom 4 inches of broccoli stalks, reserving top of stalks and heads. Place sliced stalks in a saucepan with stock, parsley, thyme, and bay leaf. Bring to a boil over high heat, reduce the heat to low, and simmer, uncovered, for 10 minutes. Strain and discard solids, and return stock to the saucepan. While stock is simmering, peel remaining stalks and slice into $\frac{1}{2}$-inch pieces, break heads into florets, and set aside.

3. Sprinkle chicken with salt and pepper. Melt butter in a large skillet over medium-high heat. Add chicken to the skillet in a single layer and cook, stirring frequently, for 2 minutes or until opaque. Remove chicken with a slotted spoon and set aside. Add onion and garlic, and cook, stirring frequently, for 3 minutes or until onion is translucent. Add rice and cook for 2 minutes, stirring constantly.

4. Add wine, increase the heat to high, and cook stirring constantly, for 3 minutes or until wine is almost evaporated. Add stock and chicken, and bring to a boil. Scrape mixture into the prepared baking pan, cover with aluminum foil, and bake for 10 minutes. Remove foil, stir in broccoli, and bake for an additional 15 to 20 minutes or until rice is soft and liquid is absorbed. Stir in Parmesan cheese, season to taste with salt and pepper, and serve immediately.

Variation: Use asparagus in place of the broccoli, and cheddar cheese for Parmesan.

Creole Curried Chicken with Dried Currants (Country Captain)

The curry flavor in this historic American dish is very subtle, and the sweetness of the currants makes the sauce distinctive.

2 to 4 chicken pieces of your choice (breasts, thighs, legs), rinsed and patted dry with paper towels

Salt and freshly ground black pepper to taste

3 TB. olive oil

1 small onion, peeled and diced

2 garlic cloves, peeled and minced

½ red bell pepper, seeds and ribs removed, and diced

1 TB. curry powder

¼ tsp. ground ginger

½ tsp. dried thyme

1 (14.5-oz.) can diced tomatoes, drained

¼ cup dry sherry

¾ cup chicken stock

⅓ cup dried currants

Active time: 20 minutes
Start to finish: 50 minutes
Each serving has:
678 calories
382 calories from fat
42 g fat
9 g saturated fat
30 g protein
38 g carbohydrates

1. Sprinkle chicken with salt and pepper. Heat olive oil in a large, deep skillet over medium-high heat. Add chicken to the skillet in a single layer and brown well on all sides turning gently with tongs. Remove chicken and set aside.

2. Add onion, garlic, and red bell pepper to the skillet, and cook, stirring frequently, for 3 minutes or until onion is translucent. Add curry powder, ginger, and thyme, and cook for 1 minute, stirring constantly.

3. Add tomatoes, sherry, stock, and currants, and bring to a boil over medium-high heat, stirring frequently.

4. Add chicken, cover, reduce the heat to medium-low, and cook for 25 to 35 minutes or until chicken is tender and no longer pink. Season to taste with salt and pepper, and serve immediately. (You can do this up to 2 days in advance and refrigerate, tightly covered. Reheat in a 350°F oven for 20 minutes or until hot.)

Variation: Substitute boneless pork chops for chicken, and cook for the same length of time.

 Déjà Two

Country Captain is a chicken dish that dates back to colonial times. Some food historians say it originated in Savannah, Georgia, a major port for the spice trade. Other sources say a British captain brought the curry-flavored dish back from India.

Indian Chicken with Cashews

While this chicken needs some time to marinate in the flavored yogurt, it's well worth the advance planning.

Active time: 20 minutes

Start to finish: 4¾ hours, including 4 hours for marinating

Each serving has:

848 calories

542 calories from fat

60 g fat

13 g saturated fat

41 g protein

42 g carbohydrates

½ cup plain yogurt

2 garlic cloves, peeled and minced

1 TB. grated fresh ginger

1½ tsp. curry powder

1½ tsp. ground *turmeric*

½ tsp. ground cardamom

¼ tsp. ground cinnamon

¼ tsp. cayenne or more to taste

2 to 4 chicken pieces of your choice (breasts, thighs, legs), rinsed and patted dry with paper towels

¾ cup roasted cashew nuts

1 cup chicken stock

2 TB. olive oil

1 small onion, peeled and chopped

1 carrot, peeled and sliced

1 cup frozen mixed vegetables, thawed

Salt and freshly ground black pepper to taste

1. Combine yogurt, garlic, ginger, curry powder, turmeric, cardamom, cinnamon, and cayenne in a heavy resealable plastic bag, and mix well. Add chicken, and turn bag to coat pieces evenly. Allow chicken to marinate, refrigerated, for at least 4 hours, preferably overnight.

2. Remove chicken from marinade, scrape off and reserve marinade. Grind ⅓ cup cashews with ¼ cup chicken stock in a food processor fitted with a steel blade or in a blender. Set aside. Coarsely chop remaining cashews and set aside.

3. Heat oil in a large skillet over medium-high heat. Add chicken to the skillet in a single layer and brown well on all sides turning gently with tongs. Remove chicken and set aside. Add onion and cook, stirring frequently, for 3 minutes or until onion is translucent. Add carrot, nut purée, remaining stock, and reserved marinade, and bring to a boil.

4. Add chicken, cover, reduce the heat to medium-low, and cook for 25 to 35 minutes until chicken is tender and no longer

pink. (You can do this up to 2 days in advance and refrigerate, tightly covered. Reheat in a 350°F oven for 20 minutes or until hot, then proceed with directions.) Stir in mixed vegetables, season to taste with salt and pepper, and cook an additional 5 minutes. Sprinkle remaining cashews on top of chicken, and serve immediately.

Duet Dialogue

Turmeric, like ginger, a rhizome, is an underground root-like plant that grows in the tropics. It has a bitter, pungent flavor and gives foods a vibrant, intense yellow-orange color. Very popular in Indian cooking, it is always found in its dried and powdered form in supermarkets. It's sometimes referred to as "poor man's saffron" because it imparts a similar color. It's also a primary ingredient in bright yellow American-style mustard.

Moroccan Chicken with Garbanzo Beans and Artichoke Hearts

The aromatic blend of cumin and coriander are what makes this stew dotted with beans and tender artichoke hearts special.

2 to 4 chicken pieces of your choice (breasts, thighs, legs), rinsed and patted dry with paper towels

Salt and freshly ground black pepper to taste

2 TB. olive oil

1 small onion, peeled and diced

2 garlic cloves, peeled and minced

1 carrot, peeled and sliced

2 TB. sweet paprika, preferably Hungarian

1 TB. ground cumin

1½ tsp. ground coriander

1 (14.5-oz.) can chicken stock

2 TB. balsamic vinegar

⅔ cup garbanzo beans, drained and rinsed

⅔ cup frozen artichoke hearts, thawed and cut into wedges

Active time: 20 minutes

Start to finish: 55 minutes

Each serving has:

639 calories

341 calories from fat

38 g fat

8 g saturated fat

36 g protein

42 g carbohydrates

1. Sprinkle chicken with salt and pepper. Heat olive oil in a large, deep skillet over medium-high heat. Add chicken to the skillet in a single layer and brown well on all sides turning gently with tongs. Remove chicken and set aside.

2. Add onion and garlic, and cook, stirring frequently, for 3 minutes or until onion is translucent. Reduce the heat to low, and add carrots, paprika, cumin, and coriander. Cook, stirring constantly, for 1 minute.

3. Add stock and vinegar, and bring to a boil over medium heat, stirring occasionally. Add chicken, cover, reduce heat to medium-low, and cook for 25 to 35 minutes until chicken is tender and no longer pink. (You can do this up to 2 days in advance and refrigerate, tightly covered. Reheat in a 350°F oven for 20 minutes or until hot, then proceed with directions.)

4. Add garbanzo beans and artichoke hearts, and simmer for 5 minutes or until artichoke hearts are tender. Season to taste with salt and pepper, and serve immediately.

Variation: Substitute thick fillets of swordfish, halibut, or cod for chicken. Reduce cooking time to 15 to 20 minutes before adding artichoke hearts.

Double Trouble

Although we credit President Herbert Hoover with the quote about "a chicken in every pot," it was first said by King Henry IV of France, born in Navarre in 1553. At his coronation, he said he hoped that every peasant could afford a "chicken every Sunday" because chicken was deemed such a luxury in those days.

Oven-Fried Chicken

Imagine crispy fried chicken without a messy stove! That's what you get using this easy method.

½ **cup buttermilk**

1 large egg, lightly beaten

1 cup *panko* breadcrumbs

1 cup vegetable oil

2 TB. Cajun seasoning

2 to 4 chicken pieces of your choice (breasts, thighs, legs), rinsed and patted dry with paper towels

Active time: 10 minutes

Start to finish: 35 minutes

Each serving has:

675 calories

419 calories from fat

46.5 g fat

10 g saturated fat

33.5 g protein

28 g carbohydrates

1. Preheat the oven to 400°F and place a 9×13-inch baking pan in the oven as it preheats. Combine buttermilk and egg in a shallow bowl, and whisk well. Combine panko, 1 tablespoon oil, and Cajun seasoning in a second large bowl, and mix well.

2. Dip chicken pieces into buttermilk mixture; let any excess drip back into the bowl. Dip pieces into panko mixture, coating all sides. Set aside.

3. Add remaining oil to the hot baking dish and heat for 3 minutes. Add chicken and turn gently with tongs to coat all sides with oil. Bake for a total of 25 minutes, turning pieces gently with tongs after 15 minutes, or until chicken is cooked through and no longer pink. Remove chicken from the pan, and pat with paper towels. Serve immediately.

Variation: Use Italian-style breadcrumbs rather than panko along with 1 tablespoon of Italian seasoning and 2 tablespoons freshly grated Parmesan cheese. Add salt and pepper to crumb mixture.

Duet Dialogue

Panko (pronounced *PAN*-koh) are Japanese breadcrumbs that are lighter, longer, and less dense than typical breadcrumbs. This texture creates a deliciously crunchy crust on baked or fried foods.

Chicken Parmesan

Chicken breasts topped with marinara sauce and creamy mozzarella are a perennial favorite, and this oven-baked method makes it so easy.

Active time: 15 minutes

Start to finish: 35 minutes

Each serving has:

863 calories

371 calories from fat

41 g fat

11 g saturated fat

69 g protein

51 g carbohydrates

2 (6-oz.) boneless, skinless chicken breast halves

2 large eggs, lightly beaten

1 TB. water

½ cup all-purpose flour

Salt and freshly ground black pepper to taste

1 cup Italian breadcrumbs

¼ cup freshly grated Parmesan cheese

½ cup olive oil

½ cup marinara sauce

⅔ cup grated mozzarella cheese

1. Preheat the oven to 400°F and place a 9×13-inch baking pan in the oven as it preheats. Rinse chicken and pat dry with paper towels. Trim all visible fat, place chicken between two sheets of plastic wrap, and pound to an even thickness of ½-inch.

2. Combine eggs and water in a shallow bowl. Season flour to taste with salt and pepper in a second bowl. Combine breadcrumbs and Parmesan cheese in a third bowl. Dust chicken with seasoned flour, shaking off any excess. Dip chicken in egg mixture, and then into breadcrumbs, pushing down to make sure crumbs adhere. Set aside.

3. Add olive oil to the hot baking pan, and heat for an additional 2 minutes in the oven. Add chicken to the pan, and turn it gently with a slotted spatula to coat both sides in oil. Bake chicken for 8 minutes.

4. Remove chicken from the oven, turn gently with a slotted spatula, and pat top of chicken with a paper towel. Top each chicken breast with ¼ cup marinara sauce and ⅓ cup mozzarella. Return chicken to the oven for an additional 8 minutes or until chicken is cooked through and no longer pink and cheese is melted. Remove chicken and drain on paper towels. Serve immediately.

Double Feature

While oven-frying significantly reduces the amount of fat used in a recipe, it can only be effective if the fat is hot when the food is added, otherwise the food will absorb the oil. That's why I heat the pan in advance and heat the oil before adding the food. Use the same technique for roasting potatoes and other vegetables.

Stuffed Cornish Game Hens

Individual game hens make such an elegant presentation, and these are stuffed with a mixture that includes vegetables and tangy dried cranberries.

2 (16- to 20-oz.) Cornish game hens, giblets removed	**1 celery rib, rinsed, trimmed, and sliced**
Salt and freshly ground black pepper to taste	**1 small carrot, peeled and grated**
½ tsp. dried thyme	**½ cup plain breadcrumbs**
2 TB. unsalted butter	**⅓ cup chicken stock**
1 small onion, peeled and diced	**2 tsp. dried sage**
2 garlic cloves, peeled and minced	**¼ cup dried cranberries**

Active time: 20 minutes
Start to finish: 70 minutes
Each serving has:
991 calories
555 calories from fat
62 g fat
21 g saturated fat
64 g protein
42 g carbohydrates

1. Preheat the oven to 375°F. Rinse hens and pat dry with paper towels. Sprinkle hens with salt and pepper and rub with thyme. Set aside.

2. Heat butter in a small skillet over medium-high heat. Add onion and garlic. Cook for 1 minute, stirring frequently. Add celery and carrot, and cook for 3 to 5 minutes or until onion is soft. Remove the pan from the heat, and stir in breadcrumbs, stock, sage, and cranberries. Season to taste with salt and pepper. Stuff mixture into cavity of hens. Close cavity with wooden toothpicks.

3. Place hens on a rack set inside a roasting pan. Roast, uncovered, for about 50 minutes or until the center of the stuffing reaches 165°F. Remove hens from oven, discard toothpicks, and serve immediately.

Double Trouble

While you can make the stuffing even a few days in advance and refrigerate it, one of the important rules of food safety is never to stuff any type of poultry until just before you put it into the oven.

Braised Cornish Hen with Bacon, Lettuce, Peas, and New Potatoes

Game hens are braised with vegetables in a delicate herbed stock to create this one-dish dinner.

Active time: 20 minutes

Start to finish: 55 minutes

Each serving has:

1147 calories

667 calories from fat

74 g fat

22 g saturated fat

77 g protein

41 g carbohydrates

2 (16- to 20-oz.) Cornish hens	½ lb. new potatoes, scrubbed and cut into 1-inch dice
Salt and freshly ground black pepper to taste	1 TB. chopped fresh rosemary or 1 tsp. dried
¼ cup all-purpose flour	1 TB. fresh thyme or 1 tsp. dried
3 slices bacon, cut into 1-inch pieces	1 cup frozen pearl onions and peas, thawed
1 shallot, peeled and diced	2 heads Bibb lettuce, rinsed, trimmed, and cut into quarters
2 garlic cloves, peeled and minced	
1 (14.5-oz.) can chicken stock	

Déjà Two

Although Rock Cornish hens are sometimes called Rock Cornish game hens, they are not game at all. These small chickens, which usually weigh about one pound, are a hybrid of Cornish and White Rock chickens that are between 4 and 6 weeks old.

1. Preheat the oven to 350°F. Sprinkle chicken with salt and pepper, dust with flour, shaking off any excess, and set aside.

2. Place bacon in an ovenproof Dutch oven over medium-high heat. Cook, stirring frequently, until bacon is crisp. Remove bacon with a slotted spoon, and set aside.

3. Add hens to the Dutch oven, and brown well on all sides turning gently with tongs. Remove hens and discard all but 1 tablespoon fat. Add shallot and garlic to the Dutch oven and cook, stirring frequently, for 3 minutes or until shallot is translucent.

4. Return hens and bacon to the pan, and add stock, potatoes, rosemary, and thyme. Bring to a boil, and transfer to the oven. Bake, covered, for 20 minutes. Add onions, peas, and lettuce. Bake for an additional 15 to 20 minutes or until hens are tender and no longer pink. (You can prepare this dish up to 2 days in advance and refrigerate, tightly covered. Reheat in a 350°F oven for 15 to 25 minutes, or until hot.) Serve immediately.

Variation: Substitute whole chicken pieces with bones for Cornish hens, and cook at the same rate.

16

From the Seas and Lakes

In This Chapter

- ◆ Crustacean creations
- ◆ Baked stuffed fish fillets
- ◆ One-dish seafood dinners

It's a chicken and egg situation. Are Americans eating more fresh fish because it's more widely available? Or is the fish department growing because people are eating more fish?

Regardless of the reason, more countries border on an ocean or major lake than are land-locked. So the majority of the world's cuisines include great fish dishes, and these are the recipes you'll find in this chapter.

Choosing the Choicest

While shops selling only fish and seafood are disappearing from the scene, searching your neighborhood for the best source of fresh fish is worth the effort. Look for a market that offers the most varied selection, that keeps its fish on chipped ice to maintain moisture, and that has a level of personal service that allows you to special-order specific varieties or cuts of fish.

When making your fish selection, remember a few simple guidelines. Above all, do not buy any fish that actually smells fishy, as this indicates it is no longer fresh or hasn't been cut or stored properly. Fresh fish has the mild, clean scent of the sea—nothing more. If possible, select a whole fish and have it cut to your specifications, such as fillets or steaks, because there are more signs to judge the freshness of a whole fish than any of the parts comprising it.

Look for bright shiny colors in the fish scales because as a fish sits, its skin becomes more pale and dull-looking. Then peer into the eyes, which should be black and beady. If they're milky or sunken, the fish has been dead too long. And the last test, if the fish isn't behind glass, gently poke its flesh. If the indentation remains, the fish is old.

Fish fillets or steaks should look bright, lustrous, and moist, with no signs of discoloration or drying. You'll find similar information for shrimp in Chapter 8.

Fish Families

Although I developed these recipes for specific fish, it's more important to use the freshest fish in the market than the particular species. All fin fish fall into three basic families, and you can easily substitute one species for another. Use the following table to make life at the fish counter easier.

A Guide to Fish

Description	Species	Characteristics
Firm, lean fish	black sea bass, cod family, flat fish (flounder, sole, halibut), grouper, lingcod, ocean perch, perch, pike, porgy, red snapper, smelt, striped bass, turbot, salmon, trout, drum family, tilefish, tilapia	Low-fat, mild to delicate flavor, firm flesh, flakes when cooked.

Description	Species	Characteristics
Meaty fish	catfish, carp, eel, monkfish (anglerfish), orange roughy, pike, salmon, shark, sturgeon, swordfish, some tuna varieties, mahi-mahi (dolphinfish), whitefish, pompano, yellowtail	Low to high fat, diverse flavors and textures, usually thick steaks or fillets.
Fatty or strong-flavored fish	bluefish, mackerel, some tuna varieties	High fat and pronounced flavor

Preparation Pointers

Rinse all fish under cold running water before cutting or cooking. With fillets, run your fingers in every direction along the top of the fillet, and feel for any pesky little bones.

You can remove bones easily in two ways. Larger bones will come out if you stroke them with a vegetable peeler, and you can pull out smaller bones with tweezers. This is not a long process, but the gesture will be greatly appreciated by all who eat the fish.

Overcooking is a common plight for fish dishes. That's why, in these recipes, we add the fish as the last ingredient. To test for doneness, flake the fish with a fork; cooked fish will flake easily, and the color will be opaque rather than translucent. While cooking, fish flakes become milky and opaque from the outside in.

Aquatic Attributes

Fish is high in protein and low to moderate in fat, cholesterol, and sodium. A 3-ounce portion of fish has between 47 and 170 calories, depending on the species. Fish is an excellent source of B vitamins, iodine, phosphorus, potassium, iron, and calcium.

The most important nutrient in fish may be the omega-3 fatty acids, which are the primary polyunsaturated fatty acids found in the fat and oils of fish. They have been found to lower the levels of low-density lipoproteins (LDL, the "bad" cholesterol) and raise the levels of high-density lipoproteins (HDL, the "good" cholesterol). Fatty fish that live in cold water, such as mackerel and salmon, seem to have the most omega-3 fatty acids, although all fish have some.

Baked Shrimp with Polenta

Polenta is a creamy corn porridge that is as delicate as the seasonings in this shrimp dish.

Active time: 20 minutes

Start to finish: 50 minutes

Each serving has:

453 calories

160 calories from fat

18 g fat

7 g saturated fat

30 g protein

43.5 g carbohydrates

1 TB. olive oil

2 shallots, peeled and chopped

2 garlic cloves, peeled and minced

½ lb. extra large (16 to 20 per lb.) raw shrimp, peeled and deveined

½ cup chopped fresh tomatoes

1 TB. chopped fresh parsley

2 tsp. chopped fresh oregano or ½ tsp. dried

1 tsp. fresh thyme or ¼ tsp. dried

¼ cup dry white wine

½ cup polenta or yellow cornmeal

1⅓ cups water

1 TB. unsalted butter

Salt and freshly ground black pepper to taste

¼ cup freshly grated Parmesan cheese

Double Feature

As long as you're making polenta, make a double batch and spread half in a greased baking sheet. Once it's chilled, cut it into squares and refrigerate it. Another evening you can fry it in unsalted butter as a side dish.

1. Preheat the oven to 350°F and grease a 9×9-inch baking pan.

2. Heat olive oil in a medium skillet over medium-high heat. Add shallots and garlic, and cook, stirring frequently, for 3 minutes or until shallots are translucent. Add shrimp, tomatoes, parsley, oregano, thyme, wine, and 1 tablespoon cornmeal. Bring to a boil, reduce the heat to low, and simmer for 3 minutes or until shrimp are pink and mixture thickens. Remove the pan from the heat and set aside.

3. Place water in a heavy 1-quart saucepan, and bring to a boil over high heat. Slowly whisk in cornmeal, whisking well between additions. When mixture boils, reduce the heat to low, and whisk until polenta is smooth. Simmer for 2 minutes or until very thick. Remove the pan from the heat, stir in butter, and season to taste with salt and pepper.

4. Spread half of polenta in the prepared pan. Top with shrimp filling and spread remaining polenta. Sprinkle with Parmesan cheese. Bake for 30 minutes or until bubbly and cheese is melted. Serve immediately.

Variation: Substitute bay scallops or 1-inch cubes of a firm-fleshed fish fillet, such as cod or halibut, for shrimp, and cook for the same length of time.

Greek Shrimp with Feta Cheese and Orzo

Orzo, a rice-shaped pasta, is baked with herbs and tomatoes and topped by shrimp and tangy feta cheese for an elegant meal.

¾ **cup orzo**

1 **TB. olive oil**

2 **shallots, peeled and diced**

2 **garlic cloves, peeled and minced**

1 **(8-oz.) can tomato sauce**

3 **TB. chopped fresh basil or 2 tsp. dried**

3 **TB. chopped fresh dill or 2 tsp. dried**

Salt and freshly ground black pepper to taste

½ **lb. extra large (16 to 20 per lb.) raw shrimp, peeled and deveined**

½ **cup feta cheese, crumbled**

2 **TB. chopped fresh oregano or 2 tsp. dried**

Active time: 15 minutes

Start to finish: 35 minutes

Each serving has:

568 calories

163 calories from fat

18 g fat

7 g saturated fat

39 g protein

62 g carbohydrates

1. Preheat the oven to 450°F and grease a 9×9-inch baking pan. Bring a large pot of salted water to a boil over high heat. Add orzo and boil for 7 minutes or until orzo doubles in size but is still slightly hard. (The amount of time depends on the brand of orzo.) Drain.

2. Heat olive oil in a medium skillet over medium-high heat. Add shallot and garlic, and cook stirring frequently, for 3 minutes or until shallot is translucent. Add tomato sauce, basil, and dill. Bring to a boil, reduce the heat to low, and simmer for 3 minutes. Add orzo, stir well, and season to taste with salt and pepper.

3. Scrape mixture into the prepared baking pan, and arrange shrimp on top. Sprinkle feta and oregano over shrimp, and cover pan with aluminum foil. Bake for 20 minutes or until shrimp are pink and cooked through and feta is melted. Serve immediately.

Variation: Substitute bay scallops, sea scallops cut into quarters, or 1-inch pieces of fish fillet for shrimp.

 **Double Feature**

Shrimp and other seafood cook in far less time than it takes even tiny pasta like orzo to reach al dente. That's why the pasta in this and many other dishes is partially cooked before baking. That par-boiling brings all the elements in the dish to the finish line at the right point.

Shrimp, Sausage, and Chicken Jambalaya

Using a commercial yellow rice mix means that this version of the Louisiana classic is on the table in a matter of minutes.

Active time: 20 minutes

Start to finish: 45 minutes

Each serving has:

755 calories

245 calories from fat

27 g fat

8 g saturated fat

56 g protein

67 g carbohydrates

1 (6-oz.) boneless skinless chicken breast

1 TB. olive oil

¼ lb. smoked sausage link, cut into ⅓-inch slices

1 small onion, peeled and diced

1 celery rib, rinsed, trimmed, and sliced

½ small red or green bell pepper, seeds and ribs removed, and sliced

2 garlic cloves, peeled and minced

1 (5-oz.) pkg. yellow rice mix, such as Carolina brand

1 (14.5-oz.) can chicken stock

2 tsp. fresh thyme or ½ tsp. dried

1 bay leaf

⅓ lb. extra large (16 to 20 per lb.) raw shrimp, peeled and deveined

1 TB. chopped fresh parsley

Salt and freshly ground black pepper to taste

1. Preheat the oven to 400°F. Rinse chicken and pat dry with paper towels. Trim all visible fat, and cut chicken into 1-inch cubes. Set aside.

2. Heat oil in an ovenproof Dutch oven over medium-high heat. Add sausage, and cook, stirring occasionally, for 3 minutes or until sausage is lightly browned. Add onion, celery, red bell pepper, and garlic. Cook, stirring frequently, for 3 minutes or until onion is translucent. Add chicken and cook, stirring frequently, for 2 minutes or until chicken is opaque.

3. Add rice, stock, thyme, and bay leaf. Bring to a boil over medium-high heat, stirring occasionally. Cover the pan, and bake for 20 minutes. (You can do this up to a day in advance and refrigerate, tightly covered. Add 15 minutes to the initial covered baking if chilled.) Remove the pan from the oven, and stir in shrimp. Bake for an additional 5 to 7 minutes or until shrimp are pink, chicken is cooked through, and liquid is absorbed.

4. Remove the pan from the oven and discard bay leaf. Sprinkle with parsley, and season to taste with salt and pepper. Serve immediately.

Déjà Two

Jambalaya is a staple of Louisiana cooking, where culinary traditions of France, Spain, Italy, the New World, and other cultures blended. Jambalaya was the local adaptation of the Spanish rice dish, paella, and became a favorite among the Cajuns, French transplants who settled in the Louisiana bayous. Some say the name of the dish comes from *jamon*, which is Spanish for ham. Others say it is from the French word for ham, *jambon*. Either way, contemporary versions of jambalaya include ham, sausage, chicken, seafood, and rice.

Bay Scallop Risotto with Sweet Peas and Corn

Tender Arborio rice is flavored with delicate peas before bay scallops add their taste.

Active time: 20 minutes

Start to finish: 40 minutes

Each serving has:

767 calories

271 calories from fat

30 g fat

11.5 g saturated fat

33 g protein

83 g carbohydrates

1 (10-oz.) pkg. frozen peas, thawed

1 (14.5-oz.) can chicken stock

2 TB. unsalted butter

2 TB. olive oil

2 shallots, peeled and minced

1 garlic clove, peeled and minced

1 celery rib, rinsed, trimmed, and thinly sliced

⅔ cup *Arborio* rice

⅓ cup dry vermouth

3 TB. chopped fresh parsley

1 TB. chopped fresh tarragon or 1 tsp. dried

⅓ lb. bay scallops, rinsed, or sea scallops cut into quarters

½ cup fresh corn kernels or frozen corn kernels, thawed

¼ cup freshly grated Parmesan cheese

Salt and freshly ground black pepper to taste

Duet Dialogue

Arborio (pronounced *ar-BORE-e-oh*) is a species of rice with short kernels and a very high starch content. It's used for risotto because the starch gives the finished dish its creamy appearance.

1. Combine half package of peas with ½ cup of stock in a food processor fitted with a steel blade or in a blender. Purée until smooth and set aside.

2. Heat butter and olive oil in a heavy 2-quart saucepan over medium-high heat. Add shallots, garlic, and celery. Cook, stirring frequently, for 3 minutes or until shallots are translucent. Stir in rice, coating all grains with fat.

3. Raise the heat to high, and add vermouth, parsley, and tarragon. Cook, stirring constantly, until wine almost evaporates. Add remaining stock, and bring to a boil. Cover the pan, reduce the heat to a simmer, and cook rice for 15 minutes or until liquid is almost absorbed, stirring occasionally. (You can do this up to 4 hours in advance; bring the mixture back to a simmer before continuing.)

4. Stir in pea purée, remaining peas, scallops, and corn. Cook for an additional 5 to 7 minutes or until scallops are cooked through, stirring occasionally. Remove the pan from the heat, and stir in Parmesan cheese. Season to taste with salt and pepper and serve immediately.

Variation: Use small shrimp or ½-inch pieces of diced cod, halibut, or salmon in place of scallops.

Monkfish with Potatoes and Summer Squash

Monkfish has the texture and sweetness of lobster, so this is a great recipe for anyone not crazy about "fishy fish."

¼ lb. white mushrooms

1 yellow summer squash

2 TB. olive oil

2 shallots, peeled and minced

2 garlic cloves, peeled and minced

2 TB. chopped fresh parsley

1 TB. chopped fresh rosemary or 1 tsp. dried

1 bay leaf

½ cup dry white wine

1 cup fish stock or bottled clam juice

⅓ lb. small new potatoes, scrubbed and cut into quarters

½ lb. *monkfish* fillets, rinsed

Salt and freshly ground black pepper to taste

1 tsp. cornstarch

1 TB. cold water

Active time: 20 minutes

Start to finish: 45 minutes

Each serving has:

411 calories

152 calories from fat

17 g fat

2.5 g saturated fat

22 g protein

34 g carbohydrates

---

1. Wipe mushrooms with a damp paper towel. Discard stems and slice mushrooms. Rinse and trim yellow squash. Cut squash in half lengthwise, and cut haves into ½-inch slices.

2. Heat olive oil in a Dutch oven over medium-high heat. Add shallots and garlic, and cook, stirring frequently, for 2 minutes. Add mushrooms, and cook, stirring frequently, for 3 minutes or until mushrooms are soft and shallots are translucent. Add parsley, rosemary, bay leaf, wine, stock, and potatoes. Bring mixture to a boil over high heat, reduce the heat to low, cover, and simmer for 15 minutes. Add squash and simmer for 5 minutes. (You can do this a day in advance and refrigerate, tightly covered. Before continuing, reheat to a simmer.)

3. Remove all membrane from monkfish by holding the thin end of each fillet and scraping away membrane with knife. Slice fillets into ½-inch slices across the grain. Add monkfish to the pan, return to a boil, and cover. Simmer for 3 to 5 minutes or until monkfish is opaque. Season to taste with salt and pepper, and remove and discard bay leaf.

4. Combine cornstarch and cold water in a small bowl. Stir cornstarch mixture into the pan, bring to a simmer, and cook for 1 minute or until mixture lightly thickens. Serve immediately.

Duet Dialogue

Monkfish is called "poor man's lobster" by many people because its sweet, mild flavor is similar to lobster. Its official name is "angler fish" because it attracts its prey by releasing a long filament that grows from its head. Smaller fish think it's a worm, or angler, and swim closer, only to be gobbled up by the angler's huge mouth. It's called *lotte* in French.

Cod Lyonnaise with Onions and Potatoes

Crispy oven-baked potatoes and onions are the foundation for this dish from southern France.

Active time: 15 minutes

Start to finish: 50 minutes

Each serving has:

418 calories

160 calories from fat

18 g fat

2.5 g saturated fat

36 g protein

28 g carbohydrates

½ lb. large red-skinned potatoes

½ lb. sweet onion (such as Vidalia or Bermuda)

¼ cup olive oil

2 garlic cloves, peeled and minced

2 tsp. fresh thyme or ½ tsp. dried

2 (6- to 8-oz.) thick cod fillets, rinsed and patted dry with paper towels

Salt and freshly ground black pepper to taste

½ tsp. Herbes de Provence

2 TB. red wine vinegar

1. Preheat the oven to 500°F and place a baking sheet in the oven as it preheats. Scrub potatoes and cut into ½-inch dice. Peel onion and cut into ½-inch dice.

2. Pour 2 tablespoons olive oil onto the baking sheet. Add potatoes, onion, garlic, and thyme. Toss to coat well with oil. Bake for 25 minutes, turning occasionally with a spatula, or until potatoes and onions are browned.

3. Rub cod with remaining olive oil, sprinkle with salt and pepper, and rub with Herbes de Provence. Place cod on top of vegetables, and bake for 10 minutes per inch of thickness or until cooked but still slightly translucent in center.

4. Remove the pan from the oven, and place cod on two serving dishes. Sprinkle vegetables with vinegar, and divide them onto the plates. Serve immediately.

Variation: Substitute salmon, swordfish, or any white firm-fleshed fish for cod, and cook according to the same formula of 10 minutes per inch of thickness.

Double Feature

Fish continues to cook after it leaves a heat source, so to avoid overcooking it's best to stop baking or grilling fish when there's still a little translucency in the center of the piece. By the time it's plated and served, it will become opaque.

Crab-Stuffed Sole Creole on Spinach

A simple cream sauce covers both the stuffed fillets and spinach to create an elegant one-dish dinner.

2 scallions

½ cup lump crab meat

3 TB. unsalted butter

1 TB. olive oil

¼ cup chopped celery

¼ cup chopped red bell pepper

1 garlic clove, peeled and minced

1 (8-oz.) bottle clam juice

2 tsp. Creole seasoning

¼ tsp. dried thyme

½ cup plain breadcrumbs

Salt and cayenne to taste

1 (10-oz.) pkg. frozen leaf spinach, thawed

2 (6-oz.) sole fillets, rinsed and patted dry with paper towels

2 TB. all-purpose flour

¼ cup heavy cream

Salt and freshly ground black pepper to taste

Active time: 20 minutes

Start to finish: 35 minutes

Each serving has:

794 calories

393 calories from fat

44 g fat

20 g saturated fat

50 g protein

52 g carbohydrates

1. Preheat the oven to 400°F. Rinse and trim scallions. Discard all but 2-inches of green tops, and slice thinly. Place crab meat on a dark colored plate and pick it over carefully to remove all shell fragments and cartilage.

2. Heat 1 tablespoon butter and olive oil in a small skillet over medium heat. Add celery, red bell pepper, scallions, and garlic. Cook, stirring frequently, for 3 minutes or until scallions are translucent. Stir in ¼ cup clam juice, 1 teaspoon Creole seasoning, and thyme. Remove the pan from the stove, and gently stir in crab meat and breadcrumbs. Season to taste with salt and cayenne and set aside.

3. Place spinach in a colander, and press with the back of a spoon to extract as much liquid as possible. Spread spinach evenly in a 9×9-inch baking pan. Divide stuffing between fillets, and place them on top of spinach.

4. Melt remaining butter in a heavy 1-quart saucepan over low heat. Stir in flour, reduce the heat to low, and cook mixture, stirring constantly, for 2 minutes. Whisk in remaining clam juice and cream, and bring to a boil over medium heat, stirring frequently. Stir in remaining Creole seasoning, and season to taste with salt and pepper.

Double Trouble

Crab is notorious for being riddled with bits of shell and hard membrane, so take the time to pick it over carefully, or you'll be crunching instead of chewing. The best way to do this is to spread it out on a dark plate and push it around gently with your fingertips so you won't break up the prized lumps.

5. Spoon sauce over fish and spinach. (You can do this up to a day in advance. Refrigerate it, tightly covered, and add 10 minutes to the baking time.) Bake uncovered for 15 to 20 minutes or until fish is opaque and stuffing is lightly brown. Serve immediately.

Variation: Substitute any thin fish fillet, such as flounder or tilapia, for sole.

Sole Almondine with Vegetable and Rice Stuffing

Herbed rice makes a flavorful stuffing with crunchy almonds added for textural interest in this easy dish.

Active time: 25 minutes

Start to finish: 45 minutes

Each serving has:

704 calories

383 calories from fat

43 g fat

13 g saturated fat

40 g protein

41 g carbohydrates

2 scallions	2 TB. all-purpose flour
2 oz. fresh shiitake mushrooms	⅔ cup whole milk
⅓ cup long-grain rice	1 tsp. Herbes de Provence
⅓ cup sliced almonds	1 TB. chopped fresh parsley
2 TB. olive oil	Salt and freshly ground black pepper to taste
2 TB. unsalted butter	4 (3-oz.) sole fillets, rinsed
1 garlic clove, peeled and minced	2 TB. *crème fraîche*
	2 TB. dry sherry

1. Preheat the oven to 375°F. Rinse and trim scallions. Discard all but 2-inches of green tops, and slice thinly. Wipe mushrooms with a damp paper towel. Discard stems and slice mushrooms.

2. Bring a large pot of salted water to a boil. Add rice and boil over medium heat, uncovered, for 15 to 18 minutes or until rice is almost cooked through. Drain and place in mixing bowl. Place almonds on ungreased baking sheet, and toast in the oven for 4 to 6 minutes or until lightly browned. Add almonds to rice.

3. Heat oil and 1 tablespoon butter in a small skillet over medium heat. Add scallions and garlic, and cook, stirring frequently, for 2 minutes. Add mushrooms, increase the heat to medium-high,

and cook, stirring frequently, for 3 to 5 minutes or until mush-rooms are soft. Scrape mixture into rice.

4. Melt remaining 1 tablespoon butter in a small saucepan over low heat. Add flour and cook, stirring constantly, for 2 min-utes. Whisk in milk, and bring to a boil over medium heat, whisking constantly. Reduce the heat to low, and simmer sauce for 2 minutes. Stir in herbes de Provence and parsley, and season to taste with salt and pepper. Add ¼ cup sauce to rice mixture, stir well, and season again with salt and pepper if necessary. Reserve remaining sauce. (You can do this a day in advance and refrigerate rice stuffing and sauce in separate con-tainers, tightly covered. Before continuing, reheat rice mixture to room temperature in a microwave oven or in a saucepan over low heat, and reheat sauce separately in the same manner.)

5. Increase the oven heat to 400°F. Grease a 9×9-inch baking pan. Place 1 sole fillet on a plate, and place one fourth rice stuff-ing in the center. Fold fillet to enclose stuffing and place in prepared baking pan seam side down. Repeat with remaining fillets and stuffing.

6. Combine remaining sauce, crème fraîche, and sherry. Pour sauce over fillets and cover the pan with aluminum foil. Bake for 10 minutes, remove foil, and bake for an additional 10 min-utes or until sole is opaque. Serve immediately.

Duet Dialogue

Crème frâiche (pronounced *krem-fresh*) is a thickened cream with a tangy taste and a rich texture. For soups and sau-ces it's better than sour cream because it can be boiled without curdling. You can easily make it at home by stirring 2 table-poons buttermilk into 1 cup heavy cream. Allow the mixture to stand at room temperature for 12 hours or until thick. Then refri-gerate the crème frâiche for up to 10 days.

Chinese-Style Sea Bass

Crunchy green asparagus and bright red bell pepper make this a visually stunning dish, and jalapeños add some heat to the Asian seasoning.

Active time: 15 minutes

Start to finish: 25 minutes

Each serving has:

362 calories

120 calories from fat

13 g fat

2 g saturated fat

41 g protein

17 g carbohydrates

3 TB. sesame seeds

⅓ lb. fresh asparagus

1 TB. Asian sesame oil

6 scallions, rinsed, trimmed, and cut into 1-inch pieces

2 garlic cloves, peeled and minced

1 TB. grated fresh ginger

½ small jalapeño chili, seeds and ribs removed, and finely chopped

½ small red bell pepper, seeds and ribs removed, and thinly sliced

2 (6-oz.) sea bass fillets, rinsed

2 TB. soy sauce

2 TB. plum wine or sweet sherry

¼ cup fish stock or bottled clam juice

1 tsp. cornstarch

1 TB. cold water

Salt and freshly ground black pepper to taste

Double Feature

Many fish fillets, such as sea bass, have a thin and a thick end. To ensure the thin end doesn't overcook, fold it up so that the fillet has an even thickness and secure it closed with a wooden toothpick.

1. Place sesame seeds in a small dry skillet over medium heat. Toast seeds for 2 minutes or until browned, shaking the pan frequently. Set aside. Rinse asparagus and discard woody stems. Slice into 1-inch pieces on the diagonal.

2. Heat sesame oil in a large skillet over medium-high heat. Add scallions, garlic, ginger, and jalapeño. Cook, stirring constantly, for 30 seconds. Add asparagus and red bell pepper and continue cooking, stirring frequently, for 2 minutes.

3. Add sea bass, along with soy sauce, wine, and stock. Bring to a boil, cover, reduce the heat to low, and cook for 5 minutes. Gently turn sea bass with a slotted spatula, and cook, covered, for an additional 3 minutes or until fish is opaque. Remove sea bass and vegetables with a slotted spatula, and keep hot.

4. Combine cornstarch and cold water in a small bowl. Add cornstarch mixture to the skillet, and simmer for 1 minute or until mixture lightly thickens. Season to taste with salt and pepper, sprinkle with sesame seeds, and serve immediately.

Variation: Substitute any thick fish fillet, such as halibut or cod, for sea bass.

From the Prairies and Plains

In This Chapter

◆ Helpers for hamburger

◆ Porcine pleasures

◆ Lusty lamb and delicate veal

Every once in a while a carnivore craving hits many of us, and nothing will satisfy except a tasty meat dish. So if you are craving some hearty dinner dish of this nature, you'll find several choice recipes here in this chapter.

While meats take longer to cook than seafood or chicken, you won't have to start these dishes too far in advance. You can have them all on the table within an hour.

The Daily Grind

While any food of animal origin can harbor bacteria, ground meats can contain a number of invisible, odor-free, illness-causing bacteria, including *salmonella* and *E coli*. Other families of bacteria can cause spoilage, with food developing a bad odor or feeling sticky on the outside. However, these are not potentially dangerous because you can detect them.

Ground meat is more prone to these problems than larger cuts. When meat is ground, the microorganisms residing on its surface can get mixed into it, so more of the meat is exposed to the harmful bacteria. Bacteria multiply rapidly in the "danger zone"—temperatures between 40°F and 140°F. To keep bacterial levels low, store ground meats at 40°F or less and use within two days or freeze. To destroy harmful bacteria, cook ground meats to 160°F.

The best way to safely thaw ground beef is in the refrigerator. Keeping meat cold while it is defrosting is essential to preventing growth of bacteria. Cook or refreeze it within one or two days after thawing.

To defrost ground beef more rapidly, you can defrost it in the microwave oven or in cold water. If you use the microwave, cook the ground beef immediately because some areas may begin to cook during the defrosting. To defrost in cold water, put the meat in a watertight plastic bag and submerge. Change the water every 30 minutes. Cook immediately. Do not refreeze ground meat thawed in cold water or in the microwave oven.

Pork's Updated Image

Fresh pork makes up only one-third of the pork supply and comes primarily from the loin and front shoulder. The remaining two thirds is sold as prepared meats, such as ham, bacon, hot dogs, and sausage.

All cuts of pork are relatively tender, and as of 1986, the U.S. Department of Agriculture (USDA) stopped inspecting fresh pork for *Trichinella spiralis* because none had been found for more than 50 years. With no fear of bacteria today, pork does not need to be dried out in the oven by high temperature cooking, so it's now quicker to cook as well.

Recent studies of randomly selected pork cuts from leading supermarkets in 15 U.S. cities have shown that today's pork is 31 percent lower in fat, 17 percent lower in calories, and 10 percent lower in cholesterol than in 1983. Professionals attribute the reduction of fat content, the other side of which is a higher protein count, in part to improvements in the breeding and feeding of pigs.

Who Had a Little Lamb?

Lamb is far more flavorful than beef and has a rosy richness that fills the house with a wonderful aroma as it cooks. Smaller than cows or pigs, a full-grown lamb of about eight months old rarely weighs more than 115 pounds. What is termed "spring lamb" comes from young animals, less than five months old, and "lamb" is from animals less than one year old. "Mutton" is lamb that comes from animals one to two years old and should only be braised or stewed because all cuts will require some tenderizing.

When choosing lamb, let its color be your guide. Look for lamb with deep pink flesh that is finely grained with white marbling and fat, although the color of the fat may vary with the species of animal and what it was fed. Avoid meat that has a dry surface or looks dark red or brown.

Versatile Veal

Pork manufacturers have built a campaign about pork being the "other white meat," but veal is even more delicate and is a luxurious meat regardless of whether it is braised, sautéed, or roasted. Veal comes from calves up to six months old that weigh no more than 200 to 250 pounds.

To ensure tender, pink meat, the animal is fed on its mother's milk rather than grain. Most milk-fed veal comes from three- to four-month-old calves, as older animals have usually started to eat grass and are on their way to becoming young cows. The meat of grass-fed veal is darker and coarser, with neither the full-flavored richness of beef nor the delicacy of milk-fed veal.

Because the meat is young, most cuts are tender, can be cooked in many ways, and will retain its delicate flavor. However, don't consider veal just a youthful version of beef; rather, treat it like chicken in the delicacy of the seasoning.

Basic Browning

The one major principle to follow for successful meat dishes is the initial browning of the meat. Browning means to cook quickly over medium-high heat, which causes the surface of the food to brown. In the case of cubes of beef for stew, browning seals in the juices and keeps the interior moist. For ground meats, the browning gives food an appetizing color, allows you to drain off some of the inherent fat, and also gives the dish a rich flavor as the sugars caramelize.

You can brown larger pieces under an oven broiler, but brown ground meats and sausage in a skillet. Crumble the meat in a skillet over medium-high heat. Break up the lumps with a meat fork or the back of a spoon as it browns; then stir it around frequently until all the lumps are brown and no pink remains. At that point, it's easy to remove it from the pan with a slotted spoon and discard the fat. You can then use the pan again without washing it for any precooking of other ingredients. The residue from browning will give whatever you're cooking more flavor.

Italian Stuffed Peppers

This is a hearty dish, with herbed beef baked right in the peppers topped with a tomato sauce.

Active time: 15 minutes	
Start to finish: 1 hour	
Each serving has:	
522 calories	
253 calories from fat	
28 g fat	
9 g saturated fat	
36.5 g protein	
30.5 g carbohydrates	

2 large red bell peppers	**¼ cup Italian breadcrumbs**
1 TB. olive oil	**2 TB. milk**
1 small onion, peeled and chopped	**¼ cup grated mozzarella cheese**
1 garlic clove, peeled and minced	**⅔ cup jarred marinara sauce**
2 TB. chopped fresh parsley	**1 large egg, lightly beaten**
1 tsp. Italian seasoning	**½ lb. lean ground beef**
Salt and freshly ground black pepper to taste	**2 TB. freshly grated Parmesan cheese**

Duet Dialogue

To **baste** is the process of brushing or spooning sauce or fat over food as it cooks. The purpose of basting is to keep food moist as well as to add flavor and color.

1. Preheat the oven to 375°F and grease a 9×9-inch baking pan. Cut off top ½ inch off red bell peppers and reserve. Scoop out seeds and ribs with your hands and discard. Discard stems, and chop pepper tops.

2. Heat oil in a large, heavy skillet over medium-high heat. Add onion, garlic, and chopped pepper pieces. Cook, stirring frequently, for 5 minutes or until onions soften. Transfer to a large mixing bowl. Mix in parsley, Italian seasoning, salt, pepper, breadcrumbs, milk, mozzarella, 3 tablespoons marinara sauce, egg, and beef. Mix well.

3. Fill pepper cavities with mixture. Stand peppers up in the prepared baking pan, and pour remaining marinara sauce over them. Cover with aluminum foil, and bake for 25 minutes. Remove foil, *baste* peppers with sauce in the pan, and sprinkle with Parmesan cheese. Bake for an additional 20 minutes. Serve immediately, spooning sauce over top of peppers.

Variation: Substitute ground turkey or some combination of ground veal and pork.

Shepherd's Pie

Shepherd's Pie, with a cheddar-flavored mashed topping, is an English comfort food classic.

½ lb. fresh shiitake mushrooms

½ lb. lean ground beef

4 TB. unsalted butter

2 TB. olive oil

1 small onion, peeled and
diced

2 garlic cloves, peeled and
minced

⅔ cup dry red wine

1 (1.1-oz.) pkg. mushroom
gravy mix

1 TB. chopped fresh rose-
mary leaves or 1 tsp. dried

2 tsp. fresh thyme or ½ tsp.
dried

½ lb. red-skinned potatoes,
scrubbed and cut into 1-inch
dice

¼ cup heavy cream

¾ cup grated sharp cheddar
cheese

1 cup frozen mixed veg-
etables

> **Active time:** 45 minutes
>
> **Start to finish:** 1 hour
>
> **Each serving has:**
>
> 1050 calories
>
> 643 calories from fat
>
> 71 g fat
>
> 36 g saturated fat
>
> 46 g protein
>
> 50 g carbohydrates

1. Grease a 9×5-inch loaf pan. Wipe mushrooms with a damp paper towel. Discard stems and slice mushrooms.

2. Heat a large skillet over medium-high heat. Add beef and cook until well browned, breaking up lumps with a fork. Remove beef from the pan with a slotted spoon and set aside. Discard fat.

3. Heat 1 tablespoon butter and 1 TB. oil in the same skillet over medium-high heat. Add mushrooms and cook, stirring constantly, for 3 minutes or until mushrooms are soft. Scrape mushrooms into the bowl with beef.

4. Heat 1 tablespoon butter and remaining 1 tablespoon oil in the skillet over medium heat. Add onion and garlic, and cook, stir-ring constantly, for 3 minutes or until onion is translucent. Add beef, mushrooms, wine, gravy mix, rosemary, and thyme. Bring to a boil, reduce the heat to low, and simmer, uncovered, for 30 minutes or until thickened. Tilt the pan to spoon off as much fat as possible. (You can do this up to two days in advance, and refrigerate, tightly covered. Before continuing, reheat over low heat, stirring occasionally, until hot.)

Déjà Two

Shepherd's Pie is a classic served at pubs in Great Britain that dates back to the eighteenth century. It was originally created as an economical way to use up leftovers from the traditional "Sunday joint," which was a leg of lamb served with potatoes and vegetables.

5. Preheat the oven to 400°F. While beef is simmering, prepare topping. Place potatoes in a saucepan, cover with salted water, and bring to a boil over high heat. Reduce the heat to medium, and boil potatoes, uncovered, for 12 to 15 minutes or until soft. Drain potatoes and set aside in a bowl. Heat cream, remaining 2 tablespoons butter, and cheddar cheese in the saucepan over medium heat until cheese melts, stirring occasionally. Return potatoes to saucepan, and mash well with a potato masher. Season to taste with salt and pepper and set aside.

6. Add mixed vegetables to beef, and return to a boil. Simmer for 3 minutes, then scrape mixture into the prepared pan. Spoon potatoes on top of beef, smoothing them into an even layer. (You can do this up to 4 hours in advance and keep at room temperature. Add 5 to 10 minutes to baking time if beef is not hot.)

7. Bake for 15 minutes or until beef is bubbly and potatoes are lightly browned. Serve immediately.

Variation: Substitute ground lamb or ground turkey.

Italian Baked Pasta with Beef and Beans (*Pasta Fazool*)

This easy pasta dish adds the flavors of Italian sausage to the beef and bean mix.

Active time: 25 minutes

Start to finish: 50 minutes

Each serving has:

905 calories

433 calories from fat

48 g fat

17 g saturated fat

45 g protein

76 g carbohydrates

¼ lb. mostaccioli or penne pasta

¼ lb. bulk hot or sweet Italian sausage (or link sausage with casings discarded)

¼ lb. lean ground beef

2 TB. olive oil

1 small onion, peeled and chopped

2 garlic cloves, peeled and minced

1 tsp. dried oregano

½ tsp. dried thyme

1 (14.5-oz.) can diced tomatoes, drained

1 TB. tomato paste

1 cup canned kidney beans, drained and rinsed

Salt and freshly ground black pepper to taste

¼ cup freshly grated Parmesan cheese

2 TB. chopped fresh parsley

⅓ cup grated fontina cheese

1. Preheat the oven to 400°F and grease a 9×9-inch baking pan. Bring a large pot of salted water to a boil. Boil pasta according to package directions until al dente. Drain and place in prepared pan.

2. Heat a large skillet over medium-high heat. Add sausage and beef, and cook, breaking up lumps with a fork, for 5 to 7 minutes or until well browned. Remove meat with a slotted spoon, and set aside. Discard fat.

3. Heat olive oil in the skillet, and add onion and garlic. Cook, stirring frequently, for 3 minutes or until onion is translucent. Add oregano and thyme, and cook, stirring constantly, for 1 minute. Add tomatoes, tomato paste, and beans, and simmer for 5 minutes. Season to taste with salt and pepper. Stir in Parmesan cheese and parsley, and stir mixture into pasta in the baking pan.

4. Cover with aluminum foil and bake for 10 minutes. Remove foil, sprinkle with fontina cheese, and bake for an additional 15 minutes or until bubbly and cheese melts. Serve immediately.

Variation: Substitute ground lamb or turkey for beef, and use any uncooked poultry sausage in place of pork.

Déjà Two

Although the names of Italian pasta shapes might sound romantic, they are merely the translation of the word for the look of the pasta. *Penne* means "quills" or "pens," while *mostaccioli* means "small mustaches." *Rotelle* are "wheels," and *farfalle* are "butterflies."

Old-Fashioned Meatloaf

The new touch to this old favorite is a crunchy coating of crushed corn flakes for added texture.

2 TB. olive oil

1 large shallot, peeled and chopped

2 garlic cloves, peeled and minced

1 carrot, peeled and chopped

¼ lb. lean ground pork

¼ lb. lean ground beef

1 large egg, lightly beaten

¼ cup grated mozzarella cheese

¼ cup Italian breadcrumbs

3 TB. milk

¼ cup *chili sauce* or ketchup

2 tsp. Worcestershire sauce

2 tsp. fresh or ½ tsp. dried thyme

Salt and freshly ground black pepper to taste

1½ cups cornflakes

Active time: 15 minutes

Start to finish: 45 minutes

Each serving has:

624 calories

334 calories from fat

37 g fat

11 g saturated fat

33 g protein

37 g carbohydrates

Duet Dialogue

Chili sauce, contrary to its name, is closer to a chunky ketchup than a fiery sauce. This tomato-based condiment contains onions, green peppers, vinegar, sugar, and spices.

1. Preheat the oven to 375°F and line a 9×13-inch baking pan with aluminum foil. Heat olive oil in a small skillet over medium-high heat. Add shallot, garlic, and carrots. Cook, stirring frequently, for 3 minutes or until shallot is translucent. Scrape mixture into a mixing bowl.

2. Add pork, beef, egg, mozzarella, breadcrumbs, milk, 2 tablespoons chili sauce, Worcestershire sauce, thyme, salt, and pepper to mixing bowl. Mix well. Form meat into a log 5-inches long and 3-inches wide in baking sheet. Spread top with remaining 2 tablespoons chili sauce. (You can do this up to a day in advance and refrigerate, tightly covered.)

3. Place cornflakes in a heavy resealable plastic bag. Crush into coarse crumbs with the flat side of a meat mallet or the bottom of a skillet. Press crumbs into top and sides of meatloaf. Bake for 30 minutes or until an instant-read thermometer registers 160°F. Serve immediately.

Variation: Substitute ground turkey for pork and beef.

Pork with Prosciutto, Mozzarella, and Sage (*Porchetta Saltimbocca*)

The pork only partially cooks before being layered with the ham, cheese, and sage so it remains tender and is on the table in a matter of minutes.

Active time: 10 minutes

Start to finish: 25 minutes

Each serving has:

456 calories

191 calories from fat

21 g fat

10 g saturated fat

60 g protein

3 g carbohydrates

1 (12- to 16-oz.) pork tenderloin

Salt and freshly ground black pepper to taste

2 garlic cloves, peeled and minced

½ tsp. Italian seasoning

8 to 10 fresh sage leaves

4 slices imported prosciutto, trimmed of visible fat

¼ lb. whole milk mozzarella cheese, thinly sliced

1. Preheat the oven to 450°F and line a 9×13-inch baking pan with aluminum foil. Rinse pork and pat dry with paper towels. Trim off all visible fat and iridescent silverskin. Sprinkle with salt and pepper, and rub with garlic and Italian seasoning. Tuck

thin tail under pork to form a cylinder of even size, and tie tail section with kitchen string or pin it with wooden toothpicks.

2. Place pork in baking pan and bake for 10 minutes. Remove pork from the oven, and discard string or toothpicks. Allow to rest 5 minutes, and then slice into ½-inch slices. Pork will still be rare.

3. Arrange pork slices in baking pan in two columns, slightly overlapping slices. Top each group with ½ of sage leaves, 2 slices prosciutto, and ½ of cheese slices. Bake for 5 to 7 minutes or until cheese is melted and bubbly. Serve immediately.

Double Feature

For small quantities of foods, like a few slices of prosciutto, it's best to visit the deli department of your supermarket. Even the smallest package of pre-packaged meats are 4- to 6-ounces.

Pork Tenderloin with Herbed Cornbread Crust

The cornbread crust is held on with sharp Dijon mustard to add a surprise flavor to this quick dish.

1 (12- to 16-oz.) pork tenderloin	**2 tsp. fresh or ½ tsp. dried thyme**
Salt and freshly ground black pepper to taste	**2 tsp. chopped fresh or ½ tsp. dried rosemary**
1 TB. olive oil	**2 tsp. chopped fresh or ½ tsp. dried sage**
1 TB. unsalted butter	
2 garlic cloves, peeled and minced	**Salt and freshly ground black pepper to taste**
1 large corn muffin, crumbled (1 cup of crumbs)	**2 TB. Dijon mustard**

Active time: 15 minutes

Start to finish: 25 minutes

Each serving has:

460 calories

199 calories from fat

22 g fat

7.5 g saturated fat

47 g protein

19 g carbohydrates

1. Preheat the oven to 425°F and line a 9×13-inch baking pan with aluminum foil. Rinse pork and pat dry with paper towels. Trim off all visible fat and iridescent silverskin. Sprinkle with salt and pepper. Tuck thin tail under pork to form a cylinder of even size, and tie tail section with kitchen string or pin it with wooden toothpicks.

2. Heat oil in a heavy large skillet over high heat. Sear pork on all sides, turning gently with tongs, for 3 minutes or until browned. Remove pork from the pan, and transfer to the baking pan. Discard string or toothpicks.

3. Reduce the heat to low, add butter to the skillet and cook garlic, stirring constantly, for 30 seconds or until fragrant. Remove the pan from the heat and stir in crumbs, thyme, rosemary, and sage. Season to taste with salt and pepper.

4. Spread mustard over pork and pat seasoned crumbs onto mustard. Roast for 10 to 15 minutes or until an instant-read thermometer registers 145°F. Allow pork to rest for 5 minutes; then slice and serve immediately.

Double Feature

The reason why it's important for roasted and sometimes grilled food to rest is to allow the juices to be reabsorbed into the fiber of the meat, thus making it juicier when sliced. During this period of resting, the internal temperature will continue to rise and finish the cooking process.

Pork Chops with Braised Red Cabbage

Apples and red currant jam add a sweet note to this savory winter dish.

Active time: 20 minutes

Start to finish: 60 minutes

Each serving has:

644 calories

201 calories from fat

22 g fat

11 g saturated fat

40 g protein

63 g carbohydrates

5 cups firmly packed shredded red cabbage

2 TB. red wine vinegar

2 TB. granulated sugar

4 (3-oz.) boneless pork loin chops, trimmed of fat, rinsed, and patted dry with paper towels

Salt and freshly ground black pepper to taste

2 TB. unsalted butter

1 large shallot, peeled and chopped

1 McIntosh or Golden Delicious apple, peeled and sliced

½ cup dry red wine

½ cup chicken stock

1 (3-in.) cinnamon stick

1 bay leaf

¼ cup red currant jelly

1. Place cabbage in a large bowl. Sprinkle with vinegar and sugar and toss. Sprinkle pork with salt and pepper.

2. Melt butter in an ovenproof Dutch oven over medium-high heat. Add pork chops and cook, turning with tongs, until browned on both sides. Remove pork chops with tongs and set aside.

3. Add shallot and apple and cook, stirring frequently, for 3 minutes or until shallot is translucent. Add wine, chicken stock, cinnamon stick, and bay leaf. Bring to a boil, and stir in cabbage with any juices from the bowl.

4. Add pork chops and cover them in cabbage, cover the Dutch oven, and cook over low heat for 30 to 45 minutes or until cabbage is tender. Remove pork chops and set aside. Remove and discard cinnamon stick and bay leaf, and stir jelly into cabbage. Cook, uncovered, over medium heat for 10 minutes or until liquid reduces in volume and becomes syrupy. Return pork chops to the Dutch oven and heat through. (You can do this up to two days in advance and refrigerate, tightly covered. Reheat over low heat until simmering.)

Déjà Two

Cabbage is one of the oldest vegetables in recorded history, although its stature has ranged from lowly to esteemed, depending on the culture. The Greek philosopher Diogenes remarked to a young man, "If you lived on cabbage, you would not be obliged to flatter the powerful." The young man's retort was, "If you flattered the powerful, you would not be obliged to live on cabbage."

Custard-Topped Greek Lamb and Eggplant (*Moussaka*)

Comfort food from the Greek tradition, with cinnamon flavoring the lamb's tomato sauce and dill scenting the creamy custard.

Active time: 30 minutes

Start to finish: 1¼ hours

Each serving has:

905 calories

542 calories from fat

60 g fat

24 g saturated fat

36.5 g protein

57 g carbohydrates

2 Italian eggplants

¼ cup vegetable oil

Salt and pepper

½ lb. ground lamb

⅓ cup olive oil

1 small onion, peeled and chopped

2 garlic cloves, peeled and minced

1 (8-oz.) can tomato sauce

¼ cup dry red wine

1 TB. chopped fresh parsley

1 TB. chopped fresh or 1 tsp. dried oregano

¼ tsp. ground cinnamon

2 TB. unsalted butter

2 TB. all-purpose flour

⅔ cup milk

1 large egg, lightly beaten

⅓ cup freshly grated Parmesan cheese

1 TB. chopped fresh dill or 1 tsp. dried

Freshly ground black pepper to taste

1. Preheat the oven to 400°F, cover a baking sheet with aluminum foil and grease a 9×5-inch loaf pan. Rinse and trim eggplants, and cut into ¼-inch slices. Spread vegetable oil on the baking sheet, and arrange eggplant slices, turning to coat both sides with oil. Sprinkle with salt and pepper. Bake eggplant for 15 to 20 minutes or until soft.

2. While eggplant is baking, heat a large skillet over medium-high heat. Add lamb, and cook until well browned, breaking up lumps with a fork. Remove from the skillet with a slotted spoon, and set aside. Discard fat.

3. Heat olive oil in the skillet, and add onion and garlic. Cook, stirring frequently, for 3 minutes or until onion is translucent. Return lamb to the skillet, and add tomato sauce, wine, parsley, oregano, and cinnamon.

4. Simmer, stirring occasionally, for about 20 minutes or until mixture thickens and is almost dry. (You can do this up to two days in advance and refrigerate, tightly covered. Before continuing, reheat over low heat until hot, stirring occasionally.)

5. Melt butter in a saucepan over low heat. Stir in flour, and stir constantly for 2 minutes. Whisk in milk, and simmer 2 minutes or until thick. Whisk a small amount of milk mixture into egg. Return egg-milk mixture to the saucepan. Bring to boil, whisking constantly to make custard. Remove from heat. Stir in ¼ cup Parmesan cheese and dill. Season to taste with salt and pepper.

6. Arrange ½ of eggplant slices in the bottom of the prepared pan. Spread meat mixture over eggplant. Top with remaining eggplant. Pour hot custard cheese sauce over eggplant. Sprinkle with remaining Parmesan cheese. Cover loosely with aluminum foil, and bake for 30 minutes. Remove foil and bake for an additional 10 minutes or until golden and bubbling on edges. Cool 5 minutes; then serve immediately.

Double Trouble

Although it might seem like a small step, whisking some of the hot liquid into the egg is crucial to the success of this dish or any dish done with an egg-enriched custard. It's called "tempering" the egg, and it makes the sauce smooth rather than like scrambled eggs.

Gratin of Veal with Wild Mushrooms and Onions

This elegant entrée is a variation on a French classic, with sautéed onions and luscious Gruyère cheese flavoring the delicate veal.

¼ **lb. fresh shiitake mushrooms**

½ **lb. veal scallops**

Salt and freshly ground black pepper to taste

2 TB. **unsalted butter**

2 **large onions, peeled and diced**

1 tsp. **granulated sugar**

1 TB. **olive oil**

⅔ **cup plain breadcrumbs**

⅔ **cup grated Gruyère**

½ **cup chicken stock**

½ **cup dry white wine**

Active time: 20 minutes	
Start to finish: 60 minutes	
Each serving has:	
755 calories	
395 calories from fat	
44 g fat	
21 g saturated fat	
43 g protein	
37 g carbohydrates	

1. Preheat the oven to 350°F. Wipe mushrooms with a damp paper towel. Discard stems and slice mushrooms. Pound veal scallops between two sheets of wax paper or plastic wrap to an even thickness of ⅛ inch. Sprinkle with salt and pepper and set aside.

2. Melt 1 tablespoon butter in a medium skillet over medium heat. Add onions and stir to coat well. Cover and cook over

low heat, stirring occasionally, for 10 minutes. Uncover, increase heat to medium-high, and sprinkle onions with salt and sugar. Cook, stirring frequently, for about 5 minutes or until onions are soft but not brown.

3. Scrape onions into a 12×7-inch *gratin* pan or a 9×9-inch baking dish. Heat remaining butter and oil in the skillet over medium-high heat. Add mushrooms, sprinkle lightly with salt and pepper, and cook, stirring frequently, for about 5 minutes or until mushrooms are soft and browned. Set aside.

4. Mix breadcrumbs with ½ cup Gruyère. Sprinkle ½ cup mixture on top of onions. Place overlapping veal slices on top of onions and crumbs. Firmly press remaining breadcrumb mixture into veal with a spatula, and then scatter mushrooms over veal. Sprinkle remaining Gruyère on top. (You can do this a day in advance and refrigerate, tightly covered. Add 10 minutes to initial bake time.) Pour stock and wine over all.

5. Cover the gratin pan with aluminum foil, and bake for 20 minutes. Remove foil and bake for an additional 20 minutes or until top is browned and veal is fork-tender. Serve immediately.

Variation: Substitute slices of turkey breast or pork tenderloin.

Duet Dialogue

Gratin (pronounced *grah-TAN*) is the French term for any dish topped with cheese and/or breadcrumbs and heated until it's brown and crispy. Gratin dishes are always cooked in a low, shallow dish to maximize their surface area; in fact, the pans known as gratin pans are typically shallow baking dishes with handles.

Part 6

The Second Time Around: Luscious Leftovers

The cliché of avoiding reinventing the wheel also applies to cooking. Often it's nice to know you've got the basis for a second meal waiting at home, and it isn't a rerun of the night before. That's how the chapters in this part work together.

In the first chapter you learn everything there is to know about roasting foods, from the perfect herbed chicken to an elegant rack of lamb. You'll also learn about roasting large fillets of fish so that they're moist and succulent.

And then comes the next step in a chapter titled "The Second Time Around." Here you'll find recipes for everything from an all-American chicken pot pie to Moroccan fish pies.

Reveling in Roasts

In This Chapter

- ◆ Perfect poultry
- ◆ Seafood savvy
- ◆ Marvelous meats

The sight of a rosy red rib roast, an elegant rack of lamb with a browned crust of mustard and bread crumbs, or the perfect roast chicken is the epitome of the celebratory dinner. And these are the recipes you'll find in this chapter.

Roasting doesn't have to take all day, however. You can cook roasted sides of fish or thin pork tenderloins in less than 30 minutes.

You'll notice that a most of the recipes in this chapter are annotated that they make four servings. Oh, you say "but this book is titled "Cooking for Two." The reason is that the leftovers from these meals for four are what you'll use when making some of the delicious dishes in Chapter 19.

Regarding Roasting

Roasting, as we use the term, is really oven baking, not roasting in the classic fashion by turning the meat on a spit of the fire. Roasting depends on the air in the oven to transfer heat from the oven walls that are heated by the gas flame or electric heating element.

Air is an inefficient heat carrier when compared to water or oil, so regardless of what temperature the oven is set, it will take the meat a long time to have that heat transferred by the air to the fibers and cook them.

The key equipment needs for a roast are a low-sided baking pan and an instant-read meat thermometer. Place the roast in the pan so that it has three inches of space on all sides. If the pan is too large, the juices will burn during cooking. If it is too small or too deep, the meat will steam rather than roast.

Insert the instant-read thermometer into the center of the meat an equal distance from both ends. Leave it in for 20 seconds, and then take the reading.

Poultry Pointers

Be it a small rock Cornish hen or a turkey for a tribe, a bird is a bird, and certain rules apply. Here's a quick guide:

- Preparing bird for roasting: all roasted poultry is far easier to carve if the wishbone has been removed. Also cut off the wing tips, and save them for stock, as they will burn before the bird is roasted.

- Trussing: tie the wings to the body by pushing a needle through the bird at the knees, where the leg joins the body. The second tie is to push the needle through the ends of the drumsticks and the tip of the breast bone in the middle. When you wrap the string around the back of the chicken and pull it taut, the cavity naturally closes.

- Carving: to add a flourish to carving that also assures crisp skin for all, first "unwrap" the breast. Use a well-sharpened knife and fork, and carve and serve one side at a time. From the neck, cut just through the skin down the middle of the breast and around the side. Hook your fork on the skin at the tail and roll the skin back to the neck. Holding the bird with the fork, remove the leg by severing hip joint. Separate the drumstick from the thigh and serve. Cut thin slices of breast at a slight angle, and add a small piece of rolled skin to each serving. Repeat all steps for other side. Remove the wings last.

Meaty Matters

It's a good rule of thumb that the further a cut of meat is from the animal's hoof or horn, the more tender it will be. The muscles in the legs and shoulders of an animal are far more developed than those around its sides.

For all animals, the loin, tenderloin and rib sections are the most tender and the ones that you should roast. Roasting the shoulder of young animals, such as veal or pork, is fine, but not for beef or lamb.

Time Out

Bring meat to room temperature before roasting, and when you take it out of the refrigerator, rub it with salt and pepper, as well as with herbs, garlic, or other flavorings so that as the meat warms, it will be absorbing flavor.

For any roast to reach room temperature takes at least three hours, and up to six hours for a piece more than five inches high. Bringing meat to room temperature is one job that you can do efficiently in the microwave.

Microwave meat on the defrost setting or LOW (20 percent power). If using the defrost setting, enter into the microwave half the weight of the meat; if using the LOW setting it should be at room temperature in two to five minutes depending on the size. Repeat in one minute intervals until it reaches room temperature.

Timing Is Everything

While most cookbooks calculate roasting times in an equation of minutes per pound, I use a different method. I roast meats by the circumference.

There is little variation in the density of different meats, and all are roasted using the same method. What makes the difference in the roasting times is how well done the meat should be. Pork is also medium rare at 130°F, but we eat pork at a far higher temperature.

Beef and lamb are both roasted along a sliding scale from rare to medium. Since cuts of both meats to be roasted are intended to be removed from the oven at the same temperature, they can be treated equally; many people prefer lamb at 130°F rather than 125°F.

To measure boneless roasts: The easiest way to calculate the circumference of a roast is with a tape measure. Stand the roast on its end, and place the tape measure snugly around what would be the waist line.

To measure standing rib roast: Stand the roast on its bones with the fatty top of the roast up. Measure the thickness of the roast from side to side, and then measure the height from the top of the bone to the top of the roast. Add those figures and multiply by 2. So if a rib is 3 inches wide and 5 inches high, the circumference equivalent is 16 inches.

Roasting Temperature for Meat

Meat	Desired Internal Temperature
Beef and Lamb	120°F—Rare 125 to 130°F—Medium Rare 135°F—Medium 145°F—Medium Well 155°F—Well Done
Pork	145 to 150°F
Veal	150 to 155°F

Roasting times for meats: These are total times for boneless roasts, with the first 15 minutes roasted at 450°F, and the oven then turned down to 350°F for the remainder of the roasting. If cooking a standing rib roast or another cut with a similar bone structure, add 5 to 7 minutes to the time listed to compensate.

Circumference	Beef/Lamb (125°F)	Veal (150°F)	Pork (145°F)
9-inches	30 to 35 min.	50 to 55 min.	55 to 60 min.
10-inches	35 to 45 min.	55 to 65 min.	60 to 70 min.
11-inches	45 to 50 min.	65 to 70 min.	75 to 85 min.
12-inches	55 to 60 min.	70 to 75 min.	85 to 95 min.
13-inches	60 to 65 min.	75 to 85 min.	95 to 105 min.
14-inches	70 to 75 min.	85 to 95 min.	105 to 115 min.
15-inches	75 to 80 min.	95 to 110 min.	115 to 125 min.
16-inches	80 to 90 min.	110 to 115 min.	125 to 130 min.

Aromatic Roast Chicken

A perfect roast chicken is a work of art, and one everyone can appreciate!

1 (3½- to 4-lb.) chicken, giblets removed

4 sprigs fresh parsley

4 sprigs fresh rosemary

6 garlic cloves, peeled

1 orange, quartered

Salt and freshly ground black pepper to taste

4 TB. unsalted butter, softened

1 small onion, peeled and roughly chopped

1 carrot, peeled and thickly sliced

1 celery rib, rinsed, trimmed, and roughly chopped

1 cup chicken stock

Serves: 4
Active time: 15 minutes
Start to finish: 2 hours
Each serving has:
711 calories
312 calories from fat
35 g fat
14 g saturated fat
5 g protein
10 g carbohydrates

1. Preheat the oven to 450°F. Rinse chicken, and pat dry with paper towels. Place 2 sprigs each of parsley and rosemary, 3 garlic cloves and orange in cavity of chicken. Sprinkle salt and pepper inside cavity.

2. Chop remaining parsley, rosemary, and garlic, and mix with butter. Season to taste with salt and pepper. Gently stuff mixture under skin of breast meat. Rub skin with salt and pepper. Truss chicken as detailed above, and place it on a rack in a roasting pan.

3. Bake for 30 minutes, reduce the heat to 350°F and add onion, carrot, and celery to the roasting pan. Cook an additional 1 to 1¼ hours or until juices run clear and the temperature of the dark meat is 180°F on an instant-read thermometer. Remove chicken from the oven, and allow it to rest on a heated platter for 10 minutes.

4. Spoon all grease out of the pan, and add stock. Stir over medium-high heat until liquid is reduced to a syrupy consistency. Strain sauce into a sauce boat, and add to it any liquid that accumulates on the platter when chicken is carved. Discard trussing string and carve chicken. Serve immediately.

Variation: Substitute tarragon for rosemary and parsley, and use white wine instead of chicken stock.

 Double Feature

Even if you don't want to serve a sauce with roasted food, it's still a good idea to deglaze the roasting pan. It makes it easier to clean.

Greek-Style Roast Chicken

The lemon, oregano, and garlic marinade gives this easy recipe it's distinctive flavor—and it's flavor without fuss.

Serves: 4

Active time: 15 minutes

Start to finish: 6 hours, including 4 hours for marinating

Each serving has:

667 calories

292 calories from fat

32.5 g fat

9 g saturated fat

89 g protein

4 g carbohydrates

1 (3½- to 4-lb.) chicken, giblets removed	6 garlic cloves, peeled and minced
½ cup dry white wine	3 TB. dried oregano
½ cup extra-virgin olive oil	1 TB. grated lemon zest
Juice of 2 lemons	Salt and freshly ground black pepper to taste

1. Rinse chicken, and pat dry with paper towels. Combine wine, oil, lemon juice, garlic, oregano, salt, and pepper in a jumbo resealable plastic bag and mix well. Add chicken, making sure marinade enters cavity, and marinate for at least 2 hours at room temperature or up to 6 hours, refrigerated, turning the bag occasionally.

2. Preheat the oven to 450°F. Remove chicken from marinade and discard marinade. Truss chicken as detailed above, and place it on a rack in a roasting pan.

3. Bake chicken for 30 minutes, reduce the heat to 350°F and cook for an additional 1 to 1¼ hours or until juices run clear and the temperature of the dark meat is 180°F on an instant-read thermometer. Remove chicken from the oven, and allow it to rest on a heated platter for 10 minutes. Discard trussing string and carve chicken. Serve immediately.

Double Feature

If you don't have any kitchen string for trussing poultry, improvise. Make some long "ropes" from rolled up aluminum foil, and tie the bird together with the foil.

Herb-Roasted Turkey Breast

Spreading the herbed butter under the turkey's skin makes it possible for the delicious flavors to permeate the meat.

1 (2- to 2.5-lb.) turkey breast half	1 TB. chopped fresh rosemary or 1 tsp. dried
6 TB. unsalted butter, softened	1 TB. fresh thyme or 1 tsp. dried
¼ cup chopped fresh parsley	Salt and freshly ground black pepper to taste
3 garlic cloves, peeled and minced	⅓ cup chicken stock or turkey stock
3 TB. chopped fresh sage or 1 TB. dried	

Serves: 4

Active time: 10 minutes

Start to finish: 1 hour, including 10 minutes for resting

Each serving has:

498 calories

281 calories from fat

31 g fat

14 g saturated fat

50 g protein

1 g carbohydrates

1. Preheat the oven to 450°F and line a roasting pan with aluminum foil. Rinse turkey and pat dry with paper towels.

2. Combine 4 tablespoons butter, parsley, garlic, sage, rosemary, thyme, salt, and pepper in a small mixing bowl. Stir well. Run your fingers underneath turkey skin, and spread butter mixture evenly over breast. Sprinkle skin with salt and pepper, place turkey in roasting pan, and pour stock into bottom of the roasting pan.

3. Cover the pan with foil, crimping it at the edges to seal it tightly. Bake breast for 30 minutes. While breast is baking, melt remaining butter. Remove the pan from the oven, and remove foil. Reduce the oven temperature to 375°F, and baste turkey with melted butter. Return turkey to the oven and bake for an additional 20 to 30 minutes or until cooked through, juices run clear, and an instant-read thermometer registers 170°F. Remove turkey and allow it to rest for 10 minutes.

4. While turkey is resting, pour juices from the roasting pan into a small saucepan. *Skim* fat from surface, and season juices to taste with salt and pepper. Carve turkey, spoon juices over meat, and serve immediately.

Variation: To give the turkey a southwestern flavor substitute cilantro for the parsley, omit the sage, rosemary, and thyme, and add 3 tablespoons chili powder and 1 tablespoon ground cumin to butter.

Duet Dialogue

To **skim** means to remove the top layer of fat from a liquid. While it can be used to describe the process of spooning off the cream that rises to the top of milk, it's most often used to describe the process of spooning fat from stocks and gravies.

Mock Peking Duck

This is perhaps the most elegant Asian dish you could make, although the extensive marinating does require some advance planning.

Serves: 4

Active time: 25 minutes

Start to finish: 16½ hours, including 12 hours for marinating

Each serving has:

1074 calories

457 calories from fat

51 g fat

15 g saturated fat

91 g protein

54 g carbohydrates

Déjà Two

This dish is "mock" because authentic Peking duck is difficult to find even in Chinese restaurants. The process begins by air being pumped between the duck's skin and flesh. After that the duck is coated with a honey mixture similar to this marinade and hung to dry until the skin is hard. Only then is it roasted.

1 (4- to 4½-lb.) duck

6 scallions, rinsed and trimmed

1 cup hoisin sauce

½ cup soy sauce

¼ cup Asian sesame oil

¼ cup dry sherry

3 garlic cloves, peeled and minced

1 TB. grated fresh ginger

8 scallions, rinsed and trimmed

8 Chinese pancakes or flour tortillas

½ cup plum sauce (or additional hoisin sauce)

1. Rinse duck and pat dry with paper towels. Prepare duck by pulling out all fat from cavity, but do not cut off neck skin. Chop 2 scallions, including 3-inches of green tops. Cut remaining scallions into julienne slices 4-inches long, and refrigerate, tightly covered.

2. Combine chopped scallions, hoisin sauce, soy sauce, sesame oil, sherry, garlic, and ginger in a jumbo resealable plastic bag, and blend well. Add duck, making sure marinade enters duck cavity, and marinate for at least 12 hours and preferably 24 hours, turning the bag occasionally. Drain duck, reserving the marinade.

3. Preheat the oven to 275°F. Pour marinade into a small saucepan, and bring to a boil over medium-high heat. Reduce heat to low, and simmer marinade for 5 minutes. Place duck on a rack in a roasting pan breast side down. Roast duck for 2½ hours, then turn it breast side up and roast for another 1½ to 2 hours or until the leg moves easily in its socket. Brush duck with marinade every 20 minutes.

4. To serve, remove skin from breast and neck, and slice into 1-inch strips. Carve meat and arrange on a warm platter. Garnish the platter with scallion slices, and serve with warm Chinese pancakes. Brush plum sauce on pancakes, and then fill with crispy skin, meat, and scallions.

Oven-Roasted Salmon

Oven-roasting keeps the delicate salmon moist and the high oven temperature makes it possible to have this dish on the table in minutes.

1 (2- to 2.5-lb.) side salmon

¼ cup olive oil

Salt and freshly ground black pepper to taste

2 garlic cloves, peeled and minced

3 TB. chopped fresh parsley

1 TB. Herbes de Provence

Serves: 4
Active time: 5 minutes
Start to finish: 22 minutes
Each serving has:
400 calories
204 calories from fat
23 g fat
3 g saturated fat
45 g protein
1 g carbohydrates

1. Preheat the oven to 425°F, and line a baking sheet with aluminum foil. Rinse salmon and pat dry with paper towels; it is not necessary to remove skin from salmon. Combine olive oil, salt, pepper, garlic, parsley, and Herbes de Provence in a small bowl. Stir well and rub mixture on top of salmon.

2. Bake salmon for 12 to 15 minutes or until cooked through but still slightly translucent in the center. Allow salmon to rest for 5 minutes; then serve immediately.

Variation: Substitute thick fillets of cod or halibut.

Double Feature

Overcooking is a common problem with fish, so the larger the piece the more it's important to allow the residual heat to finish the cooking process. The five minutes the salmon rests will allow the fish to finish cooking.

Herb-Crusted Roast Cod

The breadcrumb coating creates a crunchy texture to serve as a foil to the tender cod as well as enhancing its flavor.

Serves: 4

Active time: 10 minutes

Start to finish: 25 minutes

Each serving has:

348 calories

127 calories from fat

14 g fat

8 g saturated fat

44 g protein

9.5 g carbohydrates

2 (1-lb.) thick cod fillets

Salt and freshly ground black pepper to taste

½ cup Italian breadcrumbs

¼ cup unsalted butter, melted

¼ cup chopped fresh parsley

¼ cup freshly grated Parmesan cheese

1 TB. fresh thyme or 1 tsp. dried

2 tsp. grated lemon *zest*

1. Preheat the oven to 425°F and line a 9×13-inch baking pan with aluminum foil. Rinse cod and pat dry with paper towels. Sprinkle with salt and pepper, and place fillets into the baking pan.

2. Combine breadcrumbs, butter, parsley, Parmesan cheese, thyme, and lemon zest in a small bowl. Pat topping onto fish.

3. Bake fish for 10 to 12 minutes or until cooked through but still slightly translucent in the center. Allow cod to rest for 5 minutes; then serve immediately.

Variation: Substitute sea bass, halibut, swordfish, or salmon.

Duet Dialogue

Zest is the outermost layer of the skin of citrus fruits, where all the aromatic oils are located. But remove only the colored portion because the white pith beneath it is very bitter.

Asian Pork Tenderloin

Fragrant papaya and tangy pineapple juice add an exotic note to this marinated pork dish.

1 (12 to 16-oz.) pork tenderloin

½ cup diced papaya

⅓ cup soy sauce

¼ cup pineapple juice

6 scallions, rinsed, trimmed, and cut into 1-inch sections

¼ cup loosely packed fresh cilantro leaves

3 garlic cloves, peeled

2 TB. fresh ginger

2 TB. honey

2 TB. rice vinegar

1 TB. Asian sesame oil

1 TB. red pepper flakes

1 tsp. Chinese five-spice powder

1 TB. vegetable oil

Active time: 15 minutes
Start to finish: 1½ hours, including 1 hour for marinating
Each serving has:
487 calories
184 calories from fat
20.5 g fat
4 g saturated fat
41 g protein
37 g carbohydrates

1. Rinse pork and pat dry with paper towels. Trim off all visible fat and iridescent silverskin. Tuck thin tail under pork to form a cylinder of even size, and tie tail section with kitchen string or pin it with wooden toothpicks.

2. Combine papaya, soy sauce, pineapple juice, scallions, cilantro, garlic, ginger, honey, vinegar, sesame oil, red pepper flakes, and five-spice powder in a food processor fitted with a steel blade or in a blender. Purée until smooth. Transfer mixture to a heavy resealable plastic bag, and add pork. Marinate for at least one hour at room temperature or up to eight hours refrigerated, turning the bag occasionally. Remove pork from marinade, discard marinade and pat pork dry with paper towels.

3. Preheat the oven to 425°F, and line a 9×13-inch baking pan with aluminum foil. Heat oil in a heavy large skillet over high heat. Sear pork on all sides, turning gently with tongs, for 3 minutes or until browned. Remove pork from the pan, and transfer to a 9×13-inch baking dish.

4. Roast pork for 10 to 15 minutes or until an instant-read thermometer registers 145°F. Allow pork to rest for 5 minutes. Then slice and serve immediately.

Variation: Substitute boneless, skinless chicken breast halves pounded to an even thickness of ½-inch.

Double Feature

Always save the papaya skin when you're cooking with papaya and add it to the marinade. The skin contains an enzyme that tenderizes meat.

Beer-Basted Rib Eye Roast

This is a dish for special occasions, and the beer becomes part of the sauce as well as keeping the roast moist during cooking.

Serves: 4

Active time: 15 minutes

Start to finish: At least 1 hour, depending on thickness

Each serving has:

855 calories

411 calories from fat

46 g fat

18 g saturated fat

96 g protein

7 g carbohydrates

 **Double Feature**

A rib-eye roast is a standing rib roast that has been taken off the bone and tied. It's an incredibly tender cut of beef with more flavor and marbling than a tenderloin.

1 (3-lb.) boneless rib eye roast, at room temperature

4 garlic cloves, peeled

¼ cup soy sauce

Freshly ground black pepper to taste

1 onion, peeled and diced

1 (12-oz.) bottle dark stout beef

½ cup beef stock

1. Preheat the oven to 450°F. Cut each garlic clove into 6 long slivers. Cut slits 1-inch deep into roast at regular intervals and insert garlic into slits. Rub soy sauce over all sides of roast, and rub pepper into roast. Transfer roast to the pan, and scatter onions around it.

2. Bake for 30 minutes, basting every 10 minutes with beer, then reduce the heat to 350°F, and roast for additional time according to the chart above; continue to baste every 10 minutes. Remove roast from the oven when an instant-read thermometer registers 120°F for rare or cook to desired doneness. Allow roast to rest for 10 minutes, loosely covered with aluminum foil.

3. Skim fat from the roasting pan and discard. Add remaining beer and stock to the pan. Place the pan over medium-high heat and deglaze by stirring to dislodge the brown bits on the bottom of the pan. Simmer for 2 minutes and season to taste with salt and pepper.

4. To serve, carve beef and spoon some of pan juices over slices.

Variation: Substitute red wine for beer.

Mustard-Crusted Rack of Lamb

A rack of lamb is the perfect size for two people, and this easy coating makes it even more elegant when it comes to the table.

1 (1½-lb.) rack of lamb, trimmed	**3 garlic cloves, peeled and minced**
Salt and freshly ground black pepper to taste	**¼ cup Italian breadcrumbs**
1 TB. vegetable oil	**2 TB. freshly grated Parmesan cheese**
2 TB. Dijon mustard	**1 TB. chopped fresh rosemary**

> **Active time:** 12 minutes
>
> **Start to finish:** 25 minutes
>
> **Each serving has:**
>
> 611 calories
>
> 238 calories from fat
>
> 26 g fat
>
> 8 g saturated fat
>
> 77 g protein
>
> 14.5 g carbohydrates

1. Preheat the oven to 450°F and line a 9×13-inch baking pan with aluminum foil. Season lamb well on all sides with salt and pepper. Heat oil in a large skillet over high heat. Add lamb and brown well on all sides. Transfer lamb to the baking pan.

2. Spread mustard evenly over all sides of lamb. Combine garlic, breadcrumbs, Parmesan cheese, and rosemary in a small bowl. Press mixture onto top of lamb with your hands.

3. Bake lamb for 13 to 15 minutes for medium rare. Allow lamb to rest for 5 minutes; then carve into individual chops. Serve immediately.

Double Feature

Most racks of lamb are trimmed when you buy them, but if they aren't, here's the method. Cut between the rib bones and scrape the meat off, exposing the bottom few inches of bone. Make sure the rack is cut through at the thick end so you can carve off the individual chops.

Roast Veal with Lemon and Garlic

This recipe is a variation on the classic French Chicken with Forty Cloves of Garlic; the garlic should be popped out of the skin before eating the cloves.

Serves: 4

Active time: 15 minutes

Start to finish: 55 minutes

Each serving has:

534 calories

263 calories from fat

29 g fat

8 g saturated fat

61 g protein

4 g carbohydrates

1 (2-lb.) boneless veal loin roast, at room temperature

Salt and freshly ground black pepper to taste

¼ cup olive oil

2 heads garlic, separated into unpeeled cloves

2 cups chicken stock

½ cup freshly squeezed lemon juice

1. Preheat the oven to 450°F. Rinse veal and pat dry with paper towels. Heat olive oil in a roasting pan over medium-high heat. Add veal and brown on all sides, turning gently with tongs. Add garlic when veal is half browned and brown garlic as well.

2. Pour stock and lemon juice into roasting pan. Roast for 30 minutes or until an instant-read thermometer registers 145°F, turning veal over after 15 minutes. Remove veal from the oven, and allow it to rest for 10 minutes loosely covered with aluminum foil.

3. While veal is resting, tilt roasting pan and skim off any fat. Place pan over medium-high heat, and reduce sauce until it's thick enough to coat the back of a spoon. Season to taste with salt and pepper.

4. To serve, carve veal and scatter cooked garlic cloves over slices. Top slices with sauce.

Variation: Substitute boned chicken breasts with the skin on. Start them skin side down and then turn them over after 10 minutes and continue to bake with the skin side up for 20 minutes or until an instant-read thermometer registers 160°F and the chicken is cooked through and no longer pink.

Double Feature

Don't be frightened by the amount of garlic. It becomes incredibly sweet and nutty when it's sautéed and then braised in the stock.

Chapter 19

The Second Time Around

In This Chapter

- ◆ Poultry panoply
- ◆ Fish favorites
- ◆ Hearty hash

Leftovers are the reruns of the food world. And although the first viewing may have been riveting, the ending is predictable the second time around. But another way to look at the situation is to plan for the leftovers, and that's what you were doing when you cooked most of the recipes in Chapter 18—anticipating that you had the essential ingredient for another meal.

So check out the recipes in this chapter. They are fast to make and drawn from a variety of cuisines. And because the protein is already cooked, it becomes just another ingredient rather than central to the cooking process.

Poultry Panacea

Some of these recipes are written for chicken and others for turkey, but use the different birds interchangeably. If you have leftovers and don't plan to use them within a few days, cut them up and freeze them. You can use frozen cooked poultry for up to three months.

To defrost cut cooked poultry in a microwave oven is very quick, or you can toss the contents of the freezer bag into a dish frozen if there's a sauce simmering in which it can thaw.

Let's say you're craving a recipe in this chapter but don't have any cooked poultry on hand. Don't fret. A supermarket rotisserie chicken yields about three to four cups of shredded meat, so you're all set.

In addition to rotisserie chickens, many supermarkets also carry preroasted chickens and turkey breasts in the poultry refrigerator cases. Many also carry precooked, presliced chicken. These packages set the standard for convenience, but it's convenience you pay for on an ounce-by-ounce basis.

These recipes are very tolerant of substitutions, but keep one important caveat in mind: *do not use raw chicken or turkey in any of these recipes.* They were not formulated to cook the poultry sufficiently to make it safe, and because raw poultry gives off liquid into a dish, you will not be happy with the soupy results.

Cutting Up

You'll notice that some of these recipes specify shredded food while others have you cutting it into cubes. There is a rationale for this. In some dishes, the smaller shreds are preferable because they better absorb the sauce, and if a dish is layered, you can't see the difference. Shredding, because you can do it with your (clean, freshly washed) hands, is also faster.

But there are times, such as in the chicken pot pie, that the pieces are more visible in the finished dish. So to make it more aesthetically pleasing, these recipes call for you to dice or cube the meat or fish. But if you're low on time, shredding will work just fine.

Chicken Croquettes

These crispy patties are given more flavor than most by adding Cajun seasoning.

2 TB. unsalted butter

1 shallot, peeled and finely chopped

½ cup all-purpose flour

⅓ cup milk

⅓ cup chicken stock

Salt and freshly ground black pepper to taste

1½ cups finely chopped cooked chicken

1 TB. chopped fresh parsley

2 tsp. Cajun seasoning

1 large egg, lightly beaten

1 TB. water

½ cup breadcrumbs

1½ cups vegetable oil

Active time: 30 minutes
Start to finish: 45 minutes
Each serving has:
979 calories
682 calories from fat
76 g fat
18 g saturated fat
43 g protein
35 g carbohydrates

1. Heat butter in a small saucepan over medium heat. Add shallot and cook, stirring frequently, for 2 minutes. Add 3 tablespoons flour, reduce the heat to low, and cook for 2 minutes, stirring constantly. Whisk in milk and stock and bring to a boil over medium heat, whisking constantly. Reduce the heat to low and simmer sauce for 2 minutes. Season sauce to taste with salt and pepper.

2. Stir chicken, parsley, and Cajun seasoning into sauce and transfer mixture to a 9×13-inch baking pan. Spread mixture evenly, and refrigerate for 15 minutes or until cold, loosely covered with plastic wrap.

3. Place remaining flour on a sheet of plastic wrap, combine egg and water in a shallow bowl and place breadcrumbs on another sheet of plastic wrap. With wet hands form mixture into balls the size of golf balls, then flatten them to a thickness of ¾-inch. Dust patties with flour, dip into egg mixture, and dip into breadcrumbs, pressing to ensure crumbs adhere. (You can do this up to a day in advance and refrigerate, tightly covered with plastic wrap. Fry just prior to serving.)

4. Heat oil in a saucepan over medium-high heat to 375°F. Add patties, being careful not to crowd the pan. Cook patties for 3 minutes or until browned. Turn gently with a slotted spatula, and cook the second side. Remove from the pan with a slotted spatula and drain well on paper towels. Serve immediately.

Variation: Substitute turkey, ham, or a fish, like salmon or cod.

Double Feature

As a general rule, the thinner the layer of food the faster it chills. That's why you transfer this croquette mixture to a baking pan rather than chilling it in a saucepan. For large quantities of liquid like soups or stews, portion them into pint and quart containers to speed chilling.

Old-Fashioned American Chicken Pot Pie

Ah, chicken with vegetables in a tarragon flavored cream sauce topped with flaky puff pastry. This dish is the epitome of comfort food.

Active time: 30 minutes

Start to finish: 65 minutes

Each serving has:

730 calories

397 calories from fat

44 g fat

20 g saturated fat

46 g protein

39 g carbohydrates

¼ lb. white mushrooms

3 TB. unsalted butter

1 TB. olive oil

2 shallots, peeled and minced

1 garlic clove, peeled and minced

½ cup chicken stock

1 small carrot, peeled and thinly sliced

1 celery rib, rinsed, trimmed, and thinly sliced

1 (5-oz.) red-skinned potato, scrubbed and cut into ½-inch dice

2 tsp. fresh chopped tarragon or ½ tsp. dried

1 tsp. fresh thyme or ½ tsp. dried

1 bay leaf

½ cup frozen peas, not thawed

2 TB. all-purpose flour

½ cup half-and-half

Salt and freshly ground black pepper to taste

1½ cups cooked chicken, cut into ½-inch dice

½ sheet frozen puff pastry (¼ of a 17-oz. pkg.), thawed

1 large egg

1 TB. milk

1. Preheat the oven to 375°F. Grease a 5×9-inch loaf pan. Wipe mushrooms with a damp paper towel. Discard stems and slice mushrooms. Set aside.

2. Heat 1 tablespoon butter and olive oil in a medium skillet over medium-high heat. Add shallots and garlic and cook, stirring frequently, for 3 minutes or until shallots are translucent.

3. Add mushrooms to the skillet and cook for 2 minutes or until mushrooms begin to soften. Add stock, carrot, celery, potato, tarragon, thyme, and bay leaf. Bring to a boil, reduce heat to low, and simmer, uncovered, for 8 to 10 minutes or until potato is tender. Add peas and cook 2 minutes. Strain mixture, reserving stock. Remove and discard bay leaf, and transfer vegetables to the prepared baking pan.

4. Heat remaining butter in a saucepan over low heat. Stir in flour, and stir constantly for 2 minutes. Whisk in reserved stock, and bring to a boil over medium-high heat, whisking constantly. Add half-and-half and simmer 2 minutes. Season to taste with salt and pepper. Add chicken to the baking pan with vegetables, and stir in sauce. (You can do this a day in advance and refrigerate, tightly covered. Before continuing, reheat in a microwave oven or in a saucepan over low heat, stirring frequently.)

4. Roll puff pastry into a 7×11-inch rectangle. Beat egg lightly with milk to make egg wash. Brush egg mixture around outside edge of the baking pan. Place pastry on top of the pan, and crimp edges, pressing to seal pastry to the sides of the pan. Brush pastry with egg mixture, and cut 6 (1-inch) vents in pastry to allow steam to escape.

5. Bake for 35 minutes or until pastry is golden brown. Serve immediately.

Variation: Substitute cubes of fish, ham, or roast beef.

Double Trouble

The purpose of an egg wash is to give pastry a browned and shiny crust. But it's important to brush the crust before cutting the steam vents because the egg wash can clog the vents, which will create a soggy crust.

Turkey with Sage Cornbread Dumplings

The dumplings on top of this simmering stew have the same wonderful flavor as cornbread stuffing.

Active time: 20 minutes

Start to finish: 45 minutes

Each serving has:

730 calories

345 calories from fat

38 g fat

19 g saturated fat

41 g protein

54.5 g carbohydrates

3 TB. unsalted butter

1 TB. olive oil

1 small onion, peeled and chopped

1 garlic clove, peeled and minced

1 carrot, peeled and thinly sliced

1 celery rib, rinsed, trimmed, and thinly sliced

2 TB. dry vermouth or dry white wine

1 TB. all-purpose flour

½ cup turkey stock or chicken stock

½ cup half-and-half

2 TB. chopped fresh sage or 2 tsp. dried

1 TB. chopped fresh rosemary or 1 tsp. dried

Salt and freshly ground black pepper to taste

1½ cups cooked turkey, cut into ½-inch cubes

½ cup frozen peas, thawed

¼ cup all-purpose flour

¼ cup yellow cornmeal

½ tsp. baking soda

⅛ tsp. baking powder

⅓ cup buttermilk

1. For turkey, melt 1 tablespoon butter and olive oil in a medium skillet over medium-high heat. Add onion, garlic, carrot, and celery and cook, stirring frequently, for 3 minutes or until onion is translucent. Add vermouth and cook stirring occasionally, for 2 minutes or until wine is almost evaporated. Set aside.

2. Melt 1 tablespoon butter in a small saucepan over low heat. Stir in flour, and stir constantly for 2 minutes. Whisk in stock and bring to a boil over medium-high heat, whisking constantly. Simmer for 3 minutes; then add half-and-half, 1 tablespoon sage, and rosemary. Simmer for 2 minutes, season to taste with salt and pepper, and stir sauce, turkey, and peas into vegetable mixture in the skillet. (You can do this a day in advance and refrigerate, tightly covered. Reheat over low heat to a simmer before continuing.)

3. For dumplings, combine flour, cornmeal, baking soda, baking powder, ½ teaspoon salt, pepper, and remaining sage in a mixing bowl. Cut remaining 1 tablespoon butter into small pieces. Cut in butter using pastry blender, two knives, or your fingertips until mixture resembles coarse meal. Add buttermilk, stirring just enough so the dough holds together. (You can do this up to 30 minutes in advance and keep at room temperature.)

4. Drop 6 to 8 mounds of dough onto top of simmering turkey in the skillet, about 2 inches apart. Reduce the heat to low, cover, and cook without removing the lid for 15 to 18 minutes or until dumplings are dry on top and have puffed. Serve immediately.

Double Trouble _____

The chemical leavening agents in batters and doughs made with baking powder and baking soda are not tolerant to advance preparation of more than 30 minutes or so. They will expand right in the bowl rather than when cooked, and you'll end up with dumplings with the texture of golf balls.

Turkey Tetrazzini

Pasta, mushrooms, and turkey in a sherry-laced cream sauce are a winning combination that's kept this dish popular for almost a century.

¼ lb. white mushrooms

⅓ lb. spaghetti, broken into 2-inch lengths

2 TB. unsalted butter

1 TB. olive oil

1 shallot, peeled and minced

1 garlic clove, peeled and minced

1 celery rib, rinsed, trimmed, and thinly sliced

2 TB. all-purpose flour

¼ cup medium dry sherry

½ cup turkey stock or chicken stock

½ cup half-and-half

1½ cups shredded turkey

⅔ cup freshly grated Parmesan cheese

Salt and freshly ground black pepper to taste

¼ cup breadcrumbs

Active time: 25 minutes
Start to finish: 50 minutes
Each serving has:
910 calories
340 calories from fat
38 g fat
17.5 g saturated fat
53 g protein
81 g carbohydrates

1. Preheat the oven to 350°F. Grease a 9×9-inch baking pan. Wipe mushrooms with a damp paper towel. Discard stems and slice mushrooms. Set aside. Bring a large pot of salted water to a boil and cook spaghetti according to package directions until al dente. Drain and place in the prepared baking pan.

2. Heat 1 tablespoon butter and olive oil in a large skillet over medium-high heat. Add shallot, garlic, and celery, and cook, stirring frequently, for 3 minutes or until shallot is translucent. Add mushrooms and cook for 3 minutes or until mushrooms are soft. Add to the baking pan with spaghetti.

3. Heat remaining butter in a saucepan over low heat. Stir in flour, and stir constantly for 2 minutes. Whisk in sherry, and bring to a boil over medium-high heat, whisking constantly. Simmer for 2 minutes; then add turkey stock and half-and-half, and simmer. Add ⅓ cup Parmesan cheese, and season to taste with salt and pepper. Add mixture to pasta and vegetables in the baking pan. (You can do this a day in advance and refrigerate, tightly covered. Add 15 minutes to initial bake time.)

4. Cover the baking pan with aluminum foil and bake for 15 minutes. Combine remaining ⅓ cup Parmesan cheese with breadcrumbs. Remove foil, sprinkle breadcrumb mixture on top, and bake for an additional 15 to 20 minutes or until bubbly and top is browned. Serve immediately.

Déjà Two

This grandmother of all leftover poultry casseroles was named for Italian singer Luisa Tetrazzini, who was the toast of the American opera circuit in the early 1900s. Where the dish was created and by whom is not known.

Cold Turkey with Tuna Sauce (Turkey *Tonnato*)

Keep the turkey cold and nap the slices with a flavorful sauce made with a pantry staple, canned tuna.

1 (6.5-oz.) tuna packed in olive oil, undrained

1 TB. anchovy paste

½ cup mayonnaise

2 TB. extra-virgin olive oil

2 TB. half-and-half

1 TB. freshly squeezed lemon juice

2 TB. capers, drained and rinsed

1 TB. chopped fresh parsley

Freshly ground black pepper to taste

½ lb. thinly sliced cooked turkey

Active time: 10 minutes
Start to finish: 25 minutes, including 15 minutes for chilling
Each serving has:
918 calories
678 calories from fat
75 g fat
13 g saturated fat
55.5 g protein
1.4 g carbohydrates

1. Combine tuna, anchovy paste, mayonnaise, olive oil, half-and-half, and lemon juice in a blender. Purée until smooth. Scrape mixture into a mixing bowl, and stir in capers and parsley. Season to taste with pepper. Refrigerate for at least 15 minutes.

2. To serve, arrange turkey on two plates or a platter, and spread sauce over slices.

Variation: This dish is traditionally made with cold veal, and you can also substitute chicken.

Double Feature

Tube foods are great for small households because waste is so much less. Tubes of tomato paste should replace cans on your pantry list if you haven't discovered them.

Creole Fish Cakes

Scallions, red bell pepper, and celery enhance the texture and flavor of these easy baked cakes that can use up any sort of leftover fish.

Active time: 15 minutes

Start to finish: 30 minutes

Each serving has:

405 calories

244 calories from fat

27 g fat

11 g saturated fat

31 g protein

8.5 g carbohydrates

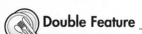 **Double Feature**

If you bought a baguette and some of it turned stale, you're not alone. That's one of the drawbacks of small household sizes. So let it get really stale, and grind it up into breadcrumbs by cutting it into 1-inch cubes and pulverizing them in the food processor.

2 TB. unsalted butter

2 scallions, rinsed, trimmed, and chopped

1 celery rib, rinsed, trimmed, and chopped

½ red bell pepper, seeds and ribs removed, and chopped

1 large egg, lightly beaten

2 TB. mayonnaise

2 TB. breadcrumbs

1 TB. Cajun seasoning

½ lb. cooked cod, halibut, or any firm-fleshed white fish, broken into ½-inch pieces

Vegetable oil spray

1. Preheat the oven to 400°F, cover a baking sheet with aluminum foil, and spray foil heavily with vegetable oil spray. Heat butter in a small skillet over medium-high heat. Add scallions, celery, and red bell pepper. Cook, stirring frequently, for 3 minutes or until scallions are translucent. Scrape mixture into a mixing bowl.

2. Add egg, mayonnaise, breadcrumbs, and Cajun seasoning. Whisk well. Add fish and stir gently to combine. Form mixture into 2 cakes 1-inch thick, and place them on prepared baking sheet. Spray top of cakes with vegetable oil spray.

3. Bake cakes for 15 minutes or until lightly brown. Remove cakes from the baking sheet with a spatula and serve immediately.

Variation: Substitute salmon or cooked ham.

Salmon Hash

This is a real hash complete with potatoes and onions, but it's lighter than most because it contains zucchini and fresh fish.

2 red-skinned potatoes, scrubbed and cut into ½-inch dice

Salt and freshly ground black pepper to taste

¼ cup olive oil

1 small onion, peeled and cut into ½-inch dice

2 small zucchini, rinsed, trimmed, and cut into ½-inch dice

2 TB. chopped fresh parsley

2 tsp. fresh thyme or ½ tsp. dried

½ lb. cooked salmon, broken into ½-inch pieces

Active time: 23 minutes
Start to finish: 25 minutes
Each serving has:
500 calories
291 calories from fat
32 g fat
5 g saturated fat
32 g protein
20.5 g carbohydrates

1. Cover potatoes with cold salted water. Bring to a boil over high heat, and *parboil* potatoes for 5 minutes. Drain and set aside.

2. Heat olive oil in a large skillet over medium-high heat. Add potatoes and onion. Cook, stirring occasionally, for 5 to 7 minutes or until vegetables are browned. Add zucchini, parsley, and thyme, and cook 3 to 5 minutes or until zucchini is crisp-tender.

3. Add salmon and stir gently. Cover the skillet and cook for 2 minutes over medium heat. Season to taste with salt and pepper and serve immediately.

Variation: Substitute cod, halibut, chicken, turkey, or ham.

Duet Dialogue

To **parboil** is to partially cook a food that takes a long time to soften, such as potatoes or carrots. The assumption is that the cooking will be completed in the finished dish.

Roast Beef Hash

Caramelizing the onion and aromatic Herbes de Provence add flavor nuances to this hearty hash.

Active time: 20 minutes

Start to finish: 30 minutes

Each serving has:

580 calories

227 calories from fat

25 g fat

12 g saturated fat

43 g protein

35.5 g carbohydrates

2 TB. unsalted butter

1 TB. olive oil

1 large sweet onion, such as Vidalia or Bermuda, peeled and diced

1 tsp. granulated sugar

½ lb. red-skinned potatoes, scrubbed and cut into ½-inch dice

1 tsp. Herbes de Provence

1½ cups diced cooked roast beef

Salt and freshly ground black pepper to taste

1. Heat butter and olive oil in a large skillet over low heat. Add onion, toss to coat, and cover the pan. Cook over low heat for 10 minutes, stirring occasionally. Uncover the pan, raise the heat to medium, sprinkle with salt, and stir in sugar. Cook for 15 to 20 minutes, stirring frequently, until onions are medium brown.

2. Preheat the oven to 450°F and grease a 9×9-inch baking pan. While onions are cooking, place potato cubes in a large saucepan of salted water. Bring to a boil over high heat. Boil potatoes for 10 to 12 minutes or until potatoes are very tender when tested with the tip of a paring knife. Drain potatoes, add Herbes de Provence, and mash roughly with a potato masher. Set aside.

3. Add roast beef and onions to potatoes and mix well. Season to taste with salt and pepper. Spread hash into prepared pan, and bake for 10 minutes or until the top is lightly brown. Serve immediately. (You can do this up to two days in advance and refrigerate, tightly covered. Reheat covered with aluminum foil for 10 minutes; then remove foil and bake for 10 minutes more.)

Variation: Substitute diced cooked ham, turkey, or chicken.

Double Feature

The smaller the cubes of hard foods, like potatoes or carrots, the faster they will cook. If you want to rush a recipe which specifies quartered potatoes, feel free to cut them into smaller pieces.

Baked Macaroni and Cheese with Ham

You can easily omit the ham and serve this perennial favorite as a side dish to four diners who will be most appreciative.

⅓ lb. elbow macaroni

2 TB. unsalted butter

2 TB. all-purpose flour

½ tsp. paprika

Pinch of cayenne

⅓ cup chicken stock

⅔ cup whole milk

⅓ lb. grated sharp cheddar cheese

1 tsp. Dijon mustard

Salt and freshly ground black pepper to taste

½ lb. ham steak, trimmed of fat and cut into ½-inch cubes

Active time: 15 minutes

Start to finish: 40 minutes

Each serving has:

909 calories

411 calories from fat

46 g fat

27 g saturated fat

55 g protein

67.5 g carbohydrates

---

1. Preheat the oven to 400°F. Grease a 9×9-inch baking pan. Bring a large pot of salted water to a boil. Add macaroni and cook according to package directions until al dente. Drain and set aside.

2. Melt butter in a saucepan over low heat. Stir in flour, paprika, and cayenne, and stir constantly for 2 minutes. Whisk in stock and bring to a boil over medium-high heat, whisking constantly. Stir in milk and all but 3 tablespoons grated cheese, stirring until cheese melts. Stir in mustard, and season to taste with salt and pepper.

3. Stir ham and macaroni into sauce, and transfer mixture to the prepared baking pan. Cover with aluminum foil, and bake for 10 minutes. Remove foil, sprinkle with remaining cheese and bake for an additional 10 to 15 minutes or until bubbly. Allow to sit for 5 minutes; then serve.

Variation: Substitute Gruyère or Swiss cheese for cheddar cheese, use cooked chicken or turkey for ham, or eliminate all meat and substitute vegetable stock for chicken stock and the dish becomes vegetarian.

 Déjà Two

When Yankee Doodle stuck a feather in his cap and called it "macaroni," he was not referring to pasta. Macaroni was a slang term in the eighteenth century for a fop or dandy; it comes from the Macaroni Club of London.

Ham, Potato, and Leek Gratin

The delicate flavor of leeks blends well with the Gruyère cheese in this layered casserole.

Active time: 15 minutes

Start to finish: 1¼ hours

Each serving has:

762 calories

334 calories from fat

37 g fat

22 g saturated fat

47 g protein

61 g carbohydrates

2 leeks

2 TB. unsalted butter

3 TB. all-purpose flour

½ cup milk

1 cup grated Gruyère

Salt and freshly ground black pepper to taste

2 large russet potatoes, peeled and thinly sliced

½ lb. thickly sliced smoked ham

1. Preheat the oven to 350°F. Grease a 9×9-inch baking pan. Trim leeks and discard all but 1 inch of light green tops. Slice thinly and rinse well in a colander. Set aside.

2. Melt butter in a saucepan over low heat. Stir in flour, and stir constantly for 2 minutes. Whisk in milk, and bring to a boil over medium-high heat, whisking constantly. Reduce the heat to low and simmer for 2 minutes. Stir in ¾ cup Gruyère, stirring until cheese melts. Season to taste with salt and pepper and set aside.

3. Arrange ⅓ of potato slices in pan and top with ⅓ of leeks. Add a layer of ½ of ham slices, and top with ⅓ of sauce. Repeat with a second layer, and end with a layer of just vegetables and sauce.

4. Cover the pan with aluminum foil, and bake for 35 minutes. Remove foil, sprinkle with remaining Gruyère, and bake for an additional 25 minutes or until potatoes are tender and liquid is thickened. Let stand 5 minutes before serving. (You can do this up to two days in advance and refrigerate, tightly covered. Reheat, covered with foil, in a 350°F oven for 20 to 30 minutes until hot.)

Variation: Substitute leftover chicken or turkey.

Double Trouble

When making a dish that contains ham, prosciutto, sausage, or any cured or spiced pork product, use salt sparingly, if at all, because all these foods have a high salt content. In a dish such as this one with potatoes, chances are you'll need to add additional salt, but that's not the case with most ham dishes.

Just Desserts

Few foods are as tired as a fruit pie on the third day when only two people have been nibbling at it. Most cookbooks just don't think about desserts for two. But that's hardly a problem here! Desserts tailor-made to the way you cook are awaiting you in these chapters.

You'll find one chapter on fast and easy desserts ranging from sweet quesadillas to decadent caramel fondue. The next chapter contains everything chocolate. Can it get any better than that?

The last dessert chapter is devoted to baking small batches. There is a difference in baking going beyond cutting down on the amounts of ingredients. You'll find everything from muffins to carrot cake with cream cheese frosting to strawberry shortcake.

Chapter 20

Homey to Haute

In This Chapter

- ◆ International apple treats
- ◆ Hot, homey puddings
- ◆ Easy-to-assemble desserts

Few cooks—including me—have time to make spun sugar swans or elaborate tortes the height of cathedrals. We want desserts that are easy and quick to prepare and can bake unattended as we're enjoying the rest of the meal.

Desserts, especially those made with fresh fruits, should be homey, and you'll find homey recipes in this chapter. Many of these recipes use apples because apples are one fruit universally available. But lots of fruits are listed both as the stars of the recipes and as supporting players.

All About Apples

With a selection of more than 300 varieties of apples grown in North America, Americans consume 18 pounds of apples each. But not all apples are created equal.

Some are better for munching raw, and others are better for cooking. Some, such as McIntosh, are good cooking apples for applesauce because they fall apart so well. But that wouldn't be an advantage in a pie or tart.

These apple varieties are good for cooking:

◆ Cortland. This medium to large all-purpose apple is crisp and juicy and has both sweet and tart flavors. It has a rich red color and is sometimes striped with green. The flesh is very white and resists browning.

◆ Empire. This is a beautiful, large, juicy red apple with a sweet, almost spicy flavor. It's wonderful baked as well as eaten fresh.

◆ Golden Delicious. This round, rich yellow apple offers a spectrum of flavors from slightly tart to mellow and sweet. The skin color ranges from light green to pale or creamy yellow, depending upon maturity. The more yellow the skin, the sweeter the apple. Avoid goldens with "russeting," a bronze-colored, rough, and scablike condition principally on the stem end of the apple.

◆ Granny Smith. This tart, all-purpose apple is gaining popularity for its tart flavor, firm flesh that retains its texture when cooked, and uniformity. The flavor tends to vary from mild to very tart, and on occasion the texture might be a bit on the dry side. Look for firm and bright-colored apples.

◆ Jonathan. This medium-size red apple with a yellow blush has firm, crisp, juicy flesh and is particularly well suited for pies and baking whole because it holds its shape very well.

◆ McIntosh. This medium-size, red-on-green apple has a crisp, sweet, aromatic flesh. It is excellent for eating and applesauce, but it does not hold its shape well for pies or baking whole.

◆ Rome Beauty. This large apple has a deep red color and is almost perfectly round. It is the best apple for baking because it retains its shape and the flavor develops best when cooked. Look for its brilliant, almost solid shade of red dotted with natural tiny white dots.

◆ Winesap. This bright, all-purpose apple with an old-fashioned tangy taste, has crisp, crunchy, juicy flesh with a sweet-tart flavor. Look for apples with smooth, glossy bright red skin with hints of purple.

Caramel Apple Quesadillas

Imagine all the flavors of apple pie on the table in minutes baked in a flour tortilla, and that's this easy dessert.

4 (6-in.) flour tortillas

12 caramel candies, unwrapped

2 TB. milk

¼ tsp. ground cinnamon

1 Golden Delicious apple, peeled, cored, and thinly sliced

2 TB. unsalted butter, melted

4 TB. granulated sugar

Active time: 10 minutes

Start to finish: 30 minutes

Each serving has:

675 calories

201 calories from fat

22 g fat

10.5 g saturated fat

9 g protein

114 g carbohydrates

1. Preheat the oven to 400°F and cover a baking sheet with aluminum foil. Soften tortillas by wrapping them in plastic wrap and heating them in a microwave oven on HIGH (100 percent power) for 10 to 15 seconds or until pliable.

2. Place caramel candies and milk in a small microwave safe bowl, and microwave for 45 seconds at MEDIUM (50 percent power). Stir and repeat as necessary until caramel is smooth. Stir in cinnamon.

3. Spread caramel mixture on tortillas to about ½-inch from the edge. Arrange apple slices over one half of each tortilla and fold over other half. Press down with the palm of your hand.

4. Place quesadillas on the baking sheet, brush with 1 tablespoon butter, and sprinkle with 2 tablespoons sugar. Bake for 10 minutes; then turn with a spatula, brush with remaining butter and sprinkle with remaining sugar. Bake for an additional 10 minutes or until quesadillas are browned. Allow to sit for 3 minutes; then cut in half and serve immediately.

Double Trouble

It's true that dessert quesadillas are not the norm, so what's really important when making them is to be sure to buy plain flour tortillas rather than flavored ones.

Easy Apple Strudel

Rice paper pancakes create a crispy shell for these juicy strudels.

Active time: 20 minutes
Start to finish: 40 minutes
Each serving has:
676 calories
194 calories from fat
22 g fat
8 g saturated fat
6 g protein
113 g carbohydrates

¼ **cup chopped walnuts**

¼ **cup raisins**

2 TB. brandy

1 Granny Smith apple, peeled, cored, and finely chopped

1 TB. freshly squeezed lemon juice

3 TB. firmly packed dark brown sugar

¼ **tsp. apple pie spice**

3 TB. unsalted butter, melted

½ **cup granulated sugar**

4 *rice paper pancakes*

1. Preheat the oven to 350°F. Place nuts on a baking sheet, and toast nuts for 5 to 7 minutes or until browned. Set aside. Combine raisins and brandy in a small bowl, and allow raisins to plump for 15 minutes.

2. Toss apple with lemon juice to prevent discoloration. Add brown sugar, apple pie spice, nuts, raisins, and 1 tablespoon melted butter. Toss to combine.

3. Increase the oven to 400°F, and cover a baking sheet with aluminum foil. Place 6 cups very hot tap water in a mixing bowl and stir in sugar.

4. Place rice paper pancakes on a large plate and cover with a damp tea towel. Place 1 pancake into hot water for 3 seconds, and then place it on a damp tea towel. Brush pancake with melted butter. Place ¼ cup apple filling in a log shape on one side of pancake, leaving a 1-inch border. Tuck ends over filling, and then roll pancake firmly. Place it seam-side down on the baking sheet, and brush top with melted butter. Repeat with remaining 3 pancakes. (You can do this up to 4 hours in advance and keep rolls at room temperature, or bake them up to a day in advance if serving at room temperature. Do not refrigerate.)

5. Bake for 20 minutes or until rolls are crisp and brown. Serve hot or at room temperature.

Duet Dialogue

Rice paper pancakes are brittle translucent sheets made from a dough of water combined with the pith of an Asian shrub, the rice-paper plant. You'll find them in the Asian aisle of supermarkets and at Asian groceries.

Upside-Down Apple Pie (*Tarte Tatin*)

The apples for this French classic are actually cooked on top of the stove and then it's baked to brown the crust.

2 Golden Delicious apples

2 TB. unsalted butter

½ cup granulated sugar

2 TB. freshly squeezed lemon juice

1 TB. brandy

¼ tsp. *apple pie spice*

1 sheet piecrust for single crust pie (homemade or purchased)

Active time: 25 minutes

Start to finish: 55 minutes, including 10 minutes for cooling

Each serving has:

712 calories

298 calories from fat

33 g fat

11 g saturated fat

3 g protein

100 g carbohydrates

1. Peel, core, and quarter apples. Slice each quarter in half lengthwise. Set aside.

2. Melt butter in an 8-inch cast-iron or other ovenproof skillet over medium-high heat. Stir in sugar, and cook, stirring frequently, for 6 to 8 minutes or until syrup is a deep walnut brown. Remove from heat and set aside.

3. Preheat the oven to 425°F. Place apple slices in a mixing bowl, and toss with lemon juice, brandy, and apple pie spice. Arrange apple slices tightly packed in a decorative pattern on top of caramel in the skillet, making several layers if necessary. Place the skillet over medium-high heat and press down on apples as they begin to soften.

4. Using a bulb baster, draw up juices from apples and pour juices over top layer of apples. Do not stir apples. After 5 minutes or when apples begin to soften, cover the skillet and cook for 10 to 15 minutes or until apples are soft and liquid is thick. Continue to baste apples during this time.

5. Remove the skillet from the stove, and roll piecrust dough into a circle one inch larger than the circumference of the skillet. Place crust on top of apples in the skillet and tuck edge of crust around apples on the sides of the skillet using the tip of a paring knife. Cut 6 (1-inch) vents in pastry to allow steam to escape.

6. Bake for 20 minutes or until pastry is golden and juice is thick. Remove from the oven and cool for 10 minutes. Using a knife, loosen edges of tart from the pan. Invert a serving plate over the pan and holding the pan and plate together firmly, invert them. Lift off the pan. Place any apples that might have stuck to the bottom of the pan on top of tart.

7. Serve tart warm or at room temperature. (You can bake tart up to six hours in advance, and keep it at room temperature.)

Duet Dialogue

Apple pie spice is a pre-blended combination of fragrant spices, but you can make your own by combining ½ teaspoon cinnamon, ¼ teaspoon nutmeg, ⅛ teaspoon allspice, ⅛ teaspoon ground cardamom, and ¼ teaspoon ground cloves. Or in a pinch, substitute cinnamon as the primary base, with a dash of any of the other spices you might have on hand.

Blue Cheese, Brie, and Caramelized Pear Quesadillas

It might seem odd to serve blue cheese for dessert but its savory flavor is balanced by creamy brie and sweetened pears.

Active time: 12 minutes

Start to finish: 20 minutes

Each serving has:

820 calories

442 calories from fat

49 g fat

22 g saturated fat

25 g protein

74 g carbohydrates

⅓ cup chopped walnuts

3 TB. unsalted butter

2 TB. firmly packed dark brown sugar

1 ripe pear, peeled, cored, and cut into ½-inch dice

4 (6-in.) flour tortillas

½ cup crumbled blue cheese

½ cup finely diced brie

2 TB. granulated sugar

1. Preheat the oven to 350°F. Place walnuts on a baking sheet and toast for 5 to 7 minutes or until browned. Set aside. Melt butter in a small skillet over medium heat. Pour off half and set aside. Add brown sugar to remaining butter and stir well. Add pear and cook, stirring occasionally, for 3 to 4 minutes or until the pear is soft. Set aside.

2. Preheat the oven to 450° F, and cover a baking sheet with aluminum foil. Soften tortillas by wrapping them in plastic wrap and heating them in a microwave oven on HIGH (100 percent power) for 10 to 15 seconds or until pliable.

3. Line tortillas out on a counter, and divide blue cheese and brie amongst them. Spread it over half the circle, and top with equal amounts of pear mixture and toasted nuts. Press quesadillas together gently into half circles and place them on the baking sheet. Brush tops with melted butter, and sprinkle with 1 tablespoon sugar.

4. Bake for 5 minutes. Turn quesadillas with a spatula, brush with butter, and sprinkle with remaining tablespoon sugar. Bake an additional 3 to 4 minutes or until quesadillas are browned. Remove from the oven and serve immediately.

Variation: Substitute Gorgonzola or Stilton for blue cheese and use Explorateur or Camembert instead of brie.

 Double Feature

This dessert is based on the way Port is traditionally served, with ripe pears, Stilton, and walnuts. As a special treat for the dessert, serve it with a glass of Port.

Peach and Blackberry Cobbler

When fruits are ripe in the summer this easy cobbler is a wonderful way to glorify them.

⅓ cup granulated sugar

1 tsp. *cornstarch*

2 TB. crème de cassis

¾ lb. ripe peaches, pitted, and cut into ½-inch slices

1 (6-oz.) pkg. fresh or frozen blackberries, rinsed

⅔ cup all-purpose flour

¾ tsp. baking powder

¼ tsp. salt

4 TB. unsalted cold butter, cut into ½-inch pieces

¼ cup whole milk

Vanilla ice cream or sweetened whipped cream (optional)

Active time: 15 minutes

Start to finish: 50 minutes

Each serving has:

664 calories

239 calories from fat

27 g fat

16 g saturated fat

8 g protein

95 g carbohydrates

---

1. Preheat the oven to 425°F. Grease a 9×9-inch baking pan. Place sugar in a mixing bowl and stir cornstarch into crème de cassis, stirring to dissolve cornstarch. Add peaches and blackberries, and toss to combine well. Transfer fruit mixture to the prepared baking pan and bake for 10 minutes or until hot.

2. While fruit is baking, combine flour, baking powder, and salt in a large bowl. Cut in butter using a pastry blender, two knives, or your fingertips until mixture resembles coarse meal. Add milk and stir just until a dough forms.

3. Drop dough onto hot fruit mixture in 6 to 8 mounds. Bake in the center of the oven for 25 to 35 minutes or until top is golden. Cool for 10 minutes, and serve topped with vanilla ice cream or sweetened whipped cream.

Variation: Substitute nectarines or plums for peaches, and use blueberries or raspberries in place of blackberries.

Duet Dialogue

Cornstarch is a powdery substance used as a thickening agent that is obtained from finely grinding the endosperm of corn kernels. Mix it with either a cold liquid or another granular powder such as granulated sugar to keep it from forming lumps in the finished dish.

Rice Pudding with Raspberries

If rice pudding is a cherished treat from your childhood it's time to dust it off and update it with the addition of vivid raspberries.

Active time: 10 minutes

Start to finish: 1¼ hours, including 1 hour for standing

Each serving has:

350 calories

31 calories from fat

3 g fat

2 g saturated fat

7 g protein

74 g carbohydrates

Double Feature

If you want to trim the fat from this recipe, use two percent milk and nonfat vanilla yogurt in place of whole milk and pudding.

1 cup water
⅓ cup long-grain white rice
Pinch salt
¼ cup granulated sugar
¼ tsp. ground cinnamon
⅔ cup whole milk
¼ tsp. pure vanilla extract
1 (6-oz.) pkg. fresh raspberries, rinsed
½ cup vanilla pudding, homemade or 1 (4-oz.) container from the supermarket refrigerator aisle

1. Bring water to boil in a medium saucepan over high heat. Add rice and salt, reduce heat to medium-low, and simmer, uncovered, for 20 minutes or until rice is very tender and water is absorbed. Add sugar and cinnamon and stir to blend. Reduce the heat to low, add milk, and simmer, stirring frequently, for 25 minutes or until mixture is very thick. Remove from the heat, and stir in vanilla extract. Cool for 1 hour or until pudding reaches room temperature.

2. Stir raspberries and vanilla pudding into rice pudding. Serve immediately at room temperature or chilled.

Variation: Substitute blueberries, blackberries, sliced strawberries, or chopped fresh peaches for raspberries.

Mexican *Dulce de Leche* Fondue

Dessert doesn't get any easier than this! Just boil a can of sweetened condensed milk and you've got it.

1 (14-oz.) can sweetened condensed milk	**½ tsp. pure vanilla extract, preferably Mexican**
1 TB. dark rum	**Variety of fruits, cookies, and/or cakes**

> **Active time:** 5 minutes
> **Start to finish:** 2 hours
> **Each serving has:**
> 611 calories
> 144 calories from fat
> 16 g fat
> 10 g saturated fat
> 15 g protein
> 100 g carbohydrates

1. Remove the label from the can, stand the can in a deep stock pot, and fill the pot with hot water. Cover the pan, and bring to a boil over high heat. Reduce the heat to low, and allow the can to simmer gently for 2 hours. Add water as necessary to keep the can covered. *It is imperative that the can is covered with water at all times or it could explode.*

2. Remove the can from water with tongs and allow it to cool for 15 minutes. Pour the can's contents into a fondue pot or other pot with a heat source, and stir in rum and vanilla extract.

3. Serve with hulled strawberries (halved if large), banana chunks, apple slices, dried coconut slices, dried apricots, crystallized ginger, donut holes, waffle squares, butter cookies, pound cake cubes, brownie cubes, coconut macaroons, or sugar cookies.

Variation: Use pure almond extract in place of vanilla. Also add chopped toasted almonds to the fondue.

Duet Dialogue

Dulce de leche means "sweet milk" in Spanish, and it's popular in all Hispanic countries. It's sometimes called *cajeta* and is used as a spread, dip, or topping. This easy method is how it's made in the Yucatan province of Mexic

New England Indian Pudding

Crystallized ginger creates a more interesting flavor for this corn-meal pudding that's older than the country.

Active time: 15 minutes

Start to finish: 65 minutes, including 10 minutes for cooling

Each serving has:

402 calories

114 calories from fat

13 g fat

7 g saturated fat

9 g protein

68.5 g carbohydrates

1 TB. unsalted butter, cut into small pieces

1 cup whole milk

3 TB. yellow cornmeal

3 TB. pure maple syrup

1 TB. firmly packed dark brown sugar

1 TB. finely chopped crystallized ginger

Pinch ground cinnamon

Pinch salt

¼ cup golden raisins

1 large egg, lightly beaten

Vanilla ice cream or sweetened whipped cream (optional)

1. Preheat the oven to 325°F and butter two (8-ounce) ramekins. Bring milk almost to a boil in a saucepan over medium-high heat; then add cornmeal in a steady stream, whisking constantly. Reduce the heat to low, and cook, stirring frequently, for 10 minutes or until mixture thickens. Stir in butter, maple syrup, brown sugar, ginger, cinnamon, and salt.

2. Remove the pan from the stove and stir constantly for 2 minutes. Stir in raisins and egg. Divide mixture into the prepared ramekins. Bake for 40 minutes or until firm. (You can do this up to two days in advance and refrigerate, tightly covered. Reheat, covered with aluminum foil, in a 300°F oven for 15 minutes or until warm.) Allow to cool for 10 minutes, then serve with ice cream or sweetened whipped cream.

Déjà Two

Because Native Americans introduced corn to the Pilgrims, anything made with corn had "Indian" as a prefix at one time or another. The other term for Indian pudding is hasty pudding, and the Hasty Pudding Club at Harvard University was named for the dessert. Recipes for Indian or hasty pudding go back to the early eighteenth century.

Espresso-Coated Coconut Flan

Coconut milk creates a creamy custard that's topped with a coffee-flavored caramel.

1 tsp. *instant espresso powder*	**1 large egg**
1 TB. very hot tap water	**1 large egg yolk**
½ cup granulated sugar	**Pinch salt**
⅓ cup coconut milk, stirred well	**3 TB. sweetened shredded coconut**
⅓ cup whole milk	

> **Active time:** 15 minutes
>
> **Start to finish:** 4 hours, including 3 hours for chilling
>
> **Each serving has:**
>
> 410 calories
>
> 167 calories from fat
>
> 18.5 g fat
>
> 13 g saturated fat
>
> 7 g protein
>
> 57 g carbohydrates

1. Preheat the oven to 325°F and grease two (6-ounce) ramekins or custard cups. Place the ramekins on a cloth tea towel in the bottom of a roasting pan. Bring a kettle of water to a boil over high heat.

2. Stir together espresso powder and water in a small saucepan until powder dissolves. Stir in ¼ cup sugar, and place over high heat. Bring to a boil, swirling the handle of the pan, but not stirring, and cook for 4 to 5 minutes or until mixture is thick and brown. Divide mixture among ramekins, tilting to coat bottoms, and let stand for about 10 minutes or until hardened.

3. While caramel is standing, bring coconut milk and whole milk just to a simmer over medium heat, stirring frequently, and remove the pan from the heat. Whisk together egg, egg yolk, salt, and remaining sugar in a large bowl. Add warm milk mixture in a steady stream, whisking as you pour. Stir in coconut, and divide mixture among ramekins.

4. Pour enough boiling water into the pan to come halfway up the sides of the ramekins. Bake for 1 hour or until set. Run a thin knife around the edge of each flan to loosen, then transfer ramekins to a rack and cool completely. Chill, covered, until cold, at least four hours. (You can do this up to two days in advance.) To unmold, invert small plates over the ramekins, and invert flans onto plates.

 Duet Dialogue

Instant espresso powder, imported from Italy, is now becoming more common in America. It's made from real espresso coffee, which is then dehydrated and ground. Look for it in the supermarket along with other instant coffees.

Baked Lemon and Dried Blueberry Pudding

Lemon has a flavor that melds beautifully with those of other fruits, as you'll see when making this easy pudding for dessert.

Active time: 10 minutes

Start to finish: 50 minutes

Each serving has:

393 calories

136 calories from fat

15 g fat

9 g saturated fat

6 g protein

60.5 g carbohydrates

2 TB. unsalted butter, softened

¼ granulated sugar

1 large egg yolk

2 TB. freshly squeezed lemon juice

1 tsp. grated lemon zest

½ cup all-purpose flour

¾ tsp. baking powder

¼ cup milk

3 TB. dried blueberries

1. Preheat the oven to 350°F. Butter two (6-ounce) ramekins and set aside. Bring a kettle of water to a boil over high heat.

2. *Cream* butter and sugar in a mixing bowl with an electric mixer on medium speed until light and fluffy. Add egg yolk, lemon juice, and lemon zest and beat well. Sift flour and baking powder directly into mixture, and stir it in. Gradually add milk, beating steadily as you add it. Stir in dried blueberries.

3. Divide mixture between the ramekins, and place ramekins in a 9×9-inch baking pan. Pour enough boiling water into the baking pan to come up the sides of the casserole an inch. Bake for 40 to 45 minutes or until pudding is firm and slightly browned. Serve warm or at room temperature.

Variation: Use lime juice and zest in place of lemon, and any dried fruit can be substituted.

Duet Dialogue

Cream, as a verb, means to beat ingredients together to form a homogeneous mixture. It's most often used as the first step in a dessert recipe because creaming together butter and sugar forms the basic structure for a dough or batter.

Chapter 21

Chocolate Cravings

In This Chapter

- ◆ Gooey fondues
- ◆ Easy baked treats
- ◆ Frosty finales

Here's a test to determine if you're a true chocoholic: did you immediately turn to this chapter from the table of contents? If so, you can join me and almost everyone I know in our passion for chocolate and enjoy the recipes you'll find in this chapter.

A benefit of chocolate addiction is that there are so many ways to get a fix. These desserts are all decadent and range from chocolate fondue to some homey dishes, like bread puddings and baked custard flans.

Chocolate 101

For all chocolate desserts, the key to success is to use a high-quality product. It's also important (with a few exceptions) to use the type of chocolate specified in the recipe because the amount of additional sugar and other ingredients are calculated according to the sweetness level of the chocolate. If you use a different chocolate, the taste of things could be off.

Now, let's consider the sweet stuff. Here's a quick guide to chocolate:

- **Unsweetened.** Also referred to as baking or bitter chocolate, this is the purest of all cooking chocolate. It is hardened chocolate liquor (the essence of the cocoa bean, not an alcohol) that contains no sugar and is usually packaged in a bar of 8 (1-ounce) blocks. According to the U.S. standard of identity, unsweetened chocolate must contain 50 to 58 percent cocoa butter.

- **Bittersweet.** This chocolate is slightly sweetened with sugar, the varying amounts depending on the manufacturer. This chocolate must contain 35 percent chocolate liquor and should be used when intense chocolate flavor is desired. It is also used interchangeably with semisweet chocolate in cooking and baking.

- **Semisweet.** This chocolate is sweetened with sugar, but unlike bittersweet, it also can have added flavorings, such as vanilla. It is available in bar form as well as chips and pieces.

- **Sweet cooking.** This chocolate must contain 15 percent chocolate liquor and almost always has a higher sugar content than semisweet chocolate. It is usually found in 4-ounce bars.

Déjà Two

Scientists named the bean of the tropical cocoa tree *Theobroma cacoa,* meaning "food of the gods."

- **Milk.** This is a mild-flavored chocolate used primarily for candy bars but rarely (except for milk chocolate chips) in cooking. It can have as little as 10 percent chocolate liquor but must contain 12 percent milk solids.

- **Unsweetened cocoa powder.** This powdered chocolate has had a portion of the cocoa butter removed. Cocoa keeps indefinitely in a cool place.

- **Dutch process cocoa powder.** This type of cocoa powder is formulated with reduced acidity and gives foods a more mellow flavor. However, it also burns at a lower temperature than more common cocoa.

- **White.** Actually ivory in color, white chocolate is technically not chocolate at all but is made from cocoa butter, sugar, and flavoring. Difficult to work with, it should be used in recipes that are specifically designed for it. Do not substitute it for other types of chocolate in a recipe.

Subbing With Success

You can use bittersweet, semisweet, and sweet chocolate interchangeably in recipes, depending on personal taste. Most chocolate desserts tend to be sweet, so it's better to go from a semisweet to a bittersweet rather than the other direction.

Do not substitute chocolate chips and bits of broken chocolate for one another. Chocolate chips are formulated to retain their shape at high heat and react differently when baked than chopped chocolate does. Chocolate chips can form gritty granules in a cooled dessert.

Sweet Savvy

Always wrap chocolate tightly after it's opened because it can absorb aromas and flavors from other foods. Store chocolate in a cool, dry place, but do not refrigerate or freeze it. If chocolate is stored at a high temperature, the fat will rise to the surface and become a whitish powder called a bloom. This will disappear, however, as soon as the chocolate is melted.

Like red wine, chocolate ages and becomes more deeply flavored after six months and can be kept for years if stored properly. However, because of the milk solids in both milk chocolate and white chocolate, these shouldn't be stored for longer than nine months.

Proper Chocolate Handling

Except when you're eating chocolate out of your hand or folding chips into a cookie dough, chocolate needs a bit of special handling. Use these tips when carrying out the common tasks associated with chocolate:

Chopping chocolate: Chopping chunks into fine pieces makes melting easier. You can do this in a food processor fitted with a steel blade. Begin by breaking it with a heavy knife rather than using your hands. Body heat is sufficiently high enough to soften the chocolate so it will not chop evenly.

Melting chocolate: Most chocolate needs careful melting because it scorches easily. You can melt it in a number of ways:

◆ Put chunks in the top of a double boiler placed over barely simmering water.

◆ Place chopped chocolate in a microwave-safe bowl, and microwave on 100 percent (HIGH) for 20 seconds. Stir and repeat as necessary.

◆ Preheat the oven to 250°F. Place chopped chocolate into the oven and then turn off the heat immediately. Stir after three minutes and return to the warm oven if necessary.

With all these methods, melt the chocolate until it is just about smooth and the heat in the chocolate will complete the process.

Fancy Flourishes

If you want to dress up a dessert, it's easy to do with melted chocolate. Here are some ideas:

◆ For random lines or drizzles, dip the tip of a knife or spatula into melted chocolate and swing it back and forth. For a more controlled look, place melted chocolate in a small, heavy plastic bag and snip off the tip; the amount you snip off will determine the thickness of your line.

◆ For an elegant chocolate garnish, brush a thick layer of melted chocolate on the underside of well-washed heavy leaves, such as lemon or holly. Chill and pull away the leaf and the chocolate will have molded into a veined pattern.

◆ To make chocolate "shells" as edible bowls, cover the back of scallop shells (available in kitchen specialty stores) or glass custard cups with foil, smoothing the foil with your hand. Brush a layer of melted chocolate on the outside, to within 1/4-inch of the edge, being careful not to get any on the edge. Chill for 5 minutes, then repeat this procedure two more times. Chill the shells for at least an hour. Remove the form, and gently pull away the foil.

Classic Chocolate Fondue

Chocolate fondue is a chocoholic's dream; melted chocolate flavored with your favorite liqueur into which you can dip just about anything!

3 TB. heavy cream

4 oz. bittersweet chocolate, chopped

1 TB. liquor or liqueur (your favorite: rum, bourbon, tequila, Cognac, brandy, triple sec, Grand Marnier, Chambord, kirsch, amaretto, Frangelico, crème de cacao, crème de banana, Irish cream liqueur, Kahlúa)

Variety of fruits, cookies, or cakes

Active time: 10 minutes
Start to finish: 10 minutes
Each serving has:
385 calories
253 calories from fat
28 g fat
17 g saturated fat
4 g protein
36 g carbohydrates

1. Combine cream and chocolate in a heavy 1-quart saucepan. Stir over very low heat to melt chocolate. When mixture is smooth and chocolate is melted, stir in liquor. (You can do this up to four hours ahead. Reheat over very low heat or in a microwave.)

2. Transfer fondue to a fondue pot or other pot with a heat source, and serve with hulled strawberries (halved if large), banana chunks, clementine segments, apple slices, donut holes, waffle squares, butter cookies, angel food cake cubes, cake cubes, brownie cubes, biscotti, or sugar cookies.

Variation: If you're serving the fondue to children or adults who cannot tolerate alcohol, substitute ¼ to ½ teaspoon pure extract for liquor or liqueur.

 Déjà Two

Chef Konrad Egli created chocolate fondue. The dish first appeared on his menu at New York's Chalet Swiss, a restaurant that popularized all fondue on this side of the Atlantic Ocean in 1964.

Mexican Chocolate Fondue

Traditional Mexican chocolate is made with almonds and cinnamon, and those are the additions to this gooey and luscious fondue.

Active time: 15 minutes

Start to finish: 15 minutes

Each serving has:

475 calories

328 calories from fat

36 g fat

18 g saturated fat

8 g protein

38 g carbohydrates

¼ **cup sliced almonds**

3 **TB. heavy cream**

4 **oz. bittersweet chocolate, chopped**

Pinch ground cinnamon

1 **TB. amaretto**

Dash **pure almond extract**

Variety of fruits and cookies or cakes

1. Toast almonds in a 350°F oven for 5 to 7 minutes or until lightly browned. Chop and set aside.

2. Combine cream, chocolate, and cinnamon in a heavy 1-quart saucepan. Stir over very low heat to melt chocolate. When mixture is smooth and chocolate is melted, stir in almonds, amaretto, and almond extract. (You can do this up to four hours ahead. Reheat over very low heat or in a microwave.)

3. Transfer fondue to a fondue pot or other pot with a heat source, and serve with hulled strawberries (halved if large), banana chunks, clementine segments, apple slices, donut holes, waffle squares, butter cookies, angel food cake cubes, spice cake cubes, brownie cubes, biscotti, or sugar cookies.

Duet Dialogue

Dash is an imprecise measurement for a very small amount of a liquid ingredient. It's equivalent to a scant ⅛ teaspoon. If measuring a dry ingredient, the word used is pinch.

Candy Bar Quesadillas

Pick your favorite candy bar, layer it with some cream cheese on a flour tortilla and you've got a dessert within minutes.

4 (6-in.) flour tortillas

1 (3-oz.) pkg. cream cheese, softened

2 TB. unsalted butter, melted

4 TB. granulated sugar

2 (1½ to 2-oz.) candy bars, each cut into thin slices (your favorite: plain or flavored chocolate bars with or without additional ingredients such as Snickers, Three Musketeers, or Almond Joy)

Active time: 5 minutes
Start to finish: 13 minutes
Each serving has:
808 calories
411 calories from fat
46 g fat
25 g saturated fat
12 g protein
90 g carbohydrates

1. Preheat the oven to 450°F and cover a baking sheet with aluminum foil. Soften tortillas by wrapping them in plastic wrap and heating them in a microwave oven on HIGH (100 percent power) for 10 to 15 seconds or until pliable.

2. Line tortillas out on a counter, and divide cream cheese amongst them. Spread cream cheese over half the circle and top with equal amounts of candy bar slices. Press quesadillas together gently into half circles, and place them on the baking sheet. Brush tops with melted butter and sprinkle with half of sugar.

3. Bake for 5 minutes. Turn quesadillas with a spatula, brush and sugar second side. Bake an additional 3 to 4 minutes or until quesadillas are browned. Remove from the oven and serve immediately.

Déjà Two

The Aztecs first discovered chocolate, and our word comes from the Aztec *xocolatl*, which means "bitter water." Famed King Montezuma believed chocolate was an aphrodisiac and is reported to have consumed some 50 cups a day.

Quick Chocolate Soufflé

Don't be afraid of a soufflé; if you can beat an egg, you can have this elegant dessert in the oven within minutes.

Active time: 15 minutes

Start to finish: 45 minutes

Each serving has:

419 calories

239 calories from fat

26.5 g fat

15 g saturated fat

10 g protein

41 g carbohydrates

1 TB. unsalted butter

¼ cup granulated sugar plus 2 TB. for the dish

2 oz. good-quality chocolate

2 TB. strong coffee

2 TB. heavy cream

2 large eggs, separated

1 egg white

Pinch salt

Sweetened whipped cream (optional)

1. Preheat the oven to 400°F. Butter a 1-quart soufflé dish and dust it well with 2 tablespoons sugar, shaking out excess. Set aside.

2. Break chocolate into small pieces and melt with coffee and cream. Beat until thick and glossy, and then add egg yolks, one at a time, beating well after each addition.

3. Beat egg whites and salt at medium speed of an electric mixer until frothy, then increase the speed to high and beat until stiff peaks form, gradually adding ¼ cup sugar. Fold egg whites into chocolate mixture and scrape mixture into the soufflé dish.

4. Place the dish in the center of the oven, and immediately turn the oven down to 375°F. Bake 30 minutes and serve immediately with sweetened whipped cream, if using.

Variation: Substitute any liquor or liqueur for coffee. Review the list given for the Classic Chocolate Fondue recipe.

Double Trouble

Egg whites will not whip if there's even a spec of anything greasy in the mixing bowl. Wash your bowl with soapy hot water and dry it with paper towels just prior to whipping the egg whites. And don't whip egg whites in a plastic mixing bowl; it's almost impossible to ensure that there's no residual grease.

Chocolate Coeurs á la Crème

Now here's a perfect ending for a Valentine's Day meal—
chocolate-flavored cream cheese with a fancy name.

⅓ **cup heavy cream**

**1 (3-oz.) pkg. cream cheese,
softened**

**2 oz. semisweet chocolate,
melted**

**Dash Grand Marnier or any
orange-flavored liqueur**

1. Place cream in a mixing bowl, and beat it with an electric
   mixer until soft peaks form. In another bowl, beat cream
   cheese, chocolate, and orange liqueur. Mix thoroughly, occasionally scraping down the sides of the bowl. Fold whipped
   cream into chocolate mixture.

2. Line two small heart-shaped ceramic molds with dampened
   cheesecloth, allowing the cheesecloth to hang over the sides
   of the mold. Fill each mold with chocolate filling. Fold
   the overlapping cheesecloth over filling, covering tightly.
   Refrigerate the molds for at least three hours. Remove hearts
   from the molds and discard the cheesecloth. Serve immediately.

Variation: For mocha hearts dissolve 2 teaspoons instant coffee in
1 tablespoon hot water. Add this to the cream cheese mixture, and
substitute a coffee liqueur for the orange.

Active time: 15 minutes
Start to finish: 3¼ hours, including 3 hours for chilling
Each serving has:
448 calories
332 calories from fat
37 g fat
23 g saturated fat
5 g protein
22 g carbohydrates

 Double Feature

Cream is easier to
whip if both the mix-
ing bowl and beater
are well-chilled.
So it's best to use
a metal rather than
glass bowl.

Chocolate Praline Bread Pudding with Cinnamon Cream

Bits of caramelized pecan candy add texture and flavor to this New Orleans classic.

Active time: 15 minutes

Start to finish: 60 minutes, including 10 minutes to cool

Each serving has:

883 calories

427 calories from fat

47.5 g fat

20.5 g saturated fat

13 g protein

113 g carbohydrates

¼ cup pecan halves

½ cup granulated sugar

2 TB. water

2 French rolls, cut into 1-inch cubes

1 cup light cream

1 large whole egg

1 large egg yolk

3 oz. bittersweet chocolate, chopped

Pinch salt

⅓ cup heavy or whipping cream

Pinch ground cinnamon

2 TB. confectioners' sugar

1. For praline, preheat the oven to 350°F. Place pecan halves on a baking sheet and toast in the oven for 5 to 7 minutes or until browned. Remove nuts from the oven and set aside.

2. Grease a baking sheet and set aside. Combine ¼ cup sugar and water in a heavy small saucepan, swirling the pan by its handle as sugar melts. Cook over medium heat without stirring for 5 to 10 minutes or until golden brown. Remove the pan from the heat, and stir in pecans. Immediately pour praline onto the prepared baking sheet and cool completely. Break praline into small pieces, and then chop it finely in a food processor fitted with a steel blade using on and off pulsing. (You can store it in an airtight container at room temperature up to one week.)

3. For pudding, preheat the oven to 350°F. Grease an 8×8-inch baking pan. Bring a kettle of water to a boil over high heat. Place bread in a large bowl and set aside.

4. Bring light cream to a boil in a saucepan over medium heat. Meanwhile, whisk together egg, egg yolk, and remaining ¼ cup sugar in a medium bowl. Slowly whisk ½ cup hot cream into egg mixture. Then, whisk hot cream-egg mixture back into cream in saucepan, and cook for 1 to 2 minutes or until sugar dissolves. Add chocolate, stirring until melted. Pour mixture over bread, stirring until bread absorbs all liquid. Stir in salt and praline.

5. Spoon mixture into the prepared baking pan. Place in a large roasting pan with at least one inch space between the sides of the baking pan and roasting pan. Pour enough hot water into roasting pan to come halfway up the sides of the baking pan.

6. Bake for 35 minutes or until a knife inserted in the center comes out clean. Remove pudding from the water bath, and cool for 10 to 20 minutes on a wire rack. (You can do this a day in advance and refrigerate, tightly covered. Remove from refrigerator 30 minutes before serving. Heat in a 350°F oven, covered with aluminum foil, for 30 minutes or until hot.)

7. For topping, beat heavy cream and cinnamon in a small bowl with an electric mixer on medium-high speed until soft peaks form. Beat in confectioners' sugar just until combined. To serve, spoon cinnamon cream over pudding and sprinkle with remaining praline.

Variation: Omit the praline, substitute white chocolate for bittersweet, and add ¼ cup dried cranberries and 2 tablespoons triple sec to the pudding.

Double Feature

Toast small nuts and seeds, such as pine nuts, sesame seeds, and slivered almonds, in a small dry skillet over medium-high heat. Toast larger nuts such as pecans, walnuts, or whole almonds, in the oven.

Mini-Molten Chocolate Tortes

These are both elegant and easy, and deliver an intense chocolate flavor.

1 TB. plus ¼ cup unsalted butter

2 TB. granulated sugar

2 oz. semisweet chocolate, chopped

1 large egg

1 large egg yolk

3 TB. confectioners' sugar

½ tsp. pure vanilla extract

2 TB. all-purpose flour

1 TB. unsweetened cocoa powder

Sweetened whipped cream (optional)

Fresh raspberries (optional)

Active time: 15 minutes

Start to finish: 30 minutes

Each serving has:

605 calories

384 calories from fat

43 g fat

25 g saturated fat

7 g protein

49 g carbohydrates

1. Preheat the oven to 400°F. Grease two (6-ounce) custard cups with 1 tablespoon butter and sprinkle with granulated sugar. Place in a shallow baking pan and set aside.

2. Combine remaining ¼ cup butter and chopped semisweet chocolate in a small saucepan and melt over low heat, stirring constantly. Remove the pan from the heat and cool. Beat egg, egg yolk, confectioners' sugar, and vanilla extract with a hand-held electric mixer set on high speed for 5 minutes or until mixture is thick and pale yellow. Beat in chocolate mixture on medium speed. Sift flour and cocoa powder over chocolate mixture and beat on low speed just until blended. Spoon batter into the prepared custard cups. (You can do this up to 2 hours in advance. Keep at room temperature.)

3. Bake for 12 to 14 minutes or until tortes rise slightly and feel firm at the edges and softer in the center when pressed gently. Cool in custard cups for 5 minutes. Invert with pot holders onto dessert plates. Cool for 5 minutes, and serve with sweetened whipped cream and top with fresh raspberries.

Variation: If you want to make this a sinfully rich dessert, place a chocolate truffle in the center of each cup before baking. The short bake time will just melt the center.

Double Trouble

Always buy pure vanilla extract. The imitation stuff is only slightly less expensive and gives food such a chemical taste.

Steamed Mocha Pudding

Steamed puddings are easy to make, and they have a wonderful dense texture that's perfect when flavored with chocolate and coffee.

Active time: 20 minutes

Start to finish: 2½ hours

Each serving has:

683 calories

348 calories from fat

39 g fat

23 g saturated fat

9 g protein

73 g carbohydrates

5 TB. unsalted butter

2 oz. semisweet or bitter-sweet chocolate, chopped

¼ cup whole milk

1 tsp. instant espresso powder

1 large egg, lightly beaten

¼ cup granulated sugar

½ cup all-purpose flour

½ tsp. baking powder

1 TB. Kahlúa or other coffee liqueur

¼ tsp. pure vanilla extract

Sweetened whipped cream or ice cream (optional)

1. Generously butter a 2 cup pudding steamer or metal mixing bowl with 1 tablespoon butter. Bring a kettle of water to a boil over high heat. Combine bittersweet chocolate and remaining butter in a small saucepan, and set over low heat. Stir frequently until liquid and smooth. Scrape chocolate mixture into a mixing bowl, and pour milk and espresso powder into the same saucepan. Heat over medium heat until coffee powder dissolves and stir into chocolate.

2. Combine egg, sugar, flour, baking powder, coffee liqueur, and vanilla extract in a mixing bowl and whisk well. Combine egg mixture with chocolate mixture and scrape batter into the prepared pan. If you're using a pudding steamer (which is airtight), clamp on the lid. If you're using a mixing bowl, top the bowl with a double layer of foil, crimping it around the edges to seal it tightly.

3. Set the mold on a wire rack in a pot or kettle large enough to accommodate it comfortably. Pour in enough boiling water to come halfway up the sides of the mold. Cover the pot, and bring water back to a boil over medium-high heat. Lower heat to a simmer and steam pudding for two hours. Add hot water to the pot as needed to maintain water level.

4. Remove pudding mold with potholders from the outer pot and remove cover. Cool on a rack for 15 minutes or until it begins to shrink away from the sides of the mold. To serve, invert pudding onto a platter and pass sweetened whipped cream or ice cream separately, if using. (You can do this up to two days in advance and refrigerate, wrapped tightly in aluminum foil. Bake in a 300°F oven for 30 to 40 minutes or until hot.)

Déjà Two

Steamed puddings date back to Medieval England, and the most famous are the plum puddings or figgy puddings served with hard sauce at Christmas time. Traditionally, steamed puddings were made with beef suet, but most modern recipes use butter.

Chocolate Sorbet

If you want a light dessert, but it must be chocolate, than this should be your choice.

1 cup water

⅔ cup *superfine sugar*

4 oz. unsweetened chocolate, chopped

2 TB. brandy

1. Combine water, sugar, chocolate, and brandy in a small saucepan, and bring to a boil over medium heat, stirring occasionally. Cool to room temperature.

2. Pour into an ice cream maker and freeze according to the manufacturer's directions. Alternatively, pour into a shallow metal bowl, place into a freezer and freeze until solid, stirring with a fork every 20 minutes after mixture starts to freeze to break up the ice crystals.

Active time: 10 minutes

Start to finish: 1 hour or longer, depending on freezing method

Each serving has:

569 calories

267 calories from fat

30 g fat

18 g saturated fat

7 g protein

81 g carbohydrates

🍴📖 **Duet Dialogue** _____

Superfine sugar, called castor sugar in England, is more finely ground than granulated sugar so it dissolves almost instantly. You can substitute it for granulated sugar on an equal basis.

White Chocolate Strawberry Coupe

Coupe is a fancy word for "doctored ice cream," and that's all there is to this easy dessert.

Active time: 10 minutes

Start to finish: 1 hour, including 50 minutes for freezing

Each serving has:

454 calories

216 calories from fat

24 g fat

15 g saturated fat

4 g protein

42 g carbohydrates

½ pt. strawberry ice cream

⅓ cup chopped white chocolate

⅔ cup sliced strawberries

4 TB. Chambord or other berry-flavored liqueur

⅓ cup heavy cream

2 TB. confectioners' sugar

1. Place ice cream in a microwave oven and microwave for 15 seconds on HIGH (100 percent power). Repeat, if necessary, until ice cream softens.

2. Scoop ice cream into a mixing bowl and stir in white chocolate, strawberries, and 2 tablespoons Chambord. Refreeze ice cream mixture for at least 50 minutes.

3. While mixture is freezing, combine cream and confectioners' sugar in a chilled mixing bowl. Beat at medium-high speed with an electric mixer until soft peaks form. To serve, divide ice cream into two bowls and drizzle with remaining Chambord. Top with whipped cream and serve immediately.

Variation: This recipe is open to endless variations; the only constant is the proportion of ice cream to chocolate. You can use any ice cream flavor, any type of chocolate, and any added additions from fruits to nuts.

🍽 **Double Feature** _____

In addition to adding flavor, the inclusion of liquor or a liqueur in a recipe means that the mixture will not freeze rock solid as alcohol doesn't freeze in a freezer.

Chapter 22

Baking Bonanza

In This Chapter

- ◆ Muffins and quick breads
- ◆ Rich cookies
- ◆ Pies and cakes

Part of wanting to cook for two is to pamper yourself and someone else. So some rich desserts—frosted layer cakes or sinfully rich cookies—are a fitting way to end the meal, and you'll find these recipes in this chapter.

But there's more to baking than desserts, so you'll also find some recipes for muffins and quick breads to start the day.

The Equipment Challenge

When I started baking the dessert recipes for this book, I encountered total frustration. Clearly baking is one area in which the hardware is hardly up to speed with the concept of the one- or two-person household. But gourmet shops do sell small tart pans, tiny loaf pans, and jumbo muffin pans, so you'll see a number of those used in these recipes.

But then improvisation became the rule of the day. I remembered as a teenager (those many decades ago) baking cakes in coffee cans. So I started to experiment and discovered that cakes can be baked in the washed out cans that entered the house holding diced tomatoes or garbanzo beans. And the benefit is that you don't have to wash the pan out for future use!

Blueberry Corn Muffins

The inherently sweet flavor of corn forms a good balance with the luscious blueberries in these muffins, a great way to start the morning.

½ **cup yellow cornmeal**	1 **TB. pure maple syrup**
1 **TB. granulated sugar**	1 **large egg white**
¼ **tsp. cream of tartar**	1 **TB. unsalted butter, melted**
⅛ **tsp. baking soda**	⅓ **cup fresh blueberries, rinsed**
Pinch salt	
⅓ **cup buttermilk**	

Active time: 10 minutes

Start to finish: 25 minutes, including 5 minutes for cooling

Each serving has:

276 calories

59 calories from fat

7 g fat

4 g saturated fat

6 g protein

56 g carbohydrates

1. Preheat the oven to 450°F and grease two jumbo (¾-cup) muffin tins. Combine cornmeal, sugar, cream of tartar, baking soda, and salt in a medium mixing bowl. Combine buttermilk, maple syrup, egg white, and melted butter in a small bowl and whisk well.

2. Add buttermilk mixture to cornmeal mixture, and stir until just blended. Stir in blueberries, and divide batter between the two greased muffin tins. Fill remaining muffin tins with water.

3. Bake muffins for 10 minutes or until a toothpick inserted in the center comes out clean. Place pan on a wire rack to cool for 5 minutes; then remove muffins and carefully pour out hot water. Serve immediately.

Double Trouble

The reason to fill the unused muffin tins with water is to keep the heat from the metal from scorching the muffins you're baking. Don't ignore this step.

Variation: Substitute raspberries or blackberries for blueberries. You can also make these savory muffins by eliminating the sugar and adding ⅓ cup grated cheddar cheese and 1 tsp. chili powder to the batter.

Apricot Ginger Muffins

Dried apricots and crystallized ginger give these muffins vivid flavor.

5 TB. unsalted butter

½ cup all-purpose flour

¼ tsp. baking soda

¼ tsp. baking powder

Pinch salt

1 medium egg

Dash vanilla extract

½ cup grated carrot

2 TB. finely chopped dried apricots

1½ tsp. finely chopped *crystallized ginger*

Active time: 15 minutes
Start to finish: 35 minutes
Each serving has:
459 calories
300 calories from fat
33 g fat
20 g saturated fat
7 g protein
34 g carbohydrates

1. Preheat the oven to 350°F and grease four standard (½ cup) muffin tins with 1 tablespoon butter. Melt remaining butter and set aside.

2. Combine flour, baking soda, baking powder, and salt in a medium mixing bowl and stir well. Combine melted butter, egg, and vanilla extract in a small mixing bowl and whisk well. Add egg mixture, carrot, apricots, and ginger to flour mixture, and stir until just blended. Divide batter into the prepared muffin tins, and fill remaining muffin tins with water.

3. Bake muffins for 15 to 17 minutes or until a toothpick inserted in the center comes out clean. Place muffin pan on a wire rack to cool for 5 minutes. Then remove muffins and carefully pour out hot water. Serve immediately.

Variation: Omit the crystallized ginger and add ½ tsp. ground cinnamon, and substitute golden raisins for dried apricots.

Duet Dialogue

Crystallized ginger is fresh ginger that has been simmered in a sugar syrup to preserve it. It's usually coated with granulated sugar to make it easier to chop.

Banana Bread

This is a rich recipe, and with some cream cheese frosting you can serve it for dessert, too!

Active time: 10 minutes

Start to finish: 35 minutes

Each serving has:

549 calories

237 calories from fat

26 g fat

16 g saturated fat

5.5 g protein

70.5 g carbohydrates

4 TB. unsalted butter

⅔ cup all-purpose flour

½ tsp. baking powder

¼ tsp. baking soda

Pinch salt

Pinch ground cinnamon

½ cup mashed banana

⅓ cup firmly packed dark brown sugar

1 large egg yolk

1 TB. dark rum

¼ tsp. pure vanilla extract

1. Preheat the oven to 350°F. Use 1 tablespoon butter to grease a 5×3-inch loaf pan and then use 1 tablespoon flour to dust inside of the pan. Shake out any extra flour. Melt remaining 3 tablespoons butter and set aside.

2. Combine flour, baking powder, baking soda, salt, and cinnamon in a mixing bowl and stir well. Combine melted butter, banana, sugar, egg yolk, rum, and vanilla in a small mixing bowl and whisk well.

3. Add banana mixture to flour mixture, and stir until just blended. Scrape batter into prepared pan, smoothing top. Bake bread for 20 to 25 minutes or until a toothpick inserted in the center comes out clean. Remove pan from the oven, and cool for 5 minutes on a wire rack. Remove bread from the pan, and serve hot or at room temperature. (You can freeze bread for up to two months, wrapped tightly in aluminum foil.)

 Double Feature

Bananas will ripen more quickly if placed in a paper bag with an over-ripe banana, an apple, or a tomato. These fruits give off a gas that aids in ripening.

Strawberry Shortcake

This is my nomination for the quintessential American dessert, and these biscuits are rich with buttery flavor.

1 cup all-purpose flour

4 TB. granulated sugar

1 tsp. *cream of tartar*

¾ tsp. baking soda

Pinch salt

5 TB. unsalted butter

½ pint strawberries

2 TB. crème de cassis or Chambord

⅔ cup heavy cream

3 TB. confectioners' sugar

1. Preheat the oven to 375°F and grease a baking sheet. Combine flour, 2 tablespoons sugar, cream of tartar, baking soda, and salt in a medium mixing bowl. Melt 1 tablespoon butter and set aside. Cut remaining butter into ¼-inch cubes.

2. Cut butter into flour mixture using a pastry blender, two knives, or your fingertips until mixture resembles coarse meal. Add ⅓ cup cream, and blend until just blended.

3. Scrape dough onto a floured surface, and knead lightly. Roll dough ¼-inch thick. Cut out 2 (4-inch) rounds and place them on the baking sheet. Brush rounds with melted butter. Cut out 2 (2½-inch) rounds, and place them on top of larger rounds. Brush tops with butter.

4. Bake for 15 to 17 minutes or until shortcakes are golden brown. Cool for at least 10 minutes on a wire rack.

5. While shortcakes are baking, rinse and slice strawberries, and toss with crème de cassis. Set aside. Just prior to serving, whip remaining ⅓ cup cream with confectioners' sugar until stiff peaks form.

6. To serve, mound strawberries on larger round, and top with whipped cream and smaller round. Serve immediately.

Variation: Substitute any berry or peeled peach slices for strawberries.

Active time: 15 minutes

Start to finish: 40 minutes, including 10 minutes for cooling

Each serving has:

787 calories

445 calories from fat

49 g fat

31 g saturated fat

7 g protein

74.5 g carbohydrates

Duet Dialogue

Cream of tartar comes from the acid deposited inside wine barrels. It's used in conjunction with baking soda to produce the same chemical reaction as that caused by baking powder.

Apricot Streusel Bars

Oats and coconut add their flavor and texture to the topping on these easy to make cookies.

Active time: 10 minutes

Start to finish: 50 minutes, including 30 minutes for cooling

Each serving has:

489 calories

183 calories from fat

20 g fat

12.5 g saturated fat

5 g protein

76 g carbohydrates

3 TB. unsalted butter

⅓ cup all-purpose flour

⅓ cup quick-cooking oats

3 TB. firmly packed dark brown sugar

1 TB. sweetened flaked coconut

⅛ tsp. baking powder

Pinch salt

¼ cup apricot preserves

2 TB. finely chopped dried apricots

1. Preheat the oven to 375°F. Line a 5×3-inch loaf pan with a strip of aluminum foil long enough to extend up the sides of the pan. Butter foil and sides of the pan with ½ tablespoon butter. Cut remaining butter into ¼-inch pieces.

2. Combine flour, oats, sugar, coconut, baking powder, and salt in a mixing bowl. Cut in butter using a pastry blender, two knives, or your fingertips until mixture resembles coarse meal. Reserve ¼ cup and pat remainder into bottom of the prepared pan.

3. Bake for 8 to 10 minutes or until crust is beginning to brown. Remove the pan from the oven, and allow to cool on a wire rack for 5 minutes. Combine preserves and chopped apricots in a small bowl and stir well. Spread mixture gently on top of crust, and sprinkle with reserved topping.

4. Bake for 20 minutes or until topping is browned. Remove the pan from the oven and cool for 20 minutes or until completely cooled. Run a knife along the edges, and then pull out of the pan by the aluminum foil. Cut into 4 bars. (You can do this up to two days in advance and keep at room temperature, tightly covered.)

Double Feature

Use this method with a loaf pan for baking small batches of any bar cookie. Bars are very tolerant of being cut back in batch size, but finding a pan to cook them in is the challenge!

Variation: Substitute any combination of flavored preserves and dried fruit, such as blueberries, cherries, or peaches, for apricots.

Chocolate Chip Cookies

There's been a proliferation of chocolate chip brand and flavors over the past few years, so use this as a base and experiment!

¼ **cup chopped walnuts or pecans (optional)**

⅓ **cup all-purpose flour**

⅛ **tsp. baking soda**

Pinch salt

3 TB. unsalted butter

⅓ **cup firmly packed light brown sugar**

1 small egg, lightly beaten

¼ **tsp. pure vanilla extract**

½ **cup chocolate chips**

Active time: 10 minutes

Start to finish: 25 minutes, including time for cooling

Each serving has:

619 calories

305 calories from fat

34 g fat

20 g saturated fat

7 g protein

79 g carbohydrates

1. Preheat the oven to 350°F. If using walnuts, toast them on a baking sheet for 5 to 7 minutes or until lightly browned. Set aside. Combine flour, baking soda, and salt, and set aside.

2. Combine butter and sugar in a medium mixing bowl. Beat at low speed with a hand-held electric mixer for 30 seconds to blend. Add egg and vanilla, and beat at medium speed for 1 minute or until light and fluffy. Add flour mixture and beat at low speed until dough is just blended. Stir in chocolate chips and nuts, if using.

3. Divide dough into 6 portions and place on an ungreased cookie sheet. Bake cookies for 12 to 15 minutes or until browned. Remove the baking sheet from the oven and allow cookies to cool for 2 minutes. Transfer cookies with a spatula to a cooling rack to cool further.

Variation: This is a master recipe for any sort of chip cookie. Feel free to use butterscotch, peanut butter, toffee, or white chocolate chips.

Double Feature

If you like cookies chewy, take them out of the oven at the minimum baking time, and if you like them crispy, leave them in the oven for another few minutes. The difference is as simple as that.

Key Lime Pie

The filling for these whipped-cream topped pies couldn't be easier to make, and they're always a hit.

<table>
<tr><td>½ cup graham cracker crumbs</td><td>1 large egg yolk</td></tr>
<tr><td>2 TB. unsalted butter, melted</td><td>3 TB. key lime juice</td></tr>
<tr><td>1 TB. granulated sugar</td><td>¼ cup heavy cream</td></tr>
<tr><td>4 TB. sweetened condensed milk</td><td>1 TB. confectioners' sugar</td></tr>
</table>

1. Preheat the oven to 350°F. Combine graham cracker crumbs, butter, and sugar in a small mixing bowl. Mix well. Divide crumbs between two (4-inch) tart pans with removable bottoms. Press crumbs onto bottom and up sides of pans. Bake crusts for 8 to 10 minutes or until set. Remove crusts from the oven and set aside.

2. Combine sweetened condensed milk, egg yolk, and lime juice in a small mixing bowl and whisk well. Pour filling on top of crusts. Bake for 8 to 10 minutes or until filling is set. Remove pies from the oven, and cool on a wire rack for 10 minutes. Refrigerate pies for at least 2 hours. (You can make these up to a day in advance, and refrigerate pies, loosely covered with plastic wrap.)

3. Combine cream and confectioners' sugar in a small mixing bowl. Beat at medium speed with a hand-held electric mixer or electric whisk until stiff peaks form. To serve, remove pies from tart pans, and top with whipped cream.

Active time: 15 minutes

Start to finish: 2½ hours, including 2 hours for chilling

Each serving has:

511 calories

283 calories from fat

31.5 g fat

18 g saturated fat

8 g protein

51 g carbohydrates

Duet Dialogue

Key limes are smaller and rounder than traditional limes, and their color is more yellow than green. The juice is more fragrant and more zesty.

Praline Cheesecakes

Brown sugar and pecans flavor these easy cheesecakes baked in graham cracker crusts.

½ cup graham cracker crumbs

2 TB. unsalted butter, melted

1 TB. granulated sugar

¼ cup chopped pecans

2 (3-oz.) pkg. cream cheese, softened

¼ cup firmly packed dark brown sugar

1 medium egg

1 TB. sour cream

2 tsp. all-purpose flour

¼ tsp. pure vanilla extract

Active time: 15 minutes
Start to finish: 3¼ hours, including 2 hours for chilling
Each serving has:
756 calories
522 calories from fat
58 g fat
29 g saturated fat
14 g protein
47.5 g carbohydrates

1. Preheat the oven to 350°F. Combine graham cracker crumbs, butter, and sugar in a small mixing bowl. Mix well. Divide crumbs between two (4-inch) tart pans with removable bottoms. Press crumbs onto bottom and up sides of pans. Bake crusts for 8 to 10 minutes or until set. Remove crusts from the oven and set aside. While crusts are baking, place pecans on a baking sheet and bake for 5 to 7 minutes or until lightly browned. Set aside.

2. Beat cream cheese and sugar in a medium mixing bowl at medium speed with a hand-held electric mixer for 2 minutes or until light and fluffy. Add egg, sour cream, flour, and vanilla extract. Beat for an additional minute or until smooth. Divide filling into baked shells, and sprinkle pecans on top.

3. Bake cheesecakes for 30 minutes or until set. Turn off and prop oven open; keep cheesecakes in the oven for an additional 30 minutes. Remove cheesecakes from the oven and cool for 10 minutes on a wire rack. Refrigerate pies for at least 2 hours. (You can do this up to a day in advance, and refrigerate pies, loosely covered with plastic wrap.)

4. To serve, unmold cheesecakes and place on individual plates.

Variation: Omit pecans and substitute granulated sugar for brown sugar. Increase vanilla to ½ teaspoon, and add 1 tsp. grated lemon zest to batter.

Duet Dialogue

Praline is both a flavor combination and a specific candy in traditional New Orleans' cooking. As a flavor, it's the combination of pecan and brown sugar, and as a candy, it's patties made by boiling those ingredients.

Carrot Cakes with Gingered Cream Cheese Frosting

Coconut, pineapple, and walnuts are added along with carrots to these cakes, and then the cream cheese frosting adds richness.

Active time: 30 minutes

Start to finish: 4 hours, including cooling times

Each serving has:

1413 calories

651 calories from fat

72 g fat

26 g saturated fat

17 g protein

182 g carbohydrates

¼ **cup chopped walnuts**

1 **TB. unsalted butter, softened**

1 **cup all-purpose flour**

⅓ **cup buttermilk**

¼ **cup vegetable oil**

Yolk of 1 large egg

½ **tsp. pure vanilla extract**

¼ **cup granulated sugar**

½ **tsp. baking powder**

¼ **tsp. salt**

½ **tsp. ground cinnamon**

½ **cup finely grated carrots**

2 **TB. raisins**

2 **TB. sweetened flaked coconut**

2 **TB. finely chopped fresh pineapple**

½ **(8-oz.) pkg. cream cheese, softened**

2 **TB. unsalted butter, softened**

2 **cups confectioners' sugar**

2 **tsp. finely chopped crystallized ginger**

½ **tsp. pure vanilla extract**

Additional toasted walnuts for garnish (optional)

---

1. Preheat the oven to 350°F. Place walnuts on a baking sheet, and toast for 5 to 7 minutes or until lightly brown. Set aside. Grease inside of cans with butter, and add 1 tablespoon flour to each. Dust inside of cans with flour, and tap out any excess. Set aside.

2. Combine buttermilk, oil, egg yolk, and vanilla in a small bowl and whisk well. Combine remaining flour, sugar, baking powder, salt, and cinnamon in a medium mixing bowl and whisk well. Add buttermilk mixture and whisk just until dry ingredients are moistened. Fold in nuts, carrots, raisins, coconut, and pineapple.

3. Divide batter between the prepared cans. Place cans on a baking sheet. Bake cakes for 35 to 40 minutes or until a toothpick inserted in the center of one comes out clean. Remove baking sheet from the oven and transfer cakes to a wire rack to cool for 10 minutes.

4. Run a thin, sharp knife around the edge of each can, and invert the cans to release cakes. Turn cakes upright and cool on the rack. (You can do this two days in advance and refrigerate them, tightly wrapped in plastic wrap.)

5. For frosting, combine cream cheese, butter, confectioners' sugar, ginger, and vanilla extract in a large mixing bowl. Beat at medium speed with a hand-held electric mixer for 2 minutes or until light and fluffy, scraping down the sides of the bowl with a rubber spatula as necessary.

6. To serve, cut each in half horizontally. Spread layer of frosting about ¼ inch thick on cut side of one cake half, then stack other half on top of it. Frost top and sides of cake. Repeat with remaining cake and frosting. Garnish with additional nuts. (Once frosted, refrigerate cakes for up to one day, loosely covered with plastic wrap.)

Double Trouble

Carrots take a long time to cook, so it's very important that they're grated on the fine side of the box grater. In a cake, carrots are used for their moisture as well as their flavor.

Appendix A

Glossary

accoutrement   An accompaniment, trapping, or garnish.

al dente   Italian for "against the teeth." Refers to pasta or rice that's neither soft nor hard, but just slightly firm against the teeth.

all-purpose flour   Flour that contains only the inner part of the wheat grain. Usable for all purposes from cakes to gravies.

allspice   Named for its flavor echoes of several spices (cinnamon, cloves, nutmeg), allspice is used in many desserts and in rich marinades and stews.

almonds   Mild, sweet, and crunchy nuts that combine nicely with creamy and sweet food items.

amaretto   A popular almond liqueur.

anchovies (also **sardines**)   Tiny, flavorful preserved fish that typically come in cans. Anchovies are a traditional garnish for Caesar salad, the dressing of which contains anchovy paste.

andouille sausage   A sausage made with highly seasoned pork chitterlings and tripe, and a standard component of many Cajun dishes.

antipasto   A classic Italian-style appetizer, usually served together as one course or plate, including an assortment of prepared meats, cheeses, and vegetables such as prosciutto, capicolla, mozzarella, mushrooms, and olives.

Arborio rice   A plump Italian rice used, among other purposes, for risotto.

artichoke hearts   The center part of the artichoke flower, often found canned in grocery stores.

arugula   A spicy-peppery garden plant with leaves that resemble a dandelion and have a distinctive—and very sharp—flavor.

au gratin   The quick broiling of a dish before serving to brown the top ingredients. When used in a recipe name, the term often implies cheese and a creamy sauce.

bain marie   A water bath that cooks food gently in the oven by surrounding it with simmering water.

bake   To cook in a dry oven. Dry-heat cooking often results in a crisping of the exterior of the food being cooked. Moist-heat cooking, through methods such as steaming, poaching, etc., brings a much different, moist quality to the food.

balsamic vinegar   Vinegar produced primarily in Italy from a specific type of grape and aged in wood barrels. It is heavier, darker, and sweeter than most vinegars.

bamboo shoots   Crunchy, tasty white parts of the growing bamboo plant, often purchased canned.

barbecue   To quick-cook over high heat or to cook something long and slow in a rich liquid (barbecue sauce).

basil   A flavorful, almost sweet, resinous herb delicious with tomatoes and used in all kinds of Italian or Mediterranean-style dishes.

baste   To keep foods moist during cooking by spooning, brushing, or drizzling with a liquid.

beat   To quickly mix substances.

Belgian endive   A plant that resembles a small, elongated, tightly packed head of romaine lettuce. The thick, crunchy leaves can be broken off and used with dips and spreads.

black pepper   A biting and pungent seasoning, freshly ground pepper is a must for many dishes and adds an extra level of flavor and taste.

blanch   To place a food in boiling water for about one minute (or less) to partially cook the exterior and then submerge in or rinse with cool water to halt the cooking.

blend   To completely mix something, usually with a blender or food processor, more slowly than beating.

blue cheese   A blue-veined cheese that crumbles easily and has a somewhat soft texture, usually sold in a block. The color is from a flavorful, edible mold that is often added or injected into the cheese.

boil   To heat a liquid to a point where water is forced to turn into steam, causing the liquid to bubble. To boil something is to insert it into boiling water. A rapid boil is when many bubbles form on the surface of the liquid.

bok choy (also **Chinese cabbage**)   A member of the cabbage family with thick stems, crisp texture, and fresh flavor. It's perfect for stir-frying.

bouquet garni   A collection of herbs including bay leaf, parsley, thyme, and others traditionally tied in a bunch or packaged in cheesecloth for cooking and subsequent removal.

braise   To cook with the introduction of some liquid, usually over an extended period of time.

breadcrumbs   Tiny pieces of crumbled dry bread, often used for topping or coating.

Brie   A creamy cow's milk cheese from France with a soft, edible rind and a mild flavor.

brine   A highly salted, often seasoned, liquid used to flavor and preserve foods. To brine a food is to soak, or preserve, it by submerging it in brine. The salt in the brine penetrates the fibers of the meat and makes it moist and tender.

broccoli rabe   An Italian vegetable more bitter than conventional broccoli with long green stems and small clusters of flowers.

broil   To cook in a dry oven under the overhead high-heat element.

broth   *See* stock.

brown   To cook in a skillet, turning, until the food's surface is seared and brown in color, to lock in the juices.

brown rice   Whole-grain rice including the germ with a characteristic pale brown or tan color; more nutritious and flavorful than white rice.

bruschetta (or **crostini**)   Slices of toasted or grilled bread with garlic and olive oil, often with other toppings.

bulgur   A wheat kernel that's been steamed, dried, and crushed and is sold in fine and coarse textures.

Cajun cooking   A style of cooking that combines French and Southern characteristics and includes many highly seasoned stews and meats.

cake flour   A high-starch, soft, and fine flour used primarily for cakes.

canapés   Bite-size hors d'oeuvres usually served on a small piece of bread or toast.

capers   Flavorful buds of a Mediterranean plant, ranging in size from *nonpareil* (about the size of a small pea) to larger, grape-size caper berries produced in Spain.

cappuccino   A coffee drink consisting of equal parts espresso and steamed milk topped with milk foam.

caramelize   To cook sugar over low heat until it develops a sweet caramel flavor. The term is increasingly gaining use to describe cooking vegetables (especially onions) or meat in butter or oil over low heat until they soften, sweeten, and develop a caramel color.

caraway   A distinctive spicy seed used for bread, pork, cheese, and cabbage dishes. It is known to reduce stomach upset, which is why it is often paired with, for example, sauerkraut.

carbohydrate   A nutritional component found in starches, sugars, fruits, and vegetables that causes a rise in blood glucose levels. Carbohydrates supply energy and many important nutrients, including vitamins, minerals, and antioxidants.

cardamom   An intense, sweet-smelling spice, common to Indian cooking, used in baking and coffee.

cayenne   A fiery spice made from (hot) chili peppers, especially the cayenne chili, a slender, red, and very hot pepper.

cheddar   The ubiquitous hard cow's milk cheese with a rich, buttery flavor that ranges from mellow to sharp. Originally produced in England, cheddar is now produced worldwide.

chevre   French for "goat milk cheese," chevre is a typically creamy-salty soft cheese delicious by itself or paired with fruits or chutney. Chevres vary in style from mild and creamy to aged, firm, and flavorful.

chili powder   A seasoning blend that includes chili pepper, cumin, garlic, and oregano. Proportions vary among different versions, but all offer a warm, rich flavor.

chili sauce   A ketchup-like condiment with a chunkier texture containing tomatoes, onions, vinegar, sugar, and spices.

chilis (or **chiles**)   Any one of many different "hot" peppers, ranging in intensity from the relatively mild ancho pepper to the blisteringly hot habañero.

Chinese chili paste with garlic   A fiery thick paste made from fermented fava beans, red chilies, and garlic.

Chinese five-spice powder   A seasoning blend of cinnamon, anise, ginger, fennel, and pepper.

chipotle   Smoked dried jalapeño chilies packed in a spicy adobo sauce.

chives   A member of the onion family, chives grow in bunches of long leaves that resemble tall grass or the green tops of onions and offer a light onion flavor.

chop   To cut into pieces, usually qualified by an adverb such as "*coarsely* chopped," or by a size measurement such as "chopped into ½-inch pieces." "Finely chopped" is much closer to mince.

chorizo   A spiced pork sausage eaten alone and as a component in many recipes.

chutney   A thick condiment often served with Indian curries made with fruits and/or vegetables with vinegar, sugar, and spices.

cider vinegar   Vinegar produced from apple cider, popular in North America.

cilantro   A member of the parsley family used in Mexican cooking (especially salsa) and some Asian dishes. Use in moderation, as the flavor can overwhelm. The seed of the cilantro is the spice coriander.

cinnamon   A sweet, rich, aromatic spice commonly used in baking or desserts. Cinnamon can also be used for delicious and interesting entrées.

clove   A sweet, strong, almost wintergreen-flavor spice used in baking and with meats such as ham.

complete protein   A food that contains all the essential amino acids.

coriander   A rich, warm, spicy seed used in all types of recipes, from African to South American, from entrées to desserts.

cornstarch   A powdery substance used for thickening obtained from finely grinding the endosperm of corn kernels.

count   In terms of seafood or other foods that come in small sizes, the number of that item that compose one pound. For example, 31 to 40 count shrimp are large appetizer shrimp often served with cocktail sauce; 51 to 60 are much smaller.

couscous Granular semolina (durum wheat) that is cooked and used in many Mediterranean and North African dishes.

cream As a verb, to beat fat and sugar together until light and fluffy.

cream of tartar An acid used in conjunction with baking soda for leavening.

crème frâiche A dairy product similar in flavor to sour cream that does not curdle if it boils.

crimini mushrooms A relative of the white button mushroom but brown in color and with a richer flavor. The larger, fully grown version is the portobello. *See also* portobello mushrooms.

croutons Chunks of bread, usually between ¼ and ½ inch in size, sometimes seasoned and baked, broiled, or fried to a crisp texture and used in soups and salads.

crudités Fresh vegetables served as an appetizer, often all together on one tray.

crystallized ginger Fresh ginger that is simmered in a sugar syrup to preserve it.

cumin A fiery, smoky-tasting spice popular in Middle Eastern and Indian dishes. Cumin is a seed; ground cumin seed is the most common form used in cooking.

curd A gelatinous substance resulting from coagulated milk used to make cheese. Curd also refers to dishes of similar texture, such as dishes made with egg (lemon curd).

curing A method of preserving uncooked foods, usually meats or fish, by either salting and smoking or pickling.

curry Rich, spicy, Indian-style sauces and the dishes prepared with them. A curry uses curry powder as its base seasoning.

curry paste A thick ingredient made with chilies, curry powder, and spices in clarified butter used in Thai cooking.

curry powder A ground blend of rich and flavorful spices used as a basis for curry and many other Indian-influenced dishes. Common ingredients include hot pepper, nutmeg, cumin, cinnamon, pepper, and turmeric. Some curry can also be found in paste form.

custard A cooked mixture of eggs and milk popular as a base for desserts.

dash A few drops, usually of a liquid, released by a quick shake of, for example, a bottle of hot sauce.

deglaze   To scrape up the bits of meat and seasoning left in a pan or skillet after cooking. Usually this is done by adding a liquid such as wine or broth and creating a flavorful stock that can be used to create sauces.

devein   The removal of the dark vein from the back of a large shrimp with a sharp knife.

dice   To cut into small cubes about ¼-inch square.

Dijon mustard   Hearty, spicy mustard made in the style of the Dijon region of France.

dill   An herb perfect for eggs, salmon, cheese dishes, and, of course, vegetables (pickles!).

dollop   A spoonful of something creamy and thick, like sour cream or whipped cream.

double boiler   A set of two pots designed to nest together, one inside the other, and provide consistent, moist heat for foods that need delicate treatment. The bottom pot holds water (not quite touching the bottom of the top pot); the top pot holds the ingredient you want to heat.

dredge   To cover a piece of food with a dry substance, such as flour or corn meal.

drizzle   To lightly sprinkle drops of a liquid over food, often as the finishing touch to a dish.

dry   In the context of wine, a wine that contains little or no residual sugar, so it's not very sweet.

emulsion   A combination of liquid ingredients that do not normally mix well beaten together to create a thick liquid, such as a fat or oil with water. Creation of an emulsion must be done carefully and rapidly to ensure that particles of one ingredient are suspended in the other.

entrée   The main dish in a meal. In France, however, the entrée is considered the first course.

extra-virgin olive oil   *See* olive oil.

fennel   In seed form, a fragrant, licorice-tasting herb. The bulbs have a much milder flavor and a celery-like crunch and are used as a vegetable in salads or cooked recipes.

fermented black beans   Tiny soy beans preserved in salt with a pungent flavor.

feta   A white, crumbly, sharp, and salty cheese popular in Greek cooking and on salads. Traditional feta is usually made with sheep milk, but feta-style cheese can be made from sheep, cow, or goat's milk.

fillet   A piece of meat or seafood with the bones removed.

flake   To break into thin sections, as with fish.

floret   The flower or bud end of broccoli or cauliflower.

flour   Grains ground into a meal. Wheat is perhaps the most common flour. Flour is also made from oats, rye, buckwheat, soybeans, etc. *See also* all-purpose flour; cake flour; whole-wheat flour.

fold   To combine dense and light mixtures with a circular action from the middle of the bowl.

frittata   A skillet-cooked mixture of eggs and other ingredients that's not stirred but cooked slowly, and then either flipped or finished under the broiler.

fritter   A food, such as apples or corn, coated or mixed with batter and deep-fried for a crispy, crunchy exterior.

fry   *See* sauté.

fusion   To blend two or more styles of cooking, such as Chinese and French.

garbanzo beans (or **chickpeas**)   A yellow-gold, roundish bean used as the base ingredient in hummus. Chickpeas are high in fiber and low in fat.

garlic   A member of the onion family, a pungent and flavorful element in many savory dishes. A garlic bulb contains multiple cloves. Each clove, when chopped, provides about one teaspoon garlic. Most recipes call for cloves or chopped garlic by the teaspoon.

garnish   An embellishment not vital to the dish, but added to enhance visual appeal.

ginger   Available in fresh root or dried, ground form, this spice adds a pungent, sweet, and spicy quality to a dish.

Gorgonzola   A creamy and rich Italian blue cheese. "Dolce" is sweet, and that's the kind you want.

grate   To shave into tiny pieces using a sharp rasp or grater.

grind   To reduce a large, hard substance, often a seasoning such as peppercorns, to the consistency of sand.

grits   Coarsely ground grains, usually corn.

Gruyère   A rich, sharp cow's milk cheese made in Switzerland that has a nutty flavor.

handful   An unscientific measurement; the amount of an ingredient you can hold in your hand.

Havarti   A creamy, Danish, mild cow's milk cheese, perhaps most enjoyed in its herbed versions such as Havarti with dill.

hazelnuts (also **filberts**)   A sweet nut popular in desserts and, to a lesser degree, in savory dishes.

herbes de Provence   A seasoning mix including basil, fennel, marjoram, rosemary, sage, and thyme, common in the south of France.

hoisin sauce   A sweet Asian condiment similar to ketchup made with soybeans, sesame, chili peppers, and sugar.

horseradish   A sharp, spicy root that forms the flavor base in many condiments from cocktail sauce to sharp mustards. Prepared horseradish contains vinegar and oil, among other ingredients. Use pure horseradish much more sparingly than the prepared version, or try cutting it with sour cream.

infusion   A liquid in which flavorful ingredients such as herbs have been soaked or steeped to extract that flavor into the liquid.

instant espresso powder   A powder made from dehydrated brewed espresso imported from Italy.

Italian seasoning   A blend of dried herbs, including basil, oregano, rosemary, and thyme.

jicama   A juicy, crunchy, sweet, large, round Central American vegetable. If you can't find jicama, try substituting sliced water chestnuts.

julienne   A French word meaning "to slice into very thin pieces."

kalamata olives   Traditionally from Greece, these medium-small long black olives have a smoky rich flavor.

Key limes   Very small limes grown primarily in Florida, known for their tart taste.

knead   To work dough to make it pliable so it holds gas bubbles as it bakes. Kneading is fundamental in the process of making yeast breads.

kosher salt   A coarse-grained salt made without any additives or iodine.

lemongrass An herb used in Asian cooking that has a lemony flavor and fragrance.

lentils Tiny lens-shape pulses used in European, Middle Eastern, and Indian cuisines.

linguicça A highly spiced Portuguese pork sausage flavored with garlic and paprika.

macerate To mix sugar or another sweetener with fruit. The fruit softens, and its juice is released to mix with the sweetener.

Manchego A Spanish sheep's milk cheese with a mellow, nutty flavor and semi-firm texture.

marinate To soak meat, seafood, or other food in a seasoned sauce, called a marinade, which is high in acid content. The acids break down the muscle of the meat, making it tender and adding flavor.

marjoram A sweet herb, a cousin of and similar to oregano, popular in Greek, Spanish, and Italian dishes.

mascarpone A thick, creamy, spreadable cheese, traditionally from Italy.

medallion A small round cut, usually of meat or vegetables such as carrots or cucumbers.

meld To allow flavors to blend and spread over time. Melding is often why recipes call for overnight refrigeration and is also why some dishes taste better as leftovers.

meringue A baked mixture of sugar and beaten egg whites, often used as a dessert topping.

mesclun Mixed salad greens, usually containing lettuce and assorted greens such as arugula, cress, endive, and others.

mince To cut into very small pieces smaller than diced pieces, about ⅛ inch or smaller.

mold A decorative, shaped metal pan in which contents, such as mousse or gelatin, set up and take the shape of the pan.

monkfish Called *lotte* in French, it's a mildly flavored fish with a texture similar to that of lobster.

mortadella An Italian cold cut similar to bologna in flavor, but with bits of fat and pistachio nuts added.

nutmeg A sweet, fragrant, musky spice used primarily in baking.

olive oil   A fragrant liquid produced by crushing or pressing olives. Extra-virgin olive oil—the most flavorful and highest quality—is produced from the first pressing of a batch of olives; oil is also produced from later pressings.

olives   The fruit of the olive tree commonly grown on all sides of the Mediterranean. Black olives are also called "ripe" olives. Green olives are immature, although they are also widely eaten. *See also* kalamata olives.

oregano   A fragrant, slightly astringent herb used in Greek, Spanish, and Italian dishes.

orzo   A rice-shape pasta used in Greek cooking.

oxidation   The browning of fruit flesh that happens over time and with exposure to air. Minimize oxidation by rubbing the cut surfaces with a lemon half. Oxidation also affects wine, which is why the taste changes over time after a bottle is opened.

oyster sauce   A Chinese condiment made from oysters and soy sauce that gives foods a rich but not "fishy" flavor.

panko   Japanese breadcrumbs that are longer and lighter than traditional bread-crumbs so foods become very crisp.

paprika   A rich, red, warm, earthy spice that also lends a rich red color to many dishes.

parboil   To partially cook in boiling water or broth, similar to blanching (although blanched foods are quickly cooled with cold water).

Parmesan   A hard, dry, flavorful cheese primarily used grated or shredded as a sea-soning for Italian-style dishes.

parsley   A fresh-tasting green leafy herb, often used as a garnish.

pecans   Rich, buttery nuts, native to North America, that have a high unsaturated fat content.

peppercorns   Large, round, dried berries ground to produce pepper.

Pernod   A French licorice-flavored liqueur.

pesto   A thick spread or sauce made with fresh basil leaves, garlic, olive oil, pine nuts, and Parmesan cheese. Some newer versions are made with other herbs.

pickle   A food, usually a vegetable such as a cucumber, that's been pickled in brine.

pilaf   A rice dish in which the rice is browned in butter or oil and then cooked in a flavorful liquid such as a broth, often with the addition of meats or vegetables. The rice absorbs the broth, resulting in a savory dish.

pinch   An unscientific measurement term, the amount of an ingredient—typically a dry, granular substance such as an herb or seasoning—you can hold between your finger and thumb.

pine nuts (also **pignoli** or **piñon**)   Nuts grown on pine trees, that are rich (read: high fat), flavorful, and a bit pine-y. Pine nuts are a traditional component of pesto and add a wonderful hearty crunch to many other recipes.

poach   To cook a food in simmering liquid, such as water, wine, or broth.

Polenta   Traditional Northern Italian cornmeal mush.

porcini mushrooms   Rich and flavorful mushrooms used in rice and Italian-style dishes.

portobello mushrooms   A mature and larger form of the smaller crimini mushroom, portobellos are brownish, chewy, and flavorful. Often served as whole caps, grilled, and as thin sautéed slices. *See also* crimini mushrooms.

praline   A combination of pecans and brown sugar as a flavor combination or as a specific candy.

preheat   To turn on an oven, broiler, or other cooking appliance in advance of cooking so the temperature will be at the desired level when the assembled dish is ready for cooking.

prosciutto   Dry, salt-cured ham that originated in Italy.

purée   To reduce a food to a thick, creamy texture, usually using a blender or food processor.

reduce   To boil or simmer a broth or sauce to remove some of the water content, resulting in more concentrated flavor and color.

render   To cook a meat to the point where its fat melts and can be removed.

reserve   To hold a specified ingredient for another use later in the recipe.

rice paper pancakes   Brittle translucent sheets made from a dough of water combined with the pith of the rice-paper plant.

rice vinegar   Vinegar produced from fermented rice or rice wine, popular in Asian-style dishes. Different from rice wine vinegar.

ricotta   A fresh Italian cheese, smoother than cottage cheese, with a slightly sweet flavor.

risotto   A popular Italian rice dish made by browning Arborio rice in butter or oil and then slowly adding liquid to cook the rice, resulting in a creamy texture.

roast   To cook something uncovered in an oven, usually without additional liquid.

Roquefort   A world-famous (French) creamy but sharp sheep's milk cheese containing blue lines of mold.

rosemary   A pungent, sweet herb used with chicken, pork, fish, and especially lamb. A little of it goes a long way.

roux   A mixture of butter or another fat and flour, used to thicken sauces and soups.

saffron   A spice made from the stamens of crocus flowers, saffron lends a dramatic yellow color and distinctive flavor to a dish. Use only tiny amounts of this expensive herb.

sage   An herb with a musty yet fruity, lemon-rind scent and "sunny" flavor.

salsa   A style of mixing fresh vegetables and/or fresh fruit in a coarse chop. Salsa can be spicy or not, fruit-based or not, and served as a starter on its own (with chips, for example) or as a companion to a main course.

sauté   To pan-cook over lower heat than used for frying.

savory   A popular herb with a fresh, woody taste.

sear   To quickly brown the exterior of a food, especially meat, over high heat to preserve interior moisture.

sesame oil   An oil, made from pressing sesame seeds, that's tasteless if clear, and aromatic and flavorful if brown.

shallot   A member of the onion family that grows as a bulb somewhat like garlic and has a milder onion flavor. When a recipe calls for shallot, use the entire bulb.

shellfish   A broad range of seafood, including clams, mussels, oysters, crabs, shrimp, and lobster. Some people are allergic to shellfish, so take care with its inclusion in recipes.

shiitake mushrooms   Large, dark brown mushrooms with a hearty, meaty flavor that can be used either fresh or dried, grilled or as a component in other recipes, and as a flavoring source for broth.

shred   To cut into many long, thin slices.

silverskin   The tough, almost iridescent membrane coating tenderloin cuts of meat that must be removed before cooking.

simmer   To boil gently so the liquid barely bubbles.

skewers   Thin wooden or metal sticks, usually about 8 inches long, used for assembling kebabs, dipping food pieces into hot sauces, or serving single-bite food items with a bit of panache.

skillet (also **frying pan**)   A generally heavy, flat-bottomed metal pan with a handle designed to cook food over heat on a stovetop or campfire.

skim   To remove fat or other material from the top of liquid.

slice   To cut into thin pieces.

steam   To suspend a food over boiling water and allow the heat of the steam (water vapor) to cook the food. A quick cooking method, steaming preserves the flavor and texture of a food.

steep   To let sit in hot water, as in steeping tea in hot water for 10 minutes.

stew   To slowly cook pieces of food submerged in a liquid. Also, a dish that has been prepared by this method.

Stilton   The famous English blue-veined cheese, delicious with toasted nuts and renowned for its pairing with Port wine.

stir-fry   To cook small pieces of food in a wok or skillet over high heat, moving and turning the food quickly to cook all sides.

stock   A flavorful broth made by cooking meats and/or vegetables with seasonings until the liquid absorbs these flavors. This liquid is then strained and the solids discarded. Can be eaten alone or used as a base for soups, stews, etc.

strata   A savory bread pudding made with eggs and cheese.

superfine sugar   Called "castor sugar" in England, it's very finely granulated so it dissolves instantly.

sweat   To cook vegetables covered over low heat in a small amount of fat to soften them.

Swiss chard   A vegetable that's a member of the beet family, grown for its celery-like stalks.

tagine   A generic term for stews from Morocco traditionally cooked in a clay pot called a "tagine."

tarragon   A sweet, rich-smelling herb perfect with seafood, vegetables (especially asparagus), chicken, and pork.

teriyaki   A Japanese-style sauce composed of soy sauce, rice wine, ginger, and sugar that works well with seafood, as well as most meats.

thyme   A minty, zesty herb.

toast   To heat something, usually bread, so it's browned and crisp.

tofu   A cheese-like substance made from soybeans and soy milk.

tomatillo   A small, round fruit with a distinctive spicy flavor, often found in south-of-the-border dishes. To use, remove the papery outer skin, rinse off any sticky residue, and chop like a tomato.

turmeric   A spicy, pungent yellow root used in many dishes, especially Indian cuisine, for color and flavor. Turmeric is the source of the yellow color in many prepared mustards.

veal   Meat from a calf, generally characterized by mild flavor and tenderness.

vegetable steamer   An insert for a large saucepan or a special pot with tiny holes in the bottom designed to fit on another pot to hold food to be steamed above boiling water. *See also* steam.

venison   Deer meat.

vinegar   An acidic liquid widely used as dressing and seasoning, often made from fermented grapes, apples, or rice. *See also* balsamic vinegar; cider vinegar; rice vinegar; white vinegar; wine vinegar.

walnuts   A rich, slightly woody-flavored nut.

wasabi   Japanese horseradish, a fiery, pungent condiment used with many Japanese-style dishes. Most often sold as a powder, add water to create a paste.

water chestnuts   A tuber, popular in many types of Asian-style cooking. The flesh is white, crunchy, and juicy, and the vegetable holds its texture whether cool or hot.

whisk   To rapidly mix, introducing air to the mixture.

white mushrooms   Button mushrooms. When fresh, they have an earthy smell and an appealing "soft crunch."

white vinegar   The most common type of vinegar, produced from grain.

whole-wheat flour   Wheat flour that contains the entire grain.

wild rice   Actually a grass with a rich, nutty flavor, popular as an unusual and nutritious side dish.

wine vinegar   Vinegar produced from red or white wine.

wok   A pan for quick cooking.

Worcestershire sauce   Originally developed in India and containing tamarind, this spicy sauce is used as a seasoning for many meats and other dishes.

yeast   Tiny fungi that, when mixed with water, sugar, flour, and heat, release carbon dioxide bubbles, which, in turn, cause the bread to rise.

zest   Small slivers of peel, usually from a citrus fruit such as lemon, lime, or orange.

zester   A kitchen tool used to scrape zest off a fruit. A small grater also works well.

Metric Conversion Chart

The scientifically precise calculations needed for baking are not necessary when cooking conventionally. This chart is designed for general cooking. If making conversions for baking, grab your calculator and compute the exact figure.

Converting Ounces to Grams

The numbers in the following table are approximate. To reach the exact amount of grams, multiply the number of ounces by 28.35.

Ounces	Grams
1 oz.	30 g
2 oz.	60 g
3 oz.	85 g
4 oz.	115 g
5 oz.	140 g
6 oz.	180 g
7 oz.	200 g
8 oz.	225 g
9 oz.	250 g
10 oz.	285 g

continues

continued

Ounces	Grams
11 oz.	300 g
12 oz.	340 g
13 oz.	370 g
14 oz.	400 g
15 oz.	425 g
16 oz.	450 g

Converting Quarts to Liters

The numbers in the following table are approximate. To reach the exact amount of liters, multiply the number of quarts by 0.95.

Quarts	Liter
1 cup (¼ qt.)	¼ L
1 pint (½ qt.)	½ L
1 qt.	1 L
2 qt.	2 L
2½ qt.	2½ L
3 qt.	2¾ L
4 qt.	3¾ L
5 qt.	4¾ L
6 qt.	5½ L
7 qt.	6½ L
8 qt.	7½ L

Converting Pounds to Grams and Kilograms

The numbers in the following table are approximate. To reach the exact amount of kilograms, multiply the number of pounds by 453.6.

Pounds	Grams; Kilograms
1 lb.	450 g
1½ lb.	675 g
2 lb.	900 g
2½ lb.	1,125 g; 1¼ kg
3 lb.	1,350 g
3½ lb.	1,500 g; 1½ kg
4 lb.	1,800 g
4½ lb.	2 kg
5 lb.	2¼ kg
5½ lb.	2½ kg
6 lb.	2¾ kg
6½ lb.	3 kg
7 lb.	3¼ kg
7½ lb.	3½ kg
8 lb.	3¾ kg

Converting Fahrenheit to Celsius

The numbers in the following table are approximate. To reach the exact temperature, subtract 32 from the Fahrenheit reading, multiply the number by 5, and then divide by 9.

Fahrenheit	Celsius
170	77
180	82
190	88
200	95
225	110
250	120
300	150
325	165
350	180

continues

continued

Fahrenheit	Celsius
375	190
400	205
425	220
450	230
475	245
500	260

Converting Inches to Centimeters

The numbers in the following table are approximate. To reach the exact number of centimeters, multiply the number of inches by 2.54.

Inches	Centimeters
½ in.	1.5 cm
1 in.	2.5 cm
2 in.	5 cm
3 in.	8 cm
4 in.	10 cm
5 in.	13 cm
6 in.	15 cm
7 in.	18 cm
8 in.	20 cm
9 in.	23 cm
10 in.	25 cm
11 in.	28 cm
12 in.	30 cm

Measurement Tables

Table of Weights and Measures of Common Ingredients

Food	Quantity	Yield
Apples	1 lb.	2½ to 3 cups, sliced
Avocado	1 lb.	1 cup mashed fruit
Banana	1 medium	1 cup, sliced
Bell peppers	1 lb.	3 to 4 cups, sliced
Blueberries	1 lb.	3⅓ cups
Butter	¼ lb. (1 stick)	8 TB.
Cabbage	1 lb.	4 cups, packed shredded
Carrots	1 lb.	3 cups, diced or sliced
Chocolate, morsels	12 oz.	2 cups
Chocolate, bulk	1 oz.	3 TB., grated
Cocoa powder	1 oz.	¼ cup
Coconut, flaked	7 oz.	2½ cups
Cream	½ pt.	1 cup, 2 cups whipped
Cream cheese	8 oz.	1 cup
Flour	1 lb.	4 cups
Lemon	1 medium	3 TB. juice

continues

Table of Weights and Measures of Common Ingredients   (continued)

Food	Quantity	Yield
Lemon	1 medium	2 tsp. zest
Milk	1 qt.	4 cups
Molasses	12 oz.	1½ cups
Mushrooms	1 lb.	5 cups, sliced
Onion	1 medium	½ cup, chopped
Peaches	1 lb.	2 cups, sliced
Peanuts	5 oz.	1 cup
Pecans	6 oz.	1½ cups
Pineapple	1 medium	3 cups, diced
Potatoes	1 lb.	3 cups, sliced
Raisins	1 lb.	3 cups
Rice	1 lb.	2 to 2½ cups, raw
Spinach	1 lb.	¾ cup, cooked
Squash, summer	1 lb.	3½ cups, sliced
Strawberries	1 pt.	1½ cups, sliced
Sugar, brown	1 lb.	2¼ cups, packed
Sugar, confectioners'	l lb.	4 cups
Sugar, granulated	1 lb.	2¼ cups
Tomatoes	1 lb.	1½ cups pulp
Walnuts	4 oz.	1 cup

Table of Liquid Measurements

Pinch	=	less than ⅛ tsp.
3 tsp.	=	1 TB.
2 TB.	=	1 oz.
8 TB.	=	½ cup
2 cups	=	1 pint
1 quart	=	2 pints
1 gallon	=	4 quarts

Pantry Checklist

These items are frequently found on the ingredient lists in this book. If you have these on hand, you can stay in the express lane when shopping.

The Basics

- All-purpose flour (2-lb. bag)
- Granulated sugar (1-lb. bag)
- Dark brown sugar (1-lb. bag)
- Confectioners' sugar (1-lb. bag)
- Salt
- Cornstarch
- Baking powder
- Baking soda

Canned Goods

- Tomato sauce (8-oz. cans)
- Diced tomatoes (14.5-oz. cans)
- Tomato paste (3-oz. tube)
- Chicken stock (14.5-oz. cans)
- Beef stock (14.5-oz. cans)
- Vegetable stock (14.5-oz. cans)
- Canned beans (15-oz. cans) such as garbanzo beans, black beans, and kidney beans

Shelf-Stable Items

- Long-grain rice
- Arborio rice
- Spaghetti, linguine, or fettuccine
- Macaroni or small shells
- Yellow cornmeal
- Couscous
- Plain breadcrumbs
- Italian breadcrumbs
- Vegetable oil (1 pt. bottle)
- Olive oil for cooking (1 pt. bottle)
- Extra-virgin olive oil (8-oz. bottle)
- Cider vinegar (1 pt. bottle)
- Distilled white vinegar (1 pt. bottle)
- Balsamic vinegar (1 pt. bottle)
- Dry sherry
- Dry marsala
- Worcestershire sauce (small bottle)
- Hot red pepper sauce (small bottle)
- Mayonnaise (1 pt. jar)
- Ketchup (20-oz. bottle)
- Dijon mustard (8-oz. jar)
- Capers
- Shallots (4 to 6)
- Onions (1 or 2 small)
- Garlic (1 head)

Asian Ingredients

- Soy sauce (8-oz. bottle)
- Hoisin sauce (small bottle)
- Oyster sauce (small bottle)
- Fish sauce (*nam pla*) (small bottle)
- Chinese chili paste with garlic (small jar)
- Asian sesame oil
- Rice vinegar
- Chinese five-spice powder
- Dried shiitake mushrooms

Dried Herbs and Spices

- Basil
- Bay leaves
- Black peppercorns
- Cinnamon (ground)
- Coriander (ground)
- Cumin (ground)
- Dry mustard

- Herbes de Provence
- Nutmeg (ground)
- Oregano
- Red pepper flakes
- Rosemary
- Sage
- Thyme

Herb and Spice Blends

- Cajun seasoning
- Chili powder
- Curry powder

- Herbes de Provence
- Italian seasoning
- Old Bay

Refrigerated Items

- Whole milk (1 pt.)
- Eggs (½ dozen)
- Unsalted butter (½ lb.)
- Heavy cream (½ pt.)
- Half-and-half (½ pt.)
- Sour cream (½ pt.)
- Parmesan cheese (½ lb.)

- Cheddar cheese (½ lb.)
- Gruyère or Swiss cheese (½ lb.)
- Parsley (1 bunch)
- Carrots (2 or 3)
- Celery (1 pkg. hearts)
- Lemons (1 or 2)

Frozen Foods

- ◆ Corn
- ◆ Green beans
- ◆ Green peas (10-oz. box)
- ◆ Mixed vegetables (10-oz. box)
- ◆ Pecan halves (6-oz. bag)

- ◆ Pearl onions (1-lb. bag)
- ◆ Pine nuts (4-oz. bag)
- ◆ Spinach, chopped (10-oz. box)
- ◆ Walnut halves (6-oz. bag)

Index

T

U–V

W-X-Y-Z

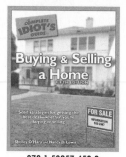

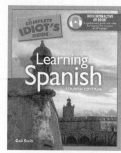

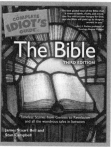
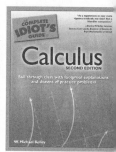

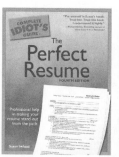
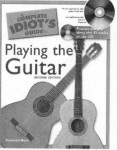